S0-AXN-766

THE JPS BIBLE COMMENTARY

RUTH רות

The JPS Torah Commentary

GENERAL EDITOR *Nahum M. Sarna*
LITERARY EDITOR *Chaim Potok*

GENESIS *Nahum M. Sarna*
EXODUS *Nahum M. Sarna*
LEVITICUS *Baruch A. Levine*
NUMBERS *Jacob Milgrom*
DEUTERONOMY *Jeffrey H. Tigay*

The JPS Bible Commentary

THE HAFTAROT *Michael Fishbane*

The Five Megillot and Jonah
GENERAL EDITOR *Michael Fishbane*

JONAH *Uriel Simon*
ESTHER *Adele Berlin*
ECCLESIASTES *Michael V. Fox*
RUTH *Tamara Cohn Eskenazi and Tikva Frymer-Kensky*

THE JPS BIBLE COMMENTARY

RUTH רות

The Traditional Hebrew Text with the New JPS Translation

Commentary by

TAMARA COHN ESKENAZI
and
TIKVA FRYMER-KENSKY

THE JEWISH PUBLICATION SOCIETY
PHILADELPHIA
2011 / 5771

The Jewish Publication Society
2100 Arch Street, 2nd floor
Philadelphia, PA 19103

Composition by El Ot Ltd. (English text) and Varda Graphics (Hebrew text)
Design by Adrianne Onderdonk Dudden
Manufactured in the United States of America

11 12 13 14 15 16 17 10 9 8 7 6 5 4 3 2 1

Library of Congress Cataloging-in-Publication Data

Bible. O.T. Ruth. Hebrew. 2011.
Ruth = the traditional Hebrew text with the new JPS translation / commentary by Tamara Cohn Eskenazi and Tikva Frymer-Kensky. – 1st ed.
p. cm. – (JPS Bible commentary series.)
Hebrew and English.
Includes bibliographical references and index.
ISBN 978-0-8276-0744-6 (alk. paper)
1. Bible. O.T. Ruth–Commentaries. I. Eskenazi, Tamara Cohn.
II. Frymer-Kensky, Tikva Simone.
III. Bible. O.T. Ruth. English. Jewish Publication Society. 2011. IV. Title.
BS1312.E85 2011
222'.35077–dc22 2011010419

GENESIS *ISBN 0-8276-0326-6*
EXODUS *ISBN 0-8276-0327-4*
LEVITICUS *ISBN 0-8276-0328-2*
NUMBERS *ISBN 0-8276-0329-0*
DEUTERONOMY *ISBN 0-8276-0330-4*
Five-volume set ISBN 0-8276-0331-2
JONAH *ISBN 0-8276-0672-9*
ESTHER *ISBN 0-8276-0699-0*
ECCLESIASTES *ISBN 0-8276-0742-3*
HAFTAROT *ISBN 0-8276-0691-5*
RUTH *ISBN 0-8276-07744-6*

Lawrence Deutsch ז״ל and Toby Deutsch

in memory of their parents,

and

in honor of their grandchildren
Silas Robert Andersen and Jemma Elizabeth Andersen

L'dor va dor

In memory of
Tikva Frymer-Kensky

Tikva Simone bat Haim Barukh Ha-levi v' Eliza

whose teaching and scholarship embodied
her passionate commitment
to honoring the legacies of biblical women

and

In memory of
Sylvia Roth Wildenstein

(sister of Tamara Cohn Eskenazi)

whose generosity, *ḥesed*, knew no bounds,
and under whose sheltering wings
much of this commentary was written

CONTENTS

PREFACE

This commentary began under trying circumstances: one of its authors died all too early, without being able to make her full contribution to life and to scholarship. In the commentary I attempted to give voice to Tikva Frymer-Kensky's view whenever her notes made it possible. This is mostly the case in chapters 1 and 2, for which she had extensive notes. I take full responsibility for chapters 3 and 4.

Yet, to write about Ruth is to find solace, even in trying circumstances. Many people have accompanied me in this journey: most of all Tikva Frymer-Kensky, whose energy, courage, intelligence, and knowledge remain an inspiration. Then come my family and friends. I am beholden to many who helped in this work: David E.S. Stein assiduously read parts of the manuscript. Rachel Adler, Carol Meyers, Dvora Weisberg, and Jacob Wright read sections, contributed their expertise, and offered most helpful comments. HUC-JIR students Joel Abramovitz and Adam Wright assisted with research. In particular, I thank Ellen Frankel, Michael Fishbane, Carol Hupping, and Leslie Rubin, who meticulously reviewed the manuscript and whose extensive comments proved an indispensable guide.

Finally, I thank my dear family and friends; without their unstinting support and love none of this would have happened.

Tamara Cohn Eskenazi
8 Kislev 5771; November 15, 2010

ABBREVIATIONS AND OTHER CONVENTIONS

Abbreviations

1 Chron.	1 Chronicles
1 Sam.	1 Samuel
2 Chron.	2 Chronicles
2 Sam.	2 Samuel
AB	Anchor Bible series
ABD	*Anchor Bible Dictionary*
B.	Babylonian Talmud
BASOR	*Bulletin of the American School of Oriental Research*
BB	Bava Batra
BDB	*The Brown-Driver-Briggs Hebrew and English Lexicon*
Ber.	Berakhot
BKAT	*Biblischer Kommentar: Alten Testament*
CBQ	*Catholic Biblical Quarterly*
CJPS	*The Contemporary Torah: A Gender-Sensitive Adaptation of the JPS Translation*
Dan.	Daniel
Deut.	Deuteronomy
Eccles.	Ecclesiastes
Exod.	Exodus
Ezek.	Ezekiel
Gen.	Genesis
HAT	Handbuch zum Alten Testament
HUCA	*Hebrew Union College Annual*
IEJ	*Israel Exploration Journal*
Isa.	Isaiah
JANES	*Journal of the Ancient Near Eastern Society*
JBL	*Journal of Biblical Literature*
Jer.	Jeremiah
JHS	*Journal of Hebrew Scriptures*
Jon.	Jonah
Josh.	Joshua

JSOT	*Journal for the Study of the Old Testament*
Jth.	Judith
Judg.	Judges
Kid.	Kiddushin
KJV	King James Version
Lam.	Lamentations
Lev.	Leviticus
M.	Mishnah
Macc.	Maccabees
Mak.	Makkot
Meg.	Megillah
Mic.	Micah
MT	Masoretic Text
Neh.	Nehemiah
NJPS	New Jewish Publication Society Translation
NRSV	New Revised Standard Version
Num.	Numbers
PdRE	Pirke de-Rabbi Eliezer
PdRK	Pesikta de-Rav Kahana
Prov.	Proverbs
Ps.	Psalms
Radak	Rabbi David Kimhi
Rashi	Rabbi Solomon ben Isaac
Ruth R.	Ruth Rabbah
Ruth Z.	Ruth Zuta
Sanh.	Sanhedrin
Songs	Song of Songs
Sot.	Sotah
VT	*Vetus Testamentum*
Yev.	Yevamot
ZAW	*Zeitschrift für die alttestamentlische Wissenschaft*
Zech.	Zechariah

Hebrew Textual Variants (Ketiv and Kerey)

The MT's *ketiv* (written tradition) and *kerey* (recited tradition) differ from each other for occasional words; and when reading the text aloud, the *kerey* is what is traditionally followed. Where differences exist, this edition first prints that word's *ketiv* letters in small type, followed by the vocalized *kerey* letters in normal text type. (This edition's biblical text is excerpted from the *JPS Hebrew-English Tanakh* [1999], as corrected in printings through 2001. For more information on the provenance and preparation of the Hebrew text, see the preface to that volume.)

Transliteration of the Hebrew Consonants

ʾ	alef
ʿ	ayin
b	bet
g	gimel
d	dalet
h	heh
v	vet, vav
w	vav (in verbal roots and in God's name)
z	zayin
ḥ	het
t	tet, tav
y	yud
k	kaf
kh	khaf
l	lamed
m	mem
n	nun
s	samekh, sin
p	peh
f	feh
tz	tzadi
k	kof
r	resh
sh	shin

Where needed to visually link the *b* sound (represented in Hebrew by the letter *bet*) with its corresponding spirantized sound (represented by *vet*), we have rendered the *v* sound as *bh*. Similarly for the *p* and *f* sounds (represented respectively by *peh* and *feh*); we have occasionally rendered the *f* sound as *ph*.

Pronunciation Guide for Vowels

a	as in *farm*
ai	as in *eye*
e	as in *dent*
ei	as in *hay*
i	as in *hit* or *heat*
o	as in *hope*
u	as in *food*

INTRODUCTION

The strangers who reside with you shall be to you as your citizens; you shall love each one as yourself... (Lev. 19:34)

You too must befriend [ve'ahavtem, "love"] the stranger, for you were strangers in the land of Egypt... (Deut. 10:19)

For love is fierce as death... (Songs 8:6)

No story in the Bible demonstrates more fully than the Book of Ruth the extraordinary power of love, channeled as *ḥesed*—kindness or generosity—that goes beyond the expected obligation. No book better models what it means to love the stranger and what it means to demonstrate *ḥesed* in a way that not only repairs a ruptured family history but also creates a community into which one wants to bring a child. Read on the holy day of Shavuot, which commemorates the giving of the Torah at Sinai, Ruth provides insights and sensitivities that frame a Jewish interpretation of the Torah.

Megillat Ruth,[1] "the Scroll of Ruth," is a book about kindness and audacity—about kindness that propels people to act audaciously for the sake of others. It is a book filled with *ḥesed* and hutzpah. Such actions bring about redemption, a notion that in the Book of Ruth expands from the personal fortunes of specific individuals to the larger thematic arc of biblical narrative, in which reconciliation reverses legacies of conflict and alienation (as between Israel and Moab). If the prophets express on a national scale what Abraham Joshua Heschel describes as "spiritual audacity and moral grandeur," then Ruth situates these powerful virtues in the domestic sphere and in the lives of ordinary people who, facing more circumscribed choices, likewise grow to such audacity and develop moral grandeur. Moreover, the book illustrates, through its depiction of Ruth, her actions and influence, just how one can cultivate such virtues so as to bring about personal and even national transformation. The book's concluding genealogy weaves this transformation into the larger tapestry of Israel's epic narrative by tying Ruth to David, Israel's most illustrious king.

The story traces a journey from Bethlehem and back, a journey from famine to fullness, from futility to fertility. Famine drives a family of four (husband, wife, and their two sons) to leave Bethlehem in Judah for the land of Moab. The husband dies, and the sons marry Moabite women. When these men also die, the three widows—Naomi and her Moabite daughters-in-law Orpah and Ruth—head back to Bethlehem. At Naomi's urging, Orpah soon returns to her home, but Ruth refuses to abandon Naomi, pledging herself with the immortal words "Wherever you go, I will go . . . your people shall be my people, and your God my God" (1:16).

In Bethlehem, Ruth the Moabite goes out to find food for the two women. She meets Boaz, a wealthy landowner, who, impressed by all that Ruth has done for her mother-in-law, graciously extends privileges and protection to her. Because Boaz is related to Naomi's family, biblical traditions entrust him with certain responsibilities toward destitute relatives. In light of these kinship obligations, Naomi instructs Ruth, at the end of the barley harvest, to approach Boaz at night and alone. Ruth does so, asking for his support, "for you are a redeeming kinsman" (3:9), and Boaz enthusiastically consents. The plot thickens when Boaz calls Ruth's attention to a complication: a closer kinsman must be approached first for support. The next day, at the city's gate, Boaz summons a public assembly to sort out the widows' situation. He succeeds in clearing all obstacles to his suit and then announces his marriage to Ruth, which the community blesses. The couple's great-grandson is King David.

The story is simple but never simplistic. Like a well-cut gem, this book has many facets that gleam brightly as one turns and turns it again. Its four gentle and elegantly crafted chapters profoundly engage difficult issues such as the complexities of love and loyalty; the challenges of finding bread (even in the "house of bread," i.e., Bethlehem) when one is a widow, a stranger, and a pauper; the nature of responsibility in a time of scarcity; the construction of community; the relation to "the other"; intermarriage; the redemptive powers of persons; and the role of God in human affairs.

Authorship and Date

Like other biblical narratives, Ruth does not disclose the identity or date of the author(s). The closing genealogy, which ends with David (4:22), places the earliest date in the tenth century B.C.E., but the preponderance of evidence points to a date in the postexilic/Persian period around the fifth century B.C.E. (see below for details).

Rabbinic sources credit the prophet Samuel with writing Ruth, along with Judges and Samuel (B. BB 14b). One tradition records that he did so to resolve a controversy that arose at the time of King Saul about David's qualification for kingship given his Moabite ancestry. Samuel, therefore, explained that the exclusion of Moabites applies only to males. Worried that this ruling would be lost after his death, Samuel wrote the Book of Ruth and secured its place as Scripture.[2] Scholars, however, acknowledge the anonymity of the author but try to discern some authorial characteristics. The erudite Hebrew and the literary sophistication of Ruth convince Jack M. Sasson that the author was highly literate.[3]

Several scholars entertain the possibility that the author was a woman. They note the unusual extent to which the book is attentive to women's lives and perspectives (comparable only to Song of Songs in this respect) as suggestive of such authorship. S. D. Goitein proposed such authorship in 1948 when he described the author as an older, "wise" woman.[4] More recently, Edward F. Campbell and Robert L. Hubbard

Jr., as well as Adrien J. Bledstein and Fokkelien van Dijk-Hemmes, have advanced arguments in favor of female authorship.[5] Mishael Caspi suggests that the story was told and retold by women and thus the "author" (which could be a circle of women) is female.[6] But as Richard Bauckham rightly notes, "Whether the real author was male or female we cannot know."[7] Suffice it to say that the book provides a female perspective in the way that the story unfolds, even though we cannot determine the author's name or gender. With its strong female perspective, the book canonizes women's experience and embeds it in the otherwise more androcentric Bible.

The fragments from the Dead Sea area show that it was in circulation by the first century B.C.E.[8] Hubbard contends that the book was written during the Solomonic era (tenth century B.C.E.) by an author who had access to royal and family archives.[9] Campbell also prefers a monarchic era date (950–700 B.C.E.).[10] But the preponderance of more recent evidence suggests a later date. Frederic W. Bush concludes that Ruth was written either in the late preexilic period or early postexilic period (sixth–fifth centuries B.C.E.),[11] and Ziony Zevit places it later, in the fifth century B.C.E.[12] For reasons indicated below, the present commentary supposes a postexilic/Persian period date in the fifth century B.C.E. although an earlier or later date cannot be ruled out entirely.

The assessment of the book's date revolves around the following major points:

1. The nature of the language in Ruth
2. The socio-legal institutions and practices reflected in the book
3. The relationship to other biblical traditions
4. The socio-political matrix, especially attitudes toward Moabites in Ruth and in Israelite history
5. The role of King David, whose birth concludes the book

The Nature of the Language in Ruth Scholars discuss three different linguistic phenomena in Ruth. First, the presence of Aramaisms (Aramaic or Aramaic-like features): these suggest a postexilic/Persian period date, the time when Aramaic became widely used in the ancient world. Aramaic is evident in the Bible beginning with the Persian period (late sixth century B.C.E.) in late works such as Ezra-Nehemiah and Daniel—books dated to the Persian or Hellenistic period. The Aramaic influence is detected in Ruth from verbs such as *s-b-r* "hope" in 1:13 (see also Esther 9:1); and *q-w-m* "confirm" occurring only in Ezek. 13:6; Ps. 119:28, 106; and Esther 9:21–32; or in forms such as *lahen,* "to them" in 1:13.[13]

Second, the presence of archaic forms: Ruth contains some archaic forms, such as *yaradeti* (*ketiv,* the "written" consonantal text) for "you go down" (3:3), to which the Masoretic tradition offers alternate reading instructions (*kerey*). For Campbell and Hubbard, for example, these archaic forms imply a preexilic hand. However, these forms can be regarded as archaisms (i.e., reflecting the deliberate use of archaic forms to indicate earlier periods). Because these archaic forms are confined to the speeches of Naomi and Boaz, they most likely signal elevated speech and the author's indication that Naomi and Boaz belong to an older generation, cohorts in terms of age and/or status.

Third, and most decisive, is the extensive presence of late biblical Hebrew in Ruth (reflective of postexilic Hebrew).[14] Although in some cases Ruth uses standard biblical Hebrew, typical of preexilic texts, Bush's systematic study cogently demonstrates the significant presence of late biblical Hebrew.[15] This occurs in syntax, forms, and vocabulary (such as the use of *n-s-ʾ* "marry" in 1:4, a term essentially limited to the postexilic era, as in Ezra 9:2). Whereas the first two linguistic phenomena could be argued as either preexilic or postexilic, Bush's study tips the scales in favor of a postexilic date, most likely in the fifth or fourth century B.C.E.[16]

The Socio-Legal Institutions and Practices Reflected in the Book Legal procedures in Ruth 4:1–10 evoke Genesis 38 and Deut. 25:5–10, which describe levirate unions, namely the union of a man with his deceased brother's wife for the purpose of producing a child. The mention of redemption (esp. Ruth 4:3–5), evokes other texts such as Leviticus 25. These points of reference have been employed in the discussion of date, but without conclusive results. The details in Ruth do not sufficiently conform to these other texts. Although scholars explain the differences as signs of development in law and practice, they disagree about the stages of the development. Some, like Hubbard, suggest that the differences can support the antiquity of Ruth in comparison with other biblical texts;[17] others, like Zevit, conversely argue that they show the lateness of Ruth. See "Levirate Marriage" below.

The Relationship to Other Biblical Traditions Several scholars observe that Ruth must be later than Genesis and Deuteronomy because it explicitly depends on them or alludes to them (see the mention of Rachel and Leah in Ruth 4:11 and the story of Judah and Tamar in Ruth 4:12).[18] See also "Ruth's Relationship to Other Biblical Books," below.

The Socio-Political Matrix, Especially Attitudes toward Moabites in Ruth and in Israelite History The socio-political matrix envisioned for the book has been important in debates about its date. The Book of Ruth exhibits no overt hostility toward foreigners in general and Moabites in particular. At the end, Ruth the Moabite is acclaimed and blessed as she enters the household of Boaz through marriage. This acceptance is in sharp contrast to the attitudes toward Moabites in Deut. 23:4–9 and Ezra-Nehemiah, which condemn Moabites for their past misdeeds (see, e.g., Neh. 13:1–3).

According to Hubbard,[19] such acceptance points to an early date for Ruth, before hostility became normative. According to other scholars such as Yair Zakovitch,[20] the Book of Ruth is a deliberate polemic against the policies of Ezra-Nehemiah and is therefore postexilic. This latter position seems more probable, especially when combined with the presence of late biblical Hebrew in Ruth. The time of Ezra-Nehemiah, which reflects necessary reconfiguration of social structures and Jewish identity after the return from exile and the demise of an indigenous monarchy, seems a most plausible context. Postexilic/Persian-period texts evince the heated debates about membership. Some sources, like Ezra-Nehemiah, opt for exclusionary measures to protect the identity of a small Jewish community in the postexilic period. Ruth is a voice in this debate. Along with Isa. 56:1–8 (also postexilic), Ruth maps processes or criteria for including worthy foreigners (see also "The Status of the Moabites," "Intermarriage," and "Conversion," below).

Hubbard's argument, that the Book of Ruth is nonpolemical in nature, does not stand as a critique against this view of the book's function. As illustrated throughout the present commentary, the Book of Ruth demonstrates a path for transformation that bypasses direct confrontation or polarizing polemics. Its protagonists achieve their goal through cooperation and by expanding a circle of *ḥesed* as generosity. It is therefore consistent with Ruth's ethos that its challenge to the exclusionary measures of Moabites in Ezra-Nehemiah would be conveyed through positive examples rather than attack.

The Role of King David, Whose Birth Concludes the Book Postexilic texts laud David as Israel's most illustrious king (see the Book of Chronicles, which cleanses his reign from wrongdoings such as the Bathsheba affair). For some scholars, concluding the Book of Ruth with the birth of David supports a date in the Solomonic era (tenth century B.C.E.), with the story either aiming to exonerate David's foreign origin or promoting popular acceptance of the Davidic dynasty with the active role of foreigners under David and Solomon.[21] The proponents of a postexilic/Persian-period date for Ruth understand the genealogy of David as support for integrating worthy foreigners into the Jewish community by showing how such inclusion benefited the entire nation.[22]

The persuasive arguments on both sides preclude a definitive conclusion. However, linguistic and legal features of the book tilt the arguments in favor of a later dating of Ruth. A more nuanced understanding of the postexilic dynamics, especially as expressed in Ezra-Nehemiah,[23] further helps to provide a social context for Ruth as a fifth-century work, and weighs the evidence in favor of a postexilic/Persian-period date, which is presumed in this commentary.

Genre/Style

The genre of the Book of Ruth has been classified in a number of ways. The most common are "short story" or "novella," terms borrowed from modern literary studies but suited, according to several scholars, for biblical narrative as well.[24] According to W. Humphries, "the short story *reveals* the nature of a character or situation;"[25] it offers an epiphany, as it were. The novel or novella, however, "*develops* characters or situations."[26] Bush leans in the direction of calling Ruth a short story, interpreting it as an unfolding revelation of the goodness and loyalty of all the protagonists. For him, Ruth and Boaz especially, but also Naomi, are "the virtual enfleshment of *ḥesed,* that quality of kindness, graciousness, and loyalty that goes beyond the call of duty."[27] I would argue that the book is something between a short story and a novella. As is typical in a short story, Ruth's *ḥesed* is revealed through her words and actions. But as in a novella, Naomi and Boaz's *ḥesed* develops as a result of their encounters with Ruth.

Because the book moors itself in a historical setting—the time of the judges or chieftains, roughly the eleventh century B.C.E.—Hubbard prefers reading Ruth as a short story. According to his understanding of these genres, "unlike the novella, the short story allows for the historical accuracy of the narrative." He assumes that the author had access to archives and preserved recognized traditions. Had David not descended from a Moabite woman, Hubbard suggests, a writer would hardly invent the idea. "While the skill of the storyteller is quite evident, the heart of the story is historical." Some other scholars likewise acknowledge the possibility that reliable traditions about David's Moabite ancestry were current, but most question or downplay the historical reliability of the book, concluding that the book is an imagined version of David's ancestry.

E. Wurtheim considers Ruth an "idyll, in which a few exemplary characters model loyalty, and a narrative to which questions of historical reliability need not be posed."[28] But calling Ruth an "idyll" underestimates the degree to which the book engages difficult social and economic issues and exposes challenges that remove it from this category.

Phyllis Trible titles her important essay on Ruth "A Human Comedy."[29] She thereby casts the book as a counterpoint to Dante's *Divine Comedy,* a hero's journey (through hell, purgatory, and paradise). Trible's title is apt also in that Ruth admirably fits the classic definition of comedy. J. William Whedbee, who applies the category to the Bible, characterizes comedy as a u-shaped plot that focuses on ordinary people (rather than heroes, kings, and divinities, as does tragedy) and that moves from tragedy to celebration and reintegration.[30]

Ruth's Place in the Canon

In contemporary Jewish Bibles, the Book of Ruth is placed with *Kethuvim,* or Writings, the third division of the Bible, as part of the Five Scrolls (*megillot*). The sequence of these five books in modern Jewish Bibles, including the JPS (Jewish Publication Society) translations, follows the Jewish liturgical calendar: Song of Songs is read first, in the spring in connection with Passover (Nisan is the first month according to the Bible), followed by Ruth on Shavuot (Feast of Weeks) fifty days later, then Lamentations (*Eikhah*) on the Ninth of Av (late summer), Ecclesiastes (Koheleth) on Sukkot (Tabernacles) in the fall, and ending with Esther on Purim in winter.[31]

However, this sequence was not the original order of these books. In the Talmud (B. BB 14b), Ruth is placed at the beginning of *Kethuvim,* preceding the Psalms, the rationale seeming to be that David's birth (Ruth 4:17–22) precedes the psalms attributed to him. Subsequent editions of the complete Bible include Ruth with the *megillot*, the five scrolls. A Jewish tradition preserved in the Leningrad Codex (eleventh century C.E.), the oldest surviving full manuscript of the Hebrew Bible, arranges the five *megillot* in a presumed chronological order: Ruth is the first scroll, since David preceded Solomon; it is followed by Song of Songs (reputedly written by Solomon as a young man); followed by Ecclesiastes (written by Solomon as an old man); then Lamentations (associated with Jeremiah and the destruction of the Temple in 586 B.C.E.); and Esther (Persian period: fifth century B.C.E.). In this sequence Ruth follows Proverbs, a book that concludes with an encomium to the *'eshet ḥayil,* a woman of valor ("capable wife," Prov. 31:1–31), linking this book to Ruth, called an *'eshet ḥayil* in Ruth 3:11 (translated as "a fine woman").[32]

In a different early tradition, Ruth is placed with the historical books, right after Judges (since Ruth is set at the time of judges or chieftains as per Ruth 1:1), and is followed by 1 Samuel which describes the rise of David, who is named at the end of Ruth (4:17 and 22). This order, with Ruth following Judges and preceding Samuel, is first attested in the Septuagint (the early Jewish Greek translation of the Bible) and is followed in non-Jewish Bibles.

Ruth's Relationship to Other Biblical Books

Genesis Ruth, like Genesis, is a story about a family destined to become great. Whereas Genesis leads to the birth of Israel and its twelve tribes, Ruth leads to David, Israel's greatest king. Ruth evokes Genesis in a number of ways. First, the book explicitly mentions some of the ancestors in Genesis by name: Rachel, Leah, Judah, Tamar, and Perez all appear in the blessings wished for Boaz and Ruth.

Second, there are some parallels and allusions. Both books focus on families who journey. Moreover, Ruth's journey to Bethlehem is praised in terms that evoke Abraham's similar journey: both left their birthplace and ancestors to come to a place or a people they did not know (compare Gen. 12:1 and Ruth 2:11). Furthermore, the language of happenstance (Ruth 2:3 and Gen. 24:18) and the mention of the mother's house (Ruth 1:8 and Gen. 24:28)[33] link Ruth with Rebekah (Gen. 24:28). In addition, Ruth's Moabite origin brings to mind the story of Lot's daughters and the birth of Moab (Gen. 19:30–37).

These intertextual connections serve many purposes. For example, they allow the story of Ruth to right wrongs—redeeming, as it were, things gone awry in Genesis: Ruth's integration into the family of Boaz repairs the breach between Abraham and his nephew Lot (Gen. 13; note esp. the repetition of *p-r-d* "separate," in Gen. 13:9,11,14, and in Ruth's pledge never to separate, *p-r-d,* from Naomi in 1:17); the seduction of Lot by his daughters that leads to the birth of Moab (Gen. 19:30–37) finds its antithesis in the chaste midnight encounter between Ruth the Moabite and Boaz, marked by reserve and responsibility; Rachel and Leah (mentioned in Ruth 4:11), who compete in Genesis 29–30, find their mirror image in the collaboration between Naomi and Ruth; even the animosity between Sarah and Hagar (Gen. 16; 21:9–11), which climaxes with the expulsion of the young foreign woman by the elderly Israelite insider, finds its resolution when the elderly Naomi and the young foreign woman, Ruth, bond and support each other.

The story of Judah and Tamar (Gen. 38) finds its complementary opposite in the story of Boaz and Ruth. Both cases reflect a breach in the expected mores. But whereas Judah transgresses by impetuously having sex with his daughter-in law, Boaz shows great restraint when confronted by a woman lying at his feet (Ruth 3:8); and whereas Tamar, Judah's daughter-in-law, accepts the invitation to have illicit sex and only later forces Judah to recognize his responsibilities, Ruth directly calls on Boaz to accept responsibility even in compromising circumstances, without, it appears, consenting to have sex with him.

Harold Fisch, who compares the story of Ruth to the stories in Genesis about Lot's daughters and Judah and Tamar, explains the importance of reading these stories in tandem:

> [T]hey are all episodes in the history of a single family. Lot is the father of Moab and thus the ancestor of Ruth, whilst Judah is the father of Perez and thus the ancestor of Boaz.... [W]e have here the story of a single clan (that of Abraham and his nephew Lot) which separates (Gen. xiii 11) at an early stage and is then reunited in the persons of Ruth and Boaz."[34]

Fisch delineates some of the striking parallels in the three stories and their significance: All three begin with a departure and feature abandoned women who initiate contact with a father or father figure. Each story involves the "bed trick," and each ends happily with the restoration of a family line.[35] Such intertextual links are not mere niceties. Rather,

> The Ruth-corpus . . . surely gives us in miniature the very essence of all Heilsgeschichte [a history of salvation]. It is . . . a process beginning with Sodom and its overthrow and ending with the birth of David, the father of a messianic dynasty. . . . We have here a drama unfolding in time and involving at each point momentous and irreversible decisions, which will weigh down upon the succeeding generations. Judah and Boaz are not interchangeable paradigms: the one represents an essential step towards the other as well as being its antitype."[36]

Fisch notes an interpretive progression in the three parallel stories: no moralizing comments are made in Gen. 19:30–38 regarding Lot's daughters; however, in Gen. 38:26, Judah affirms Tamar's rightness; and in Ruth 4:11–12, the entire community approves. These narrative details, Fisch argues, and others as well, carry political and historical significance: they validate the continuing covenantal history of David's ancestors and lineage. According to Fisch, the Ruth-Boaz story is "the means of 'redeeming' the entire corpus and of inserting it into the pattern of Heilsgeschichte."[37]

Fisch also sees an interpretive progression within Ruth itself, focused on the theme of redemption. The sequence begins with Boaz's redeeming a parcel of land, then redeeming Ruth from widowhood. Subsequently Ruth's newborn child redeems Naomi from sorrow and emptiness. Yet Fisch goes one step further, pushing back the starting point of this progression to Genesis:

> Of whom, we may ask, is Ruth the redeemer? Might it be suggested that she is the redeemer of the unnamed ancestress who lay with her father in Gen. xix?" Just as Boaz is the "redeemer" of his ancestor, Judah who, in an only slightly more edifying fashion, "went in" to the supposed prostitute at the crossroads [Tamar] leaving her his seal, his cord and his staff as a pledge. Boaz "redeems" that pledge. . . .[38]

For Fisch, this web of relationships linking Genesis and Ruth is the means by which the story of Ruth "is situated at the crossroad of history," even though the text itself seems to confine itself to domestic events.[39]

Leviticus Two different issues link the Book of Ruth with Leviticus: how to treat the stranger and how to redeem land and person. First, the love due to the stranger in Lev. 19:34 is enacted initially by Ruth herself who, in Moab, devotes herself to Naomi, the stranger in Moab, and refuses to abandon her. It finds its counterpart in Boaz who makes possible the inclusion of Ruth the Moabite in the community at Bethlehem.

Second, at a more technical level, the question of redemption in Ruth brings to mind Leviticus 25, which discusses redeeming land and certain categories of people. As noted below in "Redemption," as well as in commentaries to chapters 2, 3, and 4 of Ruth, the discussion in Leviticus serves as a backdrop for understanding some of the negotiations at the gate. The role played in Ruth by Boaz and Obed as redeemers corresponds to the directive in Leviticus that persons with means (or potential means) come to the aid of a destitute relative (Ruth and Naomi).

Deuteronomy Deuteronomy intersects with Ruth in three different ways. First, as in Lev. 19:34, Deuteronomy likewise requires that the stranger, *ger,* be loved, as it enjoins commitment to the stranger's welfare (Deut. 10:19).

Second, Ruth's Moabite status brings us back to Deuteronomy 23, which prescribes how Israel should relate to different ethnic groups in the land when they enter it; concerning Moabites, the Israelites are proscribed from admitting them into the community: "You shall never concern yourself with their welfare or benefit as long as you live" (Deut. 23:7; for further details, see "The Status of the Moabites," below). Although neither of these Deuteronomic teachings is explicitly mentioned in Ruth, readers familiar with Deuteronomy 23 can recognize the intertextual tension over the issue of Moabite status within the Israelite community. This tension helps explain the kinds of maneuvering that first Naomi and then Boaz engage in before Boaz announces his intention to marry Ruth: the obstacle blocking their union is Ruth's Moabite status, the proverbial elephant in the room. In the Book of Ruth, this elephant is implicitly circumvented. However one interprets Ruth, it is undeniable that the book recognizes the offspring of a Moabite woman and a Judahite man as legitimate members of the Israelite community, Deut. 23:4–7 notwithstanding. The Rabbis seek to reconcile the positions in Deuteronomy 23 and Ruth by interpreting the injunction against Moabites as applying only to men or by absolving/exempting converts (like Ruth) from these strictures. Many modern scholars, however, are inclined to see Ruth as an intentional challenge to the Deuteronomic law (and a criticism or an interpretation of it that illustrates the non-applicability of the law to marriage).[40]

Ruth's third connection to Deuteronomy pertains to levirate marriage, which is discussed in Deut. 25:5–10. When Naomi discourages Orpah and Ruth from returning with her to Bethlehem, pointing out that she has no more sons in her body "who might be husbands to you" (1:11), she most likely alludes to a levirate union. As her words make clear, her daughters-in-law cannot expect a levir to redeem them from widowhood; therefore, they must seek a husband by going back to their mother's house (1:8–13). Levirate laws also hover in the background of Boaz's negotiations at the gate in 4:5-10 (For more details about this topic, see "Levirate Marriage," below.)

Judges The Book of Judges forms part of the backdrop to the Book of Ruth because the latter's narrator situates the story during the time of the chieftains or judges. Judges describes this period as a series of crises, each temporarily solved by a charismatic leader, but overall a time characterized by lawlessness. Judges concludes with the worrisome statement that this was when "each man did what was right in his own eyes" (Judg. 21:25). Because Ruth unfolds in a gentle setting, free of strife, some commentators suppose that the story takes place during one of the intermittent tranquil periods (for the Rabbis, this was the time of Ibzan mentioned briefly in Judg. 12:8–10; see B. BB 91a). But hints of violence in the book suggest that the author intends to evoke the more typical image of Judges as an unruly time; the protagonists' kindness in Ruth is therefore even more striking against a background of violence. (On violence in Ruth, see comments on "molest" at 2:9 and "annoyed" at 2:22.)

Samuel The birth of David at the end of Ruth links the book explicitly with the books of Samuel, which recount David's rise and reign. For this reason some consider Ruth a story created and preserved primarily for providing background to David's monarchy. Several episodes in Samuel, however, link the books further. In 1 Samuel 22, David, still an outlaw escaping from Saul, goes to Moab: "[H]e said to the king of Moab, 'Let my father and mother come and stay with you, until I know what God will do for me.' So he led them to the king of Moab, and they stayed with him as long as David remained in the stronghold" (22:3–4). The readiness of the Moabite king to shelter David's parents suggests a prior connection between David and Moab, leading the Rabbis to conclude that Ruth was a daughter of the king of Moab. Second, key scenes in each book share similar phrasing: in 1 Sam. 24:5, David stealthily cuts off a portion of Saul's garment, a scene that evokes the language and associations of Ruth 3:7–9, where the word *kanaf,* either "wing" or "robe," also appears.

Isaiah 56 and Ezra-Nehemiah If we date Ruth to the postexilic era (fifth century B.C.E. or later), we can see it in dialogue with Ezra-Nehemiah and Isa. 56:1–7, also dated to that period. Ezra-Nehemiah describes the reconstruction of Jewish life in Judah in the aftermath of destruction and exile. It depicts a fledgling Jewish community, newly returned from exile in Babylon, seeking to safeguard its existence and identity in the midst of other inhabitants of the land. Ezra-Nehemiah opposes marriage with "peoples of the land," including Moabite women, who (it is claimed) imperil Jewish loyalty to God now that geographical and political boundaries are no longer secure. Thus, Ezra 10:2 regards the expulsion of "foreign" women as a viable strategy for Jewish survival.[41] The overriding message of the book is that neighboring nations pose a threat to Israel's identity as a people and that foreign women divert Israelite men from worshiping Israel's God (see "Intermarriage" below).

In contrast to Ezra-Nehemiah, Ruth—in tracing the journey of a Moabite woman into the household of Israel—creates an alternative or a solution to the problems that Ezra-Nehemiah seeks to address. Similarly, Isa. 56:1–7 presents an alternative to Ezra-Nehemiah (and Deut. 23:2). This prophetic work proclaims that God welcomes into the community of Israel those previously excluded, namely, eunuchs and foreigners, when they keep the covenant, especially the Sabbath. These statements in Ezra-Nehemiah, Ruth, and Isaiah most likely reflect the postexilic debates about membership in the Jewish community, now that some older criteria of such membership (such as birthplace) were less applicable.[42]

Esther Ruth and Esther are the only two women for whom a biblical book is named, a distinction that invites a comparison. While both depict genuine heroines, the two women are quite different, as are the books as a whole. The two women represent contrast: on the one hand, there is the poor, mature widow who marries a Judean man, a woman whose *ḥesed* and maternity grant her a place in Israel's memory. Her claim to fame results from her actions in the domestic and familial spheres. On the other hand, there is the young Jewish woman who marries a foreign king and lives a life of luxury, and whose offspring (if there were any) were never mentioned. Her claim to fame comes from acting on the national, even international, scale when she saves her people from slaughter. Yet, there is also complementarity: the books of Ruth and Esther function like bookends, delineating the range of women's lives, as well as the scope of women's salvific activities, moving from the domestic to the national.

Non-Israelite Biblical Heroes Ruth is one of several non-Israelites whose contribution to Israel's welfare is celebrated in the Bible. Pharaoh's daughter rescues and raises Moses (Exod. 2:5–10). The Midianite Zipporah, who marries Moses, saves their son (and perhaps Moses himself) with her quick action when she circumcises their son (Exod. 4:24–26). Zipporah's father, Jethro the Midianite priest, mentors Moses and teaches him the importance of delegating authority (Exod. 18:13–27); he also blesses Israel's God for delivering Israel (Exod. 18:8–12). Rahab the Canaanite prostitute hides the Israelite spies, gives them confidence, and helps Israel take Jericho (Josh. 2:1–21); according to Josh. 6:25, Rahab and her family are spared by the new conquerors and live among the Israelites, despite the injunction to destroy all Canaanites. (Like Ruth's story, Rahab's story conflicts with exclusionary messages elsewhere in the Bible.)

Jael (related to Jethro according to Judg. 4:11) rescues the Israelites by killing the enemy leader Sisera with a tent peg (Judg. 4:17–23; 5:24–27). Ittai the Gittite, presumably a Philistine and thus an enemy of Israel, nonetheless supports King David when the latter escapes from the coup d'état staged by his son Absalom. Furthermore, Ittai's vow of loyalty to David (2 Sam. 15:16–22) resembles Ruth's pledge to Naomi (see my comment at Ruth 1:16–17 for a comparison). The Book of Job portrays an impeccably righteous individual who is never defined as an Israelite and who may in fact be a gentile. David Perlman refers to such figures as "God's Others"[43] and illustrates their contributions to the house of Israel. These numerous depictions reflect the Bible's openness to righteous gentiles whose efforts helped secure Israel's survival.[44]

Ruth and Shavuot

It is Jewish custom to read Ruth on Shavuot (*Atzeret* in Rabbinic sources), the festival that commemorates the giving of the Torah at Sinai.[45] The practice is mentioned first in Ruth Z. 1.1. There are two traditions about the timing: one, that it is read at the conclusion of the Shabbat before Shavuot; and the other, more popular, that it is read on Shavuot. Jewish sources refer to the book as *Megillat Ruth* (the Scroll of Ruth) and offer this explanation for the practice of reading it on Shavuot:

1. Both the Torah, which was given on Shavuot, and Ruth are all about *ḥesed.*[46]

2. At Sinai, Israel took upon itself obedience to the Torah; Ruth likewise takes this obligation to the Torah upon herself.

3. According to one tradition, David was born and died on Shavuot; Ruth ends with the lineage of David.

4. Shavuot is connected to the barley harvest (also called *bikkurim* in the Bible); so, too, is the story of Ruth.

5. A midrash (Ruth Zuta) claims that the Torah can be adequately grasped only by those who have suffered; Ruth suffers poverty and hardship.

6. The Hasidic master known as the Sefat Emet[47] offers additional explanations for the link between Shavuot and Ruth: (*a*) Reading Ruth teaches us that actions, not mere study, are the essence of "righteous living" or "goodness" (as per Pirkei Avot 1.17); Boaz exemplified this teaching through his actions of *ḥesed* and his observance of *mitzvot;* (*b*) having received the Torah at Sinai, Israel is now ready to bring near anyone who seeks to receive it (as per Deut. 10:19), including proselytes like Ruth—the welcoming of Ruth is an example of this readiness; (*c*) the Torah helps Israel gather the holy sparks scattered among the nations, such is the case with Ruth; (*d*) In taking the Torah upon themselves at Sinai, the Jewish people all became proselytes.[48]

7. A more specific historical explanation hypothesizes that the Rabbinic decision to connect Ruth and Shavuot was made in response to the Karaites (a Jewish movement that began in the eighth century C.E. and challenged the legitimacy of the Oral Torah). According to this last view, the Book of Ruth validates the Oral Torah publicly, making possible (through its re-interpretation of Deut. 23:4, which excludes Moabites from the community of Israel) the marriage of Boaz and Ruth the Moabite, a union that established the line of David and the Messiah.[49]

Background Issues and Themes

The Family The Bible presents the family or household as the basic and central institution in ancient Israel. Familial relationships often serve as metaphors to express the most intimate and enduring bonds of care and love (even though the narratives themselves frequently illustrate strife among family members). Thus, references to God often depict God as parent and spouse (see Exod. 4:22–23; Isa. 54:1–11), and brotherly relationships are invoked to unify the nation (see Neh. 5:7–8).

Most families in the biblical period lived in an agrarian society (an estimated 90 percent), where land was the main certain source of economic security and therefore was protected by extensive laws.[50] The Bible includes complex traditions intended to protect the household unit socially, economically, and spiritually/religiously. Biblical laws carefully demarcate the scope of the family, establish lines of kinship through these laws, and delineate family obligations. Leviticus 18 and 20, for example, map family relations by listing prohibited sexual liaisons. The Decalogue commands individuals to care for their parents (see Exod. 20:12; Deut. 5:16); other texts presuppose parental obligations for their offspring, and spouses for each other. Redemption laws in Lev. 25:48–49 further extend the lines of kinship beyond these primary relationships by assigning responsibilities for redemption to more distant relatives.

KINSHIP TERMS

The *bayit,* "house" or "household" (see most often *beit 'av,* "father's house," but also *beit 'em,* "mother's house," as in Ruth 1:8) was both a spatial and a relational unit. As a relational unit, it was a subset of the *mishpaḥah,* the considerably larger kinship agnatic unit best rendered as "clan" (larger than what the modern Hebrew term *mishpaḥah* connotes) and of the *sheivet/matteh* "tribe." The *beit 'av* or just *bayit,* the ancestral household, often refers to the smallest unit.[51] Persons could be identified as *ben* (plural *banim*), namely son(s) or descendant(s);[52] or as *bat* (plural *banot*), namely daughter(s) of immediate parents; or as *benei,* "children of," a more distant relationship expressed through an assumed eponym (the person after whom the group is named, e.g., Israel); thus the frequent designation *benei yisra'el* refers to the nation as a whole.

Likewise, the common term *'aḥ* (plural *'aḥim*), usually translated as "brother," can designate either biological or adoptive relationships but can also refer to all Israelites who share a presumed ancestor, namely Jacob/Israel. Other kinship terms include *ḥoten*, referring to a father-in-law (Exod. 18:1), *ḥatan,* usually referring to a son-in law (Gen.19:12), as well as *kallah,* usually used for a daughter-in-law (Gen. 38:11). (References to *ḥatan* and *kallah* as groom and bride typically appear in texts dealing with later periods, as in the time of Jeremiah [Jer. 33:11]). The Book of Ruth augments this customary terminology with additional references to female kin relationships. Terms like "her mother-in-law," *ḥamotah* (e.g., 2:19), and "your sister-in-law," *yevimteikh* (1:15), appear only in Ruth. Mention of "mother's house" (instead of the more typical biblical references to "father's house") appears only in Ruth 1:8, Gen. 24:28, and Songs 3:4 and 8:2 and is likewise exceptional (see comment at 1:8).

STRUCTURE OF THE HOUSEHOLD UNIT

Literary, archaeological, and ethnographic sources converge in portraying biblical families, like most other families in the ancient world, as patrilineal and patrilocal households: the head of the household was usually male, and the woman joined the husband's family upon marriage. However, we learn from certain texts that senior females in the household also had important spheres of authority and power (as is suggested by the references to the "mother's house" in Ruth 1:8 and elsewhere).[53] The household unit usually included an extended family of grown sons, together with their spouses and children, unmarried daughters, as well as other relatives (such as aging parents), sometimes living under the same roof.

The household also included slaves and indentured laborers. Female slaves were also available for sex and procreation (as is reflected in biblical narratives; e.g., Rachel offers her maid to Jacob to produce a child in Gen. 30:3. Cf. also the laws in Exod. 21:7–11). Concubinage was accepted. Genesis, Samuel, and Kings describe polygynous families, with several wives or concubines providing legitimate sons; but most likely such marriages were typically reserved for the affluent few, such as kings.

Biblical genealogies and lineage are reckoned through the male line. However, when the male line is disrupted, special strategies, such as surrogacy and adoption, are employed. So, for example, the name of Barzillai, who has only daughters, is preserved through his adopted son-in-law, who takes his name (Ezra 2:61; 7:63). Surrogacy is another way to preserve the family line and name. Thus, levirate marriage provides a surrogate heir for a deceased childless man through his brother; slave women provide surrogate children for a barren wife. Sarai, for instance, plans to be "built up" (i.e., become a mother) through Hagar's union with Abraham (Gen. 16:2). A different strategy is depicted in the case of Zelophehad, who leaves behind only daughters when he dies (see "Inheritance" below).

Inheritance Because biblical households were primarily agricultural, with land as the most essential basis for economic survival, biblical laws, like other ancient Near Eastern laws, focus on protecting land rights and regulating its transmission across generations. Israelite family land was in principle inalienable.[54] Redemption of land lost to the household was one of several safeguards against a permanent loss of inherited land (Lev. 25:25–45). Usually sons inherit. Numbers 27:8–11 demarcates additional lines of property transmission when a person dies: "If a man dies without leaving a son, you shall transfer his property to his daughter. If he has no daughter, you shall assign his property to his brothers. If he has no brothers, you shall assign his property to his father's brothers. If his father had no brothers, you shall assign his property to his nearest relative in his own clan [his *mishpaḥah*], and he shall inherit it."

The question of inheritance arises in Ruth 4 when Boaz reports that Elimelech's land must be redeemed (i.e., restored or preemptively acquired) to keep it within the family. Although biblical laws make clear the priority of keeping the land in perpetuity within the family (see Lev. 25:25–34; Num. 27, 36), they do not specifically address situations comparable to that in Ruth, namely that of widows (including a foreign widow) without living sons. Consequently, Naomi's and Ruth's right to the family's land has been subject to debate (see also "Widowhood" below).

It is noteworthy, however, that the land in the Book of Ruth does not automatically revert to the male relatives (such as Boaz and the nearer kin of Elimelech). Some biblical narratives mention widows who own land (see 2 Kings 8:3,6), possibly because they inherited it. According to Numbers 27 and 36, daughters inherit when there are no sons. But daughters' rights to the family inheritance under other circumstances are not clear. Deuteronomy 21:15–17 illustrates that a parent has some discretion in allocating inheritance. Thus, S. J. Osgood observes, the laws show some flexibility in the descent system, allowing for brothers and even daughters to inherit.[55] From Josh. 15:18–19 and Judg. 1:14–15, we learn that daughters could be beneficiaries of family property during their lifetime, for Achsah's father gives her some property when she requests it.

In an ostracon (clay fragment) from eighth-century-B.C.E. Judah, a woman addresses an officer concerning land that came to her by his decision after the death of her childless husband.[56] This ostracon demonstrates that a childless widow could petition and receive her husband's or the family's land. The debate about the authenticity of the ostracon makes this evidence uncertain, but it conforms to other biblical and extrabiblical data in presuming that arrangements for transmitting inheritance to women were possible. Contracts from the Jewish colony in Elephantine, Egypt, show that in the fifth century B.C.E. Jewish women could inherit, own, or sell property. They could also bequeath it to sons and daughters and in all ways control their inheritance.[57]

Zevit concludes that "the fact that Naomi disposed of property that once belonged to her husband poses no historical difficulty within the general ancient Near Eastern or specifically Israelite milieu of the *author* of Ruth."[58] Osgood likewise concurs that Naomi had the right to dispose of family property. Although Elimelech and both his sons died in Moab, the property that was previously allotted to him was "still the inalienable right of the surviving members of his *beit 'av* ["father's house" or "ancestral household"] even though they were women. The land was still regarded as Elimelech's, but to Naomi, as his widow, remained the right of disposing of it by leasing it either to an outsider or to a kinsman."[59]

Marriage The most common purpose of marriage in the Bible, as in other ancient societies, is to produce children, provide labor for economic survival, and preserve the household's resources (property, status, etc.) across the generations, primarily through the male line. These social and economic underpinnings of matrimony do not exclude emotional attachment and love. Genesis 2 characterizes the bond between a woman and a man as a couple's attempt to restore a primordial unity: "Hence a man leaves his father and mother and clings to his wife, so that they become one flesh" (Gen. 2:24). The Bible states that Isaac loves Rebekah when they cohabit (Gen. 24:67) and that Jacob marries Rachel for love (Gen. 29:18). Although procreation is constantly emphasized, and the birth of sons viewed as among the greatest of blessings, spousal relations do not exist merely for procreation and a growing workforce. Thus Elkanah tries to convince his wife Hannah that she need not bear a child (1 Sam. 1:8), pointing out to her that he is "more devoted to you than ten sons."

Biblical marriages are typically endogamous, that is, Israelites are expected to marry Israelites. But there are exceptions. Moses, for example, marries a Midianite woman (see Exod. 2:21). Whereas some texts oppose certain marriages with outsiders (Deut. 7:3), others reflect no such objections (see "Intermarriage" and "Conversion," below). Unfortunately, the Bible provides very little information about the procedures that constituted a legal marriage. Although there are some details concerning legal divorce in certain cases (Deut. 24:1–4), nothing definitive is said about the process of marriage. And because the Hebrew word for "woman," *ishah*, designates both wife and unattached woman, it is often difficult to ascertain when a woman's status has been formally changed.

The predominant language for marriage in the Bible and ancient Near Eastern sources is expressed simply as the giving or taking of a daughter or a woman. This "give" (*natan*) and "take" (*lakaḥ*) vocabulary is present in almost all texts connected with Israel's preexilic period. These terms of conveyance describe the movement of the woman to her husband's household. A different term, *nasa'*, appears in texts dating from the postexilic period, often describing marriages with non-Judean/Israelite women (as in Ruth 1:4). The word's basic meaning is "to lift up," and it becomes a common term for marrying in postbiblical Hebrew. (Some have related the Rabbinic *nissu'in* ceremony to the physical act of raising the bride over the threshold.)

We can only hypothesize about the formal steps of marriage during the biblical period, based on a few hints from the Bible and from cultural patterns in surrounding societies. Genesis 24 is the most fully delineated depiction of the process leading to marriage. But it may also be exceptional in that it is conducted by a proxy, Abraham's servant, who acts as an agent of the groom's father. Other biblical narratives show marriages brokered by a parent (in the case of Samson, both father and mother; see Judg. 14:5) or male siblings (see Gen. 34:7–14). All these marriages are presented as solely family affairs, resulting from an agreement between two households, requiring no other confirmation.

The Bible mentions the *mohar,* a betrothal gift from the groom to the bride's father (Exod. 22:15–16; 1 Sam. 18:25, translated as "bride-price"). Extra-biblical sources, however, also mention a dowry that the bride retains if the marriage is terminated, in addition to the *mohar.*[60] (In Rabbinic sources, the *mohar* is transmuted into a promise guaranteed by the ketubah to provide for the woman in cases of divorce or widowhood; see, e.g., B. Ket. 82b).

From Elephantine, Egypt, we learn that in the fifth century B.C.E., Jewish marriages were at times accompanied by a legal contract in which economic arrangements were recorded and witnessed, including provisions for the dissolution of the marriage. These documents, the oldest extant Jewish marriage contracts, show that a woman could inherit her husband's possessions, and that a daughter, as well as a son, could inherit parents' possessions.[61]

Even more remarkable, the contracts disclose that either the wife or the husband could initiate a unilateral divorce (a tradition, incidentally, that does not conflict with biblical sources). However, because these documents come from Jews living in a foreign military installation in Egypt, it is not possible to determine the extent to which their more urban situation and greater affluence, as well as the surrounding Egyptian culture, influenced such arrangements.

Ruth 4:9–13 may be depicting a marriage ceremony. If so, it is the only biblical example, although it may be describing a typical marriage for its time. Even though the ceremony does not include a written agreement, it contains all the other elements considered necessary in later Rabbinic sources to constitute a legal marriage (and its features also mirror the contracts in Elephantine): the announcement of intent by the groom in the presence of witnesses (4:9–10), the transfer of material possessions, and affirmation by witnesses (4:11); followed by consummation, after the woman has joined the man's domicile (4:13). Ruth is the only biblical example in which the community or its representatives, rather than the immediate family, plays a role in formalizing a marriage.

Widowhood Ruth is the most detailed biblical narrative about widows. Their precarious position in the ancient world forms an important backdrop for understanding the challenges that Naomi and Ruth face. The legal status of widows in the Bible is unclear. On the one hand, they are shielded by biblical law. Levirate marriage is one of the ways in which a childless widow's place in society is reinstated so that she receives support for her needs (see "Levirate Marriage," below). The widowed Tamar, for instance, is sent back to her father's house to wait until her levir (her deceased husband's brother) reaches majority and provides her with a child (Gen. 38:11). Leviticus 22:13 provides paternal support for a priest's daughter if she is a childless widow (*'almanah*) or a divorcée.

But the Bible's frequent warnings against the oppression of widows (e.g., Exod. 22:21; Jer. 7:6; Zech. 7:10), the prophets' frequent demands to plead their cause (e.g., Isa. 1:17), and the gleaning provisions enjoined upon the community (Deut. 24:19–21) demonstrate that widows were generally at a great social disadvantage and needed economic and legal protection. Certain stories bear this out, as in the cases of the impoverished widow whom the prophet Elijah helps (1 Kings 17:10–16) and the widow whose children are about to be seized to pay her deceased husband's debts, but whom the prophet Elisha rescues (2 Kings 4:1–7). Some widows fare better than others, it seems, as does Abigail, the widow of the wealthy Nabal (1 Sam. 25:40–42), whom David woos and marries, but such instances seem to be the exception.

Jewish marriage contracts from Elephantine (fifth century B.C.E.) provide evidence that some legal and financial protection was offered to a widow by bequeathing to her, her husband's possessions as well, upon her husband's death. Thus we read: "If tomorrow or another day Ananiah should die, Tamut shall have power over all the goods which there may be between Anani and Tamut."[62] A second-century-C.E. Jewish marriage contract from the region of the Dead Sea likewise makes provision for the widow.

Here Babatha's husband guarantees: "If I go to my eternal home before you, you will dwell in my house and be provided for from my house and from my estate until the time that my heirs wish to give you your *ketubah* money" (lines 15–16).[63] Thus, extra-biblical sources indicate that some in Second Temple Jewish society were concerned about the vulnerability of widows and took measures to protect them.

Levirate Marriage

Levirate marriage refers to a union between a man and the childless widow of his deceased relative, arranged expressly for the purpose of producing a child. The English term "levir" comes from the Latin, meaning "brother-in-law." The Hebrew noun and verb for this act are forms of the root *y-b-m*. Levirate marriage (mentioned in Deut. 25:5–10) is a practice well attested in ancient cultures and even in some societies today (including ones in Africa and India).[64]

Levirate marriage has been normative in some Jewish communities until the modern era. Today this practice applies in certain Orthodox circles, where it is considered obligatory only if the brother is a bachelor—and is usually dissolved by means of the release ritual described in Deut. 25:5–10 and developed in Rabbinic law. Rabbinic sources refer to levirate marriage as *yibbum* and to the release from such a marriage as *ḥalitzah*. Levirate laws aim to regulate the transmission of family status, rights, and property upon the death of a childless married man and to "normalize" the status of his widow. In the Bible, the child of the union between a man and his deceased brother's widow provides a posthumous heir for the deceased and preserves the inheritance of the deceased for the widow and her child. This assures men in the society that their name and memory continue after death even if they did not have a child. In addition, the widow benefits because "the birth of a son improves her status, fulfills her obligations to her husband, and provides her with a source of support."[65]

Ancient Near Eastern sources and contemporary ones show that the specific possibilities and restrictions concerning levirate marriage differ from culture to culture around the world, reflecting countless variations. Different societies consider different male relatives as a qualified levir (in some, only a biological brother; in others any male relative within a larger kinship constellation).[66] Thus, according to Willis, a number of Hittite sources refer to levirate union as one of several ways to determine the status of a widow. Hittite Laws numbers 192–193 state that the responsibility falls to the deceased man's brother or (if there is no brother) to the father.[67] However, it is not clear whether this legislation is optional (he may marry) or obligatory (he must marry).[68] Middle Assyrian Laws number 30 refers to giving a childless widow to her brother-in-law or placing her under the care of a second son's father-in-law.[69] But it is not certain whether these conform to a definition of a levirate union.[70]

Studies show that different regulations apply to the woman's familial status, and expectations are different regarding the status of the offspring. For example, the widow in some societies may leave her husband's family and return to her former home; in others, she must remain with the deceased husband's family. In some, the union is permanent whereas in others it lasts only until the child is born. In some communities, either the widow or the brother can forgo the union; in others, it remains mandatory. In some, the child is reckoned as the deceased's offspring; whereas in others, he or she is considered the child of the biological father. Ideally, levirate marriage benefits the entire family and the larger community. After all, it repairs the break in the lines of continuity resulting from the man's death and secures the status of a childless widow. But it is also evident that this union can create certain tensions by imposing a burden on the levir or the widow or by uniting a couple who may not be suitable for each other. Moreover, there may be conflicts with incest taboos that have to be resolved.[71]

Whereas Rabbinic sources include lengthy discussions of levirate marriage (an entire Talmudic tractate, *Yevamot*, is devoted to it, and additional discussions appear elsewhere as well), the Bible provides only rudimentary evidence for how it was understood and practiced. Only two texts explicitly deal with a levirate obligation: the narrative in Genesis 38 and the law in Deut. 25:5–10. These texts deserve a close reading given the (problematic) tendency to interpret the marriage of Boaz and Ruth as an example of a levirate marriage. In what follows I examine these laws in order to show why they do not apply to the marriage of Boaz and Ruth.

Levirate Marriage in Genesis 38 The following is the account in Gen. 38:6–11:

> Judah got a wife for Er his first-born; her name was Tamar. But Er, Judah's first-born, was displeasing to the LORD, and the LORD took his life. Then Judah said to Onan, "Join with your brother's wife and do your duty by her as a brother-in-law [*yabem*], and provide offspring for your brother." But Onan, knowing that the seed would not count as his, let it go to waste whenever he joined with his brother's wife, so as not to provide offspring for his brother. What he did was displeasing to the LORD, and He took his life also. Then Judah said to his daughter-in-law Tamar, "Stay as a widow in your father's house until my son Shelah grows up"—for he thought, "He too might die like his brothers." So Tamar went to live in her father's house.

The expression: "do your duty by her as a brother-in-law" (Gen. 38:8) is expressed by a single word in Hebrew, *yabem,* the technical term for levirate marriage. Its meanings and consequences in this passage are fairly clear: to provide offspring for the deceased brother. Onan, the younger brother, accepts the responsibility of having sex with his sister-in-law but avoids providing her (and thus his dead brother) with a child. The narrator is explicit that Onan does not want his child to be credited to his brother. Upon his death, the responsibility falls to the youngest brother. Judah, however, fearing that Tamar is somehow the cause of his sons' deaths, avoids having his youngest son impregnate her. These details are important in showing how *yibbum* (the later technical term for levirate marriage) is construed in this text.

Gen. 38:6–11 makes it clear that the levir's child will be credited to his deceased brother. But things get muddled as the story progresses. Tamar waits in vain for Judah to fulfill his promise to give her his son. According to Gen. 38:12–30, Tamar then veils herself and places herself strategically in Judah's path. Thinking her a prostitute (*zonah*), Judah procures her services and unknowingly impregnates his own daughter-in-law. When confronted later with evidence that his daughter-in-law is carrying his own child, Judah declares her more righteous than himself (Gen. 38:26). This story concludes with the birth of twins, Perez and Zerah.

How is this story to be understood? Is this union between Judah and Tamar a levirate union or is it incest that is nonetheless justified? This uncertainty influences our interpretation of Ruth's marriage to Boaz. Some Rabbinic sages consider this sexual union a legitimate *yibbum* and use it as evidence to prove that other males in the family can undertake the role of a levir (in this case, a man's father). But this conclusion is questionable. First, the technical vocabulary of *y-b-m* is not employed in describing Tamar and Judah's relation. Moreover, the sons of Tamar and Judah are reckoned as Judah's, not Er's (Tamar's first husband).

When one assumes, as some do, that the union of Tamar and Judah is a version of levirate marriage recognized after the fact, then the door opens to considering Boaz and the other redeemer in Ruth 4 as qualified potential levirs. But such a strategy is problematic. It seems driven by apologetic goals, seeking to exculpate both Tamar and Judah from their violation of an incest taboo and to explain how Boaz can violate biblical prohibitions against Moabites (see Deut. 23; and "Intermarriage," "Conversion," and "The Status of the Moabites" below).[72]

Levirate Marriage in Deuteronomy Deuteronomy 25:5–10 offers the most detailed treatment of levirate marriage, or *yibbum:*

> When brothers dwell together and one of them dies and leaves no son, the wife of the deceased shall not be married to a stranger, outside the family. Her husband's brother [*yebhamah*] shall unite with her: he shall take her as his wife and perform the levir's duty [*yibemah*]. The first son that she bears shall be accounted to the dead brother, that his name may not be blotted out in Israel. But if the man does not want to marry his brother's widow [*yebhimto*], his brother's widow [*yebhimto*] shall appear before the elders in the gate and declare, "My husband's brother [*yebhami*] refuses to establish a name in Israel for his brother; he will not perform the duty of a levir [*yabemi*]." The elders of his town shall then summon him and talk to him. If he insists, saying, "I do not want to marry her," his brother's widow [*yebhimto*] shall go up to him in the presence of the elders, pull the sandal off his foot, spit in his face, and make this declaration: Thus shall be done to the man who will not build up his brother's house! And he shall go in Israel by the name of "the family of the unsandaled one."

The reference to brothers who live together unmistakably refers to a situation such as that of Judah's sons, who share the same father (Genesis 38) and presumably live on the same land. The words "her husband's brother" are a translation of the Hebrew noun consisting of the letters *y-b-m,* the same root letters that spell *yibemah,* the "levir's duty," that is, "to perform *yibbum* with her." Forms of this word appear seven times in this passage, referring to the deceased's brother, the widow, and the action to be taken. For our purpose, it is important to remember that the goal of this institution is to keep the widow in the family (25:5), so that the child will be reckoned as the deceased man's child ("to establish a name for his brother;" v. 7). It is also important to keep in mind that there exists a process of release from such a union, initiated at the discretion of the levir, but performed publicly by the widow through a ritual using a sandal.

Rabbinic tradition changes the practice of levirate marriage as described in Deuteronomy. The Talmudic tractate *Yevamot* establishes the parameters as to who may be a levir (only a brother who shares a father with the deceased), as well as the nature and extent of the union; it also examines many other elements in the laws. "The Mishnah states that after a man marries his brother's widow, 'she is like his wife in every way,' insisting that a levirate union operates like a 'regular' marriage. The children of the union are recognized as the children of the woman's new husband rather than of the deceased, *thus contravening the biblical view.*"[73] Further legal developments allow only an unmarried man to serve as a levir, in line with the establishment of monogamy as the norm among Ashkenazic Jews; a different pattern applied to Sephardic communities in Islamic countries. The Rabbis recognize the fact that these later laws differ from the biblical ones about levirate union. An awareness of the difference guards against interpreting the marriage of Boaz and Ruth in terms of postbiblical practices.

Levirate Marriage and Ruth Most ancient and modern interpreters, with Rashi as an important exception, have assumed that the marriage between Ruth and Boaz is a levirate union. They base their conclusion on Gen. 38 and Deut. 25:5–10, together with the scenes on the threshing floor (3:9) and at the gate (esp. 4:5,7–8,10).[74] Even though this conclusion has been widely accepted for a long time, it is increasingly difficult to support and is best relinquished.[75] Frederic Bush sums up the prevailing views of those who interpret the marriage of Ruth and Boaz as a levirate union: "in general almost all commentators have argued as follows: (1) Ruth 4:5, 10 show that Boaz's marriage to Ruth was a levirate type of marriage, similar at least to that prescribed in Deut 25:5–10.... (2) In 3:9 Ruth bases her request that Boaz accept the levirate marriage responsibilities on the fact that he is a...'redeemer.' (3).... Boaz uses the implications of the redeemer's double responsibilities of 'levirate' marriage to Ruth...to induce the unnamed גאל,...to cede those rights and responsibilities to him."[76]

Such interpreters understand Ruth's request in 3:9 as an overt or oblique reference to levirate marriage, claiming that Boaz counts as a "brother" even though he and Elimelech (Naomi's husband) are not sons of the same father (the Rabbis go on to identify him as her husband's first cousin; see Ruth R. 6.3). The argument then continues in reference to 4:5 where Boaz announces the acquisition of Ruth "so as to perpetuate the name of the deceased upon his estate." The Hebrew phrase *lehakim shem,* "to perpetuate the name," seems at first glance to be identical with the Hebrew describing the purpose of the levirate union in Deut. 25:7 (*lehakim...shem*), translated there as "establish the name."

However, the pervasive assumption that Ruth's marriage to Boaz represents a levirate marriage is nowadays challenged by a number of scholars, who base their arguments against this interpretation on the differences between how levirate marriage is depicted in Ruth and elsewhere in the Bible, and on the fact that the Book of Ruth does not refer to the union of Ruth and Boaz as a levirate marriage. The following are some of the central points of this alternative position:

1. The key word for levir or levirate marriage—a form of *y-b-m* or *yibbum*—is missing from the negotiations concerning this marriage of Boaz and Ruth.

2. Nothing indicates that Boaz is an actual brother of Mahlon or that there is an expectation that a distant kin act as a levir. The one time when levirate union plays a role in Ruth, it forms the backdrop to Naomi's plea to her daughters-in-law in 1:11–15. Naomi bemoans the fact that she is no longer able to produce husbands for the younger women (1:11–14). Explicitly, she refers to Orpah's relationship to Ruth by using the noun form of *y-b-m* (1:15; twice)—the technical term specific to levirate marriage; but in this case it means "sister-in-law." This is the only place this technical term appears in the Bible aside from Deut. 25:5–10 and Gen. 38:8. But here Naomi makes it very clear that a levirate union is impossible for her widowed daughters-in-law because no qualified levir exists or can be produced. She recognizes no potential levir in Bethlehem, which is why she urges them to return to their mothers' houses (1:8–13).

3. Ruth's one unambiguous request to Boaz on the threshing floor is redemption, not marriage. Any reference to matrimony is at best allusive. The redemption of land in the Bible never entails marriage with the widow whose land it is; and redemption of persons from slavery, likewise, does not entail marriage.[77]

4. The only two definite biblical examples of levirate marriage indicate that the offspring of such a union are reckoned as the deceased husband's child (Gen. 38:8–9 and Deut. 25:6). However, the son of Boaz and Ruth is reckoned in the book's genealogy as Boaz's son, not as the son of Elimelech (Naomi's husband) or Mahlon (Ruth's husband). In other words, he is not regarded as the child of a levirate marriage and does not perpetuate the name of the deceased.

5. Neither the narrator, Naomi, or Boaz refers to Boaz as a levir.

6. To complicate the situation further, the plain meaning of Boaz's public announcement regarding his acquisition of Ruth in 4:5 is uncertain. In particular, it is uncertain whether the unnamed redeemer is told that he has acquired Ruth—or will acquire her, when he redeems the land—or whether Boaz himself is acquiring Ruth. The interpretation depends upon whether one follows the written consonantal text (*ketiv*), *kaniti,* which seems to mean, "I will acquire" (namely I, Boaz) or whether one follows the Masoretic reading instructions (*kerey*), *kanita,* which means "you will acquire" (i.e., the other man). The latter would mean that the redeemer, as a redeemer, is obligated to take the widow, an expectation not connected with any biblical law of redemption. Because redemption, not levirate marriage, has been the only subject discussed by Ruth (3:9) and Boaz (3:10–13 and 4:3–5), and because nothing indicates that either the other redeemer or Boaz is a levir, Boaz's statement stands in tension with all known biblical laws.

7. The ritual that Boaz and the other potential redeemer enact to establish their agreement (4:7–8) differs from that mandated by Deut. 25:5–10. Many interpreters rely on the ritual of the sandal in Ruth 4:7–8 as proof that levirate marriage is in play in

Ruth as per Deut. 25:5–10. But the only connection between the ritual in Ruth 4:7–8 and the ritual in Deut. 25:5–10 is the mention of the sandal, which as Ruth 4:7 indicates, is used for establishing *any* contractual agreement. Ironically, then, the reference to a sandal thus negates a specific association with levirate marriage. In addition, the ceremony in Ruth decisively differs from that in Deut. 25:5–10. Ruth 4 does not include the role prescribed for the woman in Deuteronomy, namely, loosening the levir's shoe and shaming him in public. Furthermore, the deceased man's name is not preserved in the genealogy of Boaz and Ruth, as prescribed in Deuteronomy.

Despite all the compelling evidence against interpreting Ruth 3–4 as a levirate marriage, the Rabbinic sages, the Targum, and many modern commentators nonetheless conclude that the marriage in Ruth is a levirate marriage of sorts. The Rabbis seem motivated by the need to justify the book's blatant disregard of the prohibition concerning the Moabites, and by their wish to explain Boaz's words in 4:5. Some modern scholars, however, attempt to reconcile the differences between Ruth and the levirate unions in Genesis 38 and Deut. 25:5–10 by postulating an evolution in these laws over time. Based on a supposed early dating for Ruth, a few scholars propose that Ruth preserves a pre-monarchic tradition, with Genesis predating that tradition, and Deuteronomy following it, making it more restrictive.[78] Zevit, however, considers Ruth postexilic and proposes a different historical sequence: the Judah-Tamar story in Genesis 38 reflects a ninth- or eighth-century-B.C.E. perspective, whereas Deuteronomy 25 offers a seventh-century-B.C.E. perspective; and Ruth complements the Deuteronomic legislation.[79] For Zevit, Judah acts as a proxy, something conceivable in earlier periods of Israelite history. But Deuteronomy restricts the circle of potential redeemers, with the goal of keeping the property intact (rather than benefiting the widow). Robert Gordis likewise sees the law evolving, changing from Genesis 38, to Deut. 25:5–10, to Lev. 18:16 and 20:21, but considers something other than a levirate union in Ruth.[80]

Like the author of the present commentary, a number of modern scholars now conclude that Ruth is not about levirate marriage (these include R. G. Beattie, Gordis, and Sasson).[81] Bush offers a middle position: "Even though the obligation presumed had no legal standing and accorded no legal rights to the parties involved, . . . Ruth 4:5 clearly implies that a communally recognized *moral* obligation, a family responsibility, on the part of the next of kin *did* exist" (Bush's emphasis).[82] According to Bush, this communally sanctioned obligation accounts for Boaz's claim.

Although most Rabbinic texts approach the union between Boaz and Ruth as a form of levirate marriage (even though it does not meet the standards of Rabbinic laws), a few do not. Commenting on Naomi's disclosure that "Boaz is one of our redeeming kinsmen" (Ruth 2:20), Ibn Ezra differentiates between redemption here and levirate marriage. With this he avoids the conflation that typifies other interpretations. Rashi also indicates that he does not regard the union as a levirate marriage. In his comment on 3:9, he places certain words in Ruth's mouth, having her explain that if Boaz marries her, people will say: "There goes Mahlon's wife," whenever they see her in the field. Such declarations, according to Rashi, will serve to perpetuate the name of the deceased. Moreover, Rashi interjects into Boaz's speech in 4:5 a statement that

Ruth will not relinquish the field unless the redeemer marries her. These additions eliminate the need to construe Boaz's announcement as pertaining to levirate marriage; they also indicate that Rashi understood that levirate marriage was not being represented in chapters 3 and 4 of Ruth.

But if levirate marriage does not serve as the rationale for the union between Boaz and Ruth, why does Boaz marry Ruth? And why does he go about it in the complicated, confusing manner described in the book? The next section, "The Marriage of Boaz and Ruth," addresses this question.

The Marriage of Boaz and Ruth

Why does Boaz marry Ruth? He is surely under no legal obligation to do so. As Avivah Gottlieb Zornberg rightly notes, "in marrying Ruth, Boaz does not fulfill a law."[83] He marries Ruth not because he has to but because he wants to, because her acts of *ḥesed* and her virtues as "a fine woman" (*'eshet ḥayil,* in 3:11) have captivated him. These inspire him to act likewise. Earlier he had hoped that she would find shelter under God's wings (mentioning *kanaf,* "wing," *kenafav,* 2:12), meaning that God will secure her needs, but then she invites him to provide shelter for her, asking him to spread his wing (*kanaf*) over her (3:9). He had promised to redeem her but at the end also offers marriage, the best protection in the ancient world for a woman in Ruth's otherwise precarious position.

In 4:1–10 Boaz grandly introduces his intention to marry Ruth in a roundabout manner. Why? As we have seen, Boaz is not a levir required to marry a widowed kin; and as a redeemer he is, likewise, not obliged to marry the widow. But Boaz extends the responsibilities to widows beyond the expected practice and announces this in a complicated manner to circumvent a likely obstacle. That obstacle is Deut. 23:4, the directive to exclude Moabites from the congregation of Israel. In contrast to Ezra-Nehemiah, which prohibits marriage with foreign women, including Moabites (Ezra 9–10; Neh. 13:23–27), the Book of Ruth permits a Moabite woman to enter the community. To justify this apparent break with other biblical teachings, Boaz repeatedly insists that he is marrying Ruth to preserve the name of the deceased (Ruth 4:5 and 10), thus providing a moral counterweight to any objections to such a union.

Boaz thereby is portrayed as a man who does not unilaterally use his clout to brush aside communal norms. Rather, he shrewdly builds community support for his intentions by expanding the communally sanctioned tradition of the redeeming kinsman. Ruth's own admirable reputation (3:11) helps pave the way for such support. Although the people of Bethlehem hint at the irregular nature of the couple's union, referring in their blessing to the incestuous liaison of Judah and Tamar that produced Boaz's ancestor, Perez (4:12), they nonetheless affirm this new union (see Genesis 38 and the commentary on Ruth 4:12). The Book of Ruth thus models a process to make constructive change possible. The resulting marriage and the birth of David are products of this process.

Intermarriage

The story of Boaz and Ruth is the most fully depicted example in the Bible of the incorporation of a foreigner through marriage into the community. It raises the question of whether the book reflects a period in Israel's history when intermarriage was unproblematic or whether the work seeks to support intermarriage and define the processes or criteria that would legitimize such marriages in the face of competing positions. As Shaye J. D. Cohen notes, the Bible has no general prohibition against intermarriage.[84] It is the case that the preferred marriage pattern in the Bible is endogamy, namely, marriage with members from within the group. It is also the case that certain portions of the Tanakh explicitly oppose exogamous marriages, namely, marriage to an outsider. The most frequent marriage prohibition in the Bible concerns marrying the local Canaanites (see, e.g., Deut. 7:1–4). Yet, some other texts describe marriages with outsiders with no apparent objections, and a number of texts that frown on such marriages also recognize them as legitimate. The different traditions reflect changing social, geographical, and political circumstances. They can be construed, as well, as a part of the negotiation of norms when ideas about membership in the community had to be adjusted in light of developments such as exile and return.

The Bible includes examples of intermarriage contracted by leading figures, such as Abraham, who marries the Egyptian Hagar (Gen. 16:3); Joseph, who marries an Egyptian priest's daughter, Asenath (Gen. 41:45); Moses, who marries the Midianite Zipporah (Exod. 2:21); and Esther, who is married to the Persian King Ahasuerus. According to Cohen, the proscriptions of, and polemics against, all forms of intermarriage are postbiblical and emerge in the Hasmonean era (second century B.C.E.

In the early stages of Israel's history and also in some postbiblical sources, a person's identity was established according to the father's status. When a man married a non-Israelite, she may have remained a foreigner, but their offspring were reckoned as Israelites.[85] Consequently, Joseph and Asenath's sons become the eponyms of two major Israelite tribes, Ephraim and Manasseh, even though the mother (according to the Bible) is Egyptian. None of these marriages is presented as problematic. And although Miriam criticizes Moses in Numbers 12 on account of his Cushite wife, it is not clear to what extent his wife's foreignness is the cause of her criticism. The text indicates another reason for Aaron and Miriam's rebellion.

In contradistinction to these stories of tolerance for strangers, there are other stories in Genesis that show opposition to marrying local Canaanite women. For example, Abraham sends his servant to fetch a wife for Isaac from his own kin, categorically forbidding Isaac to marry the local inhabitants (Gen. 24:3–4). Isaac and Rebekah also object to Esau's marriages to Canaanite women (27:46–28:9). The story of the rape of Dinah (Jacob's daughter) in Genesis 34 begins with a negotiation for intermarriage between Canaanites and Israelites, but ends in making such a union impossible. According to the story, Dinah is raped by the local Canaanite prince Shechem who then wishes to keep her as his wife. His father approaches Dinah's family to make the arrangements and says, "My son Shechem longs for your daughter. Please give her to him in marriage. Intermarry with us: give your daughters to us, and take our daughters for yourselves..." (34:8–9).

Dinah's brothers pretend to agree but require that first all the males in the town of Shechem be circumcised. "Then we will give our daughters to you and take your daughters to ourselves; and we will dwell among you and become as one kindred." (34:15–16). When the men of the town comply, Dinah's brothers kill all the men and take Dinah back. Interpreters long regarded this gruesome story as a polemic against intermarriage with local inhabitants; although it describes potential criteria for an intermarriage (circumcision), it ultimately cancels that possibility.

The dangers of union with foreign women is also depicted in Numbers 25 and 31, which record the seduction of Israelite men who consort with Moabite (25:1) and Midianite (25:6) women when Israel is about to reach the promised land. As a result of this intermixing, the Israelites worship Baal, and God unleashes upon them severe punishments.

The strongest opposition to intermarriage in the Bible emerges in texts that present Israel as a people at risk, a vulnerable nation surrounded by more powerful populations. Many warnings against such marriages are found in Deuteronomy, which focuses in large measure on the Israelites' upcoming settlement of a land filled with foreign nations, whose practices pose a deadly threat to the people and faith of Israel. Deuteronomy 7 is a case in point. It describes Israel as "the smallest of nations," which is why God chose it (Deut. 7:7–8). This smallness is the reason given for God's demand that Israel, upon entering the land, should utterly destroy its Canaanite inhabitants. Israelites must "doom them to destruction: grant them no terms and give them no quarter. You shall not intermarry with them: do not give your daughters to their sons or take their daughters for your sons. For they will turn your children away from Me to worship other gods,..." (Deut. 7:2–4).

1 Kings depicts King Solomon as succumbing to such danger: "King Solomon loved many foreign women in addition to Pharaoh's daughter—Moabite, Ammonite, Edomite, Phoenician, and Hittite women, from the nations of which the Lord had said to the Israelites, 'None of you shall join them and none of them shall join you, lest they turn your heart away to follow their gods.'... and his wives turned his heart away" (1 Kings 11:1–3).

Deuteronomy 23:4–7, although not specifically addressing intermarriage, expresses the importance of excluding certain groups from the Israelite community: "No Ammonite or Moabite shall be admitted into the congregation of the Lord; none of their descendants, even in the tenth generation, shall ever be admitted into the congregation of the Lord... You shall never concern yourself with their welfare or benefit as long as you live" (Deut. 23:4–7).

Yet despite these harsh prohibitions against mixing with certain foreign peoples, there are also biblical passages that point in the opposite direction. For example, Deut. 21:10–14 describes a process by which a woman captured in war can become a wife of an Israelite man. Although the woman's ethnic identity is not specified, it can be supposed that she is non-Israelite and that the circumstances resemble those depicted in Numbers 31, when Midianite women are given to Israelite men as booty. And Deut. 23:8–9 follows the exclusion of Ammonites and Moabites by stating that offspring of Edomites and Egyptians (presumably with Israelite spouses) can be included in the third generation.

The question of intermarriage looms large in texts that depict Judah in the fifth-century B.C.E., when the Jewish people return from Babylonian exile after the destruction of the Temple in 586 B.C.E. The conditions of the fledgling, newly restored Jewish life in Judah are still precarious. The texts show that new religious and sociopolitical structures emerged to cope with changed circumstances: the vacuum left by the demise of an indigenous monarchy, the reality of Diaspora, the Israelis' status as a subject people in the vast Persian Empire, and the presence of other nationalities/ethnicities in the land. The struggle to define and maintain a distinct identity in the midst of a more diverse population made the question of legitimate citizenship a bone of contention.

Biblical sources indicate a lively internal community debate. Strongly opposing intermarriage are Ezra, the priest and scribe (Ezra 9–10), and Nehemiah, the Jewish governor of Judah and a contemporary of Ezra (Neh. 13:23–30). In an episode set in the fifth century B.C.E., Ezra concludes that unions with "foreign" women who are of "the people of the land" conflict with God's teachings and pose an imminent threat to the community's survival (Ezra 9:1–15);[86] in response to his exhortations, the community agrees to separate from foreign wives and the offspring of such marriages (Ezra 10). Later, Nehemiah chastises men who have married foreign women. He likewise focuses on the religious consequences of intermarriage, recalling that King Solomon deserted God on account of his foreign wives. But he also criticizes the fact that the children of such intermarriages speak the foreign languages of their mothers, and not Hebrew (*yehudit*); 13:23–24.[87]

In addition, according to Neh. 13:1–3, the reconstituted community that has now rededicated itself to the Torah applies Deut. 23:4–7 to itself and accordingly separates itself from all foreigners in its midst (not only Moabites). (Because this passage does not mention spouses, we can only infer its application to intermarriage.) These latter writings demonstrate the conviction that Israel's survival demands separation from other ethnicities and religions to maintain the integrity and the distinctiveness enjoined by the Torah and Israel's commitment to its God. It should be noted that the issue is not whether foreigners may or may not live with Jews, but rather whether they may be reckoned as members of the Jewish community. Indeed, it is precisely the difficulty of securing extensive independent physical space for Jewish life (both in the land and in the Diaspora) that undergirds the drive for creating a separate social and religious sphere.

Whereas Ezra 9–10 and Neh. 13 oppose intermarriage and any inclusion of "foreigners" in the community, another postexilic voice welcomes foreigners who seek to enter the community. Thus, Isa. 56:3–7 (also likely from the fifth or fourth century B.C.E.) promises the foreigner a venerable place in God's house.

Let not the foreigner say,
Who has attached himself to the LORD,
"The LORD will keep me apart from His people";
And let not the eunuch say, "I am a withered tree."
For thus said the LORD:. . . .
"As for the foreigners
Who attach themselves to the LORD,
To minister to Him,
And to love the name of the LORD,
To be His servants—
All who keep the sabbath and do not profane it,
And who hold fast to My covenant—
I will bring them to My sacred mount
And let them rejoice in My house of prayer.
Their burnt offerings and sacrifices
Shall be welcome on My altar;
For My House shall be called
A house of prayer for all peoples."

Although intermarriage is not the specific focus of this passage, it can be surmised that such enthusiastic acceptance of foreigners would include foreign-born spouses.

The marriage of Boaz and Ruth, then, is an example of intermarriage. This integration of a Moabite woman into a Judean household unfolds in a peaceful fashion, and the entire community welcomes her as a worthy heir to Israel's ancestral mothers (4:11).

Conversion

The question of conversion looms large in the interpretation of Ruth because the book illustrates the incorporation of a Moabite woman into the Judean community. The Rabbinic sages considered Ruth a convert. Yet, conversion as we know it today is a product of the Rabbinic world, which also set forth the terms and processes of conversion that are followed, although with some contemporary differences among the various movements within Judaism. To understand the issues as they unfold in the Ruth, we review here the relevant biblical material regarding membership in the community and assess its relation to the notion of conversion.

"Conversion" in the Biblical World In the earlier biblical world, a person's social identity was constructed and recognized by the following markers: father's (at times also mother's) name, place of origin and/or domicile (the two being the same in most agrarian societies in the ancient world), and the larger clan affiliation. The biblical *ben* (translated typically as "son of," or "offspring of," and in the plural inclusive of females as well) can be followed by a parent's name or place name (as in Ezra 2).

From biblical texts that depict the preexilic period, it appears that a woman joined her husband's household and was thereby absorbed into his community. This pattern corresponds to those of other ancient Near Eastern cultures. There was no expected protocol to mark a wife's changed ethnic status or social identity. As noted above, Joseph, Moses, and Solomon all married foreign wives. In Joseph's case, his sons with Asenath, his Egyptian wife, became eponyms for two of Israel's most prominent tribes: Ephraim and Manasseh.[88] After the Babylonian exile questions of individual identity became problematic, complicated by the emergence of Israelite and Judean diasporas, as well as by the presence of numerous nationalities in the provinces of Samaria and Judah. After the exile, where one was born no longer always corresponded to one's ethnic or social affiliation.

The multinational, ethnic, and cultural settings following the deportation and return of the population of Judah and the emergence of the Diaspora brought the issue of membership within the Jewish community to the fore and stimulated debates about exclusion and inclusion. As noted above ("Intermarriage"), several biblical books reflect this struggle for definition.

Cohen's extensive analysis of "becoming Jewish" in the ancient world offers an excellent summary of some of the issues.[89] According to him, the notion of conversion and the processes of conversion are essentially absent from the Hebrew Bible. Although priestly material (such as Leviticus) makes reference to the resident alien, the *ger* (often translated in later, postbiblical sources as "proselyte"), Cohen rightly concludes that in the Torah the *ger* is not considered a convert who is to be integrated into Israelite society.[90] Moreover, even though a number of foreigners or foreign-born persons did live among the Israelites, there is no indication that at some point they "converted" and blended with the Israelites. Furthermore, there appears to have been no formal way for them to make such a move.

Cohen himself dates the "harbingers of the idea of conversion in both its religious and cultural sense" to the Persian period (sixth to fourth centuries B.C.E.) when the changed circumstances gave rise to the idea that "gentiles could somehow attach themselves to the people of Israel by attaching themselves to Israel's God."[91] But he claims that conversion was not formalized until the Hellenistic era, around the second century B.C.E. Formal conversion, Cohen points out, is the product of centuries-long processes, and an innovation that "had already begun by the time of Ezra and Nehemiah was well under way by the time of the Maccabees and was substantially complete by the time of the Talmud." It is only in the second century B.C.E. that the idea takes root. The Hellenistic book of Judith is one that explicitly—or nearly so—describes a person who actively joins the people Israel by means of a ritual (Jth. 14:10; see also 2 Macc. 9:13–17, where this idea is contemplated).

Cohen's analysis of "becoming Jewish" establishes important guidelines for reflecting on what is called conversion and its place in the ancient world. However, his insights and conclusions about the process and its dating must be modified to shed light on the dynamics in Ruth. It remains the case (as Cohen argues) that the Hebrew Bible, with the possible exception of Ruth, shows very little evidence that what the Rabbis later call "conversion" was an option. However, the issue was brought to the fore earlier than Cohen supposes. Ezra 9–10, Nehemiah 13, and Isaiah 56 are more than mere "harbingers" (as Cohen claims). Rather, the fifth century, as depicted in these texts, already reflects the heated debate about membership. This crisis forces the question of Jewish identity in a new way, and the various postexilic responses are competing strategies for dealing with the new question. Furthermore, whereas the *ger* is not to be construed as a convert, the idea of becoming a Jew is explicit in Esther—another narrative set in the Persian period—when non-Jews *mityahadim,* that is, "professed to be Jews" (Esth. 8:17); a more literal translation would be "made themselves into Jews."[92]

These debates in the texts indicate that there was not as yet a process in place by which such tensions about communal boundaries could be adjudicated. The Book of Ruth may be a response to such a dilemma about foreigners' relations to Jews and an illustration of how to address the problem.

If, as Cohen argues, formal conversion does not come into play until the second century B.C.E. and if Ruth is dated to the Persian period or earlier, how are we to understand Ruth's status in the book? Neil Glover's study of ethnicity in postexilic texts offers a possible explanation.[93] He reviews three basic views about ethnic identity that anthropologists (specifically ethnologists) identify in cultures: (1) a view that allows a person to unilaterally choose an identity, in which case Ruth's words in 1:16–17 could constitute a "conversion"; (2) a "constructive" view of ethnicity that supposes that biological descent is not always necessary for ethnic belonging and that constructs specific criteria for membership; and (3) the view that ethnicity is immutable and therefore excludes the possibility of changed ethnic identity,[94] in which case Ruth could never erase her Moabite "gene," as it were.

According to Glover, the Book of Ruth reflects the middle position: that ethnicity is mutable. Ruth becomes a member of the Judean community by undergoing stages of assimilation into the community. She begins as a Moabite and remains so for most of the book. Her "Moabiteness" is highlighted by the narrator (1:22; 2:2, 21) and by Boaz (4:5; 4:10). This epithet characterizes her long after she proclaims her commitment to Naomi, Naomi's people, and Naomi's God—an act that many interpret as a conversion (Ruth 1:16–17). But despite retaining her Moabite marker, the book also charts her journey through specific stages whereby her initial pledge is gradually affirmed by others—by Boaz, by the people of Bethlehem, and finally, by God. In this process, Ruth's unilateral pledge is but a first step. Her declaration requires others' response.

Boaz first affirms her decision when he generously welcomes her—a foreigner, as she indicates (2:10)—because she has chosen to come under God's protecting wings (2:12). Next Boaz affirms Ruth's well-known reputation as an *'eshet ḥayil* "a fine woman" (3:11) and the legitimate wife of a deceased Judean man. The elders and people's blessings in 4:11–12 signal their collective acceptance of her as a member of their community, joining her to the matriarchs Rachel and Leah (4:11). Finally, her pregnancy testifies to God's approbation, as we can infer from the unique phrasing in 4:13: "The LORD let her conceive" or more literally, "YHWH gave her pregnancy." This phrase is unique to Ruth and more directly implicates God in her pregnancy than is true of other biblical birth accounts (where God typically remembers a woman and she conceives, as with Sarah in Gen. 21:1–2). It should be noted that Ruth's pregnancy is the only action in the book that the narrator attributes directly to God, a detail that highlights God's validation of Ruth's union with Boaz. Most significantly, the very last time that she is named, in 4:13, Ruth is no longer labeled as a Moabite.

However we understand Ruth's social status, her story functions as a counterpoint to the negative attitude toward Moabite and other foreign women in the biblical accounts in Ezra-Nehemiah. In its own biblical context, then, the Book of Ruth exemplifies a way that a Moabite woman can marry a Judean and join the community, despite what we read in Deut. 23. Rabbinic sources will seek a basis for reconciling explicitly the tension between Ruth's place in the Jewish community and Deut. 23:4–7 regarding Moabites.

Rabbinic Views of Intermarriage and Conversion in Response to Ruth Prohibition of intermarriage does not appear in the Mishnah,[95] but later Rabbinic texts are concerned with the subject and approach it in different ways. Many early Rabbinic texts typically presume that foreign wives of biblical figures have converted to the religion of Israel. Consequently, not only do they propose that Joseph's Egyptian wife, Asenath, is a daughter of Dinah, adopted by an Egyptian couple, but they also claim that she undergoes a formal conversion because of her attraction to Joseph.[96] As for an Israelite soldier's marriage to a beautiful captive, discussed in Deut. 21:13, Targum Jonathan adds that the foreign woman has to follow conversion ritual in accordance with Rabbinic procedures.

Usually, the Babylonian Talmud considers the biblical prohibition against intermarriage as applicable only to the seven Canaanite nations that Deuteronomy 23 mentions. Yet, although the Talmud seems to recognize that the Bible is not a definitive source for the general prohibition against intermarriage, some Rabbinic sages nonetheless do read Deuteronomy 7 as a general prohibition against marrying *all* gentiles, and the issue continues to be debated by medieval scholars.[97]

The Rabbinic sages consider Deut. 23:3–6—the ban against admitting Moabites and Ammonites into the Israelite community—to be a prohibition against marrying them, but they debate the prohibition's application to the Book of Ruth and to the circumstances of their own time. The sages get around the biblical exclusion of Moabites in Deut. 23:4 by means of two strategies. One is to claim that the law applies only to Moabite men. They point out that the collective noun, translated as "the Moabite," *mo'avi,* refers strictly to a Moabite man; according to this view, the noun does not refer to Moabite women (a Moabite woman would be *mo'aviah,* or as the Rabbis render it, *mo'avit*) and thus does not exclude such women from the community. A second Rabbinic strategy, sometimes combined with the first, is to claim that Ruth converted, either prior to marrying Mahlon or through her declaration to Naomi in Ruth 1:16–17. The Targum (like a number of Rabbinic sources) embed these verses as Ruth's responses to Naomi's instructions in the Book of Ruth (the italics represent the biblical verses):

> But Ruth said: "*Do not urge me to leave you, to turn back and not follow you,* for I desire to become a proselyte." Said Naomi: "We are commanded to keep the Sabbaths and holidays, not to walk more than two thousand cubits." Said Ruth: "*Wherever you go I will go.*" Said Naomi: "We are commanded not to spend the night together with non-Jews." Said Ruth: "*Wherever you lodge I will lodge.*" Said Naomi: "We are commanded to keep six hundred thirteen commandments." Said Ruth: "That which your people keep, that I shall keep, as though they had been my people before this." Said Naomi: "We are commanded not to worship idols." Said Ruth: "*Your God . . . my God.*"

Although this procedure does not conform to the subsequent Rabbinic ritual of conversion, it is nonetheless invoked as evidence of Ruth's conversion to Judaism.

Pesikta de-Rav Kahana, a midrashic work from the sixth century C.E., is one of several Rabbinic texts that deal with Ruth's conversion by asserting that Moabite women may convert (unlike Moabite men). More specifically, it acknowledges that limiting the exclusion in Deut. 23:3–6 solely to Moabite men is a Rabbinic revision of the consequence of the original Mosaic law. According to the midrash, Boaz explains to Ruth when they meet in the field (in 2:11): "Had you come a short time ago, we could not have accepted you as a proselyte because the new interpretation of the law concerning proselytes had not yet been established, the new interpretation being as follows: 'A . . . Moabite man may not marry an Israelite woman, but a Moabite woman [who had been converted] may marry an Israelite.'"[98] The issue of Ruth's conversion appears in the Talmud in a debate about David's qualifications raised by his enemy Doeg the Edomite; the sages retort that the halakhah (legal ruling) permits marriage with Moabite women (B. Yev. 76b–77a), and Ruth Rabbah reiterates, in the case of a different challenge, God's specific choice of David (1 Sam. 16:12) as further proof of his qualification (Ruth R. 8.3). But other situations as well prompt the Rabbinic sages to discuss the notion of the "righteous proselyte," *ger tzedek*, who is to be welcomed and guided, with virtuous Ruth as a model (see, e.g., Ruth R. 2.12).

The Status of the Moabites

The repeated references to Ruth as a Moabite call attention to her origins, obliging us to assess what messages the book seeks to convey.

Moab was a territory east of the Dead Sea, in the southern part of what is today the country of Jordan. It was a state that emerged approximately at the same time as the kingdom of Israel. Biblical and extrabiblical sources concur that Israelites and Moabites were culturally related. The large Mesha Stone, discovered in Jordan in 1868, preserves a thirty-four-line inscription in Moabite from the ninth century B.C.E. that illustrates the linguistic similarities between paleo-Hebrew and Moabite, both in terms of script and vocabulary.

According to Gen. 19:30–37, Moabites are the descendants of Abraham's nephew Lot. Yet, despite this relation to Abraham, the predominant perception of Moabites in the Bible is negative. There are, however, exceptions, and one is evident in the Book of Ruth. Another major exception is 1 Sam. 22:3–4, recounting how David, while a fugitive from King Saul's wrath, sends his parents to the king of Moab to secure their safety. (The Rabbis, therefore, hold that Ruth was in fact the daughter of the king of Moab. See, e.g., the Targum to Ruth 1:4.)

Genesis 19:30–37 traces the origin of the Moabites to the incest between Lot and his older daughter, following the destruction of Sodom. Presuming that no other men are still alive, Lot's two daughters get their father drunk in order to produce a child through him. Lot's older daughter names her son Moab, *mo'abh*—a pun on *mei'abh*, "from a father"—a name that identifies the boy's origin. (The son of the other daughter is the ancestor of the Ammonites, Moab's neighbors to the north and the other nation also closely related to Israel.)

According to Numbers 21–22, the king of Moab seeks to destroy the Israelites in the wilderness; and in Num. 25:1, Israelite men profane themselves with Moabite women just as the Israelites are about to enter the land. As a result of this shameful history, the Moabites are denounced. In Deuteronomy the Moabites are specifically excluded from the Israelite community in a passage especially relevant to the Book of Ruth:

> No Ammonite or Moabite shall be admitted into the congregation of the LORD; none of their descendants, even in the tenth generation, shall ever be admitted into the congregation of the LORD, because they did not meet you with food and water on your journey after you left Egypt, and because they hired Balaam son of Beor, from Pethor of Aram-naharaim, to curse you.—But the LORD your God refused to heed Balaam; instead, the LORD your God turned the curse into a blessing for you, for the LORD your God loves you.—You shall never concern yourself with their welfare or benefit as long as you live. (Deut. 23:4–7)

With Ruth in mind, the Rabbinic sages interpreted the passage as applying solely to males (see Ruth R. 2.9), which is a problematic solution given that the singular "Moabite" often serves as a collective noun referring to an entire people, as does Israel. In B. Yev. 77a an additional explanation is offered: because the exclusion results from the Moabites' refusal to welcome the Israelites with bread and water, it must refer to the men only; no one would have expected Moabite women to bring bread and water. But some Rabbinic sources acknowledge that this ingenious interpretation is likely to be a late innovation. So, for example, in Pesikta de-Rav Kahana, Boaz assures Ruth that she is fortunate to have come when she did, because the halakhah only recently determined that the Deuteronomic ban refers only to Moabite men (PdRK, Nachamu 16.1). Despite this later Rabbinic view, it is almost certainly the case that Deuteronomy 23 excludes from community membership the children of a union between Israelites and Ammonites or Moabites. This law bears directly on the status of the descendants of Boaz and Ruth, on David's status in particular.

Interestingly, Deuteronomy also preserves a different tradition about the Moabites, in which the Moabites welcome the Israelites during their wilderness trek (Deut. 2:26–29). The coexistence of competing traditions suggests that the debate about Moabite status was already embedded within Deuteronomy and reflects different hands or changes in attitudes over time.

In the Prophets and Writings, Israel fights with Moab on a number of occasions (e.g., see Judg. 11). Other wars with Moab are recorded in 2 Kings 3 and 13, and several prophets castigate Moab for its treatment of Israel, especially when Judah was under attack; these texts forecast Moab's doom (Isa. 14, Jer. 48, Zeph. 2). In addition, 2 Chron. 24:26 implicates the sons of two Moabite mothers in the coup against the Judean king Joash.

These contradictory references complicate interpreting the Book of Ruth. The fact that Ruth herself is repeatedly introduced as a Moabite, even when that information does not seem necessary for identification (1:4,22; 2:2,6,21; 4:5,10), underscores the importance of her Moabite status in the book. The ancient readers of Ruth would have been familiar with the largely negative picture of Moabites in the Bible and with their exclusion from the community (according to Deut. 23). Therefore, it is logical that Ruth's Moabite status would have been regarded as a problem, even though no pejorative reference to Moabites appears in the book. The complex route that Boaz takes before announcing his marriage to Ruth (4:10) can be understood as a response to this problem. His references to establishing the name of the deceased may serve to justify and legitimize his marriage to a Moabite. Some Jewish sources understand Ruth's conversion and her "return" (as per 1:22) as a mending of the history of animosity between Israel and Moab.[99]

Ḥesed

In her notes for this commentary, Tikva Frymer-Kensky devoted considerable thought to the issue of *ḥesed* as it plays out in the Bible and in the story of Ruth. The section immediately below, "*Ḥesed* in the Bible," is an edited version of her longer essay on the subject. The subsequent section, "*Ḥesed* in Ruth," like the rest of this introduction, is by Tamara Cohn Eskenazi.

***Ḥesed* in the Bible** *Ḥesed* is an important concept in the Bible and plays a key role in Ruth, where it explicitly describes the actions of Ruth and of God (Ruth 1:8; 2:20; 3:10). Often translated as "lovingkindness," *ḥesed* refers to acts of benevolence that one does out of kindness, not out of any obligation. Yet despite its ostensibly selfless nature, a particular act of goodness, or *ḥesed,* often sets up an expectation of reciprocation, and this may be the reason for one's own benevolent action; the first action can set off a chain of good deeds. *Ḥesed* can also be applied to the benevolent payback for past favors. Thus, David sends messengers to the people of Jabesh-Gilead to tell them that he wishes to do good things for them because they performed a great *ḥesed* for Saul in burying him (2 Sam. 1:5–6). David also mentions *ḥesed* in his "last will and testament": he charges Solomon to show the sons of Barzillai *ḥesed* by supporting them financially because they sided with David when he fled before Absalom (1 Kings 2:7).

Ḥesed sometimes entails forgiveness. The Israelite practice of *ḥesed* is assumed in 1 Kings 2:31, where the Arameans tell their king that Israel's kings are known as kings of *ḥesed* because they will forgive those enemies who show true repentance. *Ḥesed* most often describes God's actions (see Ps. 136, which mentions God's *ḥesed* twenty-six times). In surveying the Bible, we see that divine *ḥesed* can spring from unmerited generosity that typically generates a chain of goodwill. Normally, such divine favor is expressed in a formal promise that God makes to heroes and their descendants. God performs *ḥesed* for Abraham (Gen. 24:12,26) and for Jacob (Gen. 32:11), and Deuteronomy explains that God has also taken an oath to perform *ḥesed* for the ancestors (Deut. 7:12). God later performs an act of great *ḥesed* for David in granting him a dynastic heir (1 Kings 3:5) and will always do *ḥesed* for his descendants (Ps. 62:13).

Although God in the Bible is depicted both as rewarding and punishing people according to their actions, we more often see the merciful face of God acting in Israel's history. According to the Ten Commandments, God performs acts of *ḥesed* toward God's adherents for a thousand generations (Exod. 20:6, Deut. 7:9, and Jer. 32:18). In the divine bookkeeping of *ḥesed,* God can reckon acts of *ḥesed* accumulated over thousands of generations as sufficient to overwhelm any bad deeds, and thus bring forgiveness instead of punishment (Num. 14:18–19). God's unique relationship with Israel, and especially with David, continually infuses benevolence into the historical chain of events (even if such beneficence has not been earned by the human chain of *ḥesed*).

Ḥesed might seem self-contradictory. On the one hand, God is said to have *ḥesed* "because you requite for each person according to his deeds" (Ps. 62:13), and the psalmist associates *ḥesed* with justice: "you love righteousness and justice, your *ḥesed* fills the earth" (Ps. 33:5). On the other hand, God will always perform good acts for the Davidic house, whether or not David's descendants deserve it (2 Sam. 22:51), and Moses invokes *ḥesed* to prevent God from giving Israel the punishment that they justly deserve (Num. 14:19). But this seeming contradiction actually conveys a profound message. The greatest act of benevolence God can do for us is to give us a sense that there is justice in the world, that there is some degree of predictability, and therefore that we can control our fate (at least to some extent) by controlling how we treat each other and how we act toward God. Yet, sometimes we don't want justice because we have acted unjustly. Rather, we want compassion—we want to be forgiven, or to have our broken deeds fixed. In these moments, true benevolence chooses to suspend justice. It is as if *ḥesed* has cumulative force: one good deed provokes another and another, and each adds goodness to the world. Benevolence toward others and toward the world generates good acts even when they are not earned, and it certainly demands good acts when they are. But sometimes this force weakens and even fades away. Then, both we and God need to forget about the idea of measure for measure and simply perform good deeds—acts of random lovingkindness.

Ḥesed in Ruth According to R. Zeira (Ruth R. 2.14), Ruth was written to teach about *ḥesed* and its rewards. Maimonides[100] defines *ḥesed* as "good deeds [performed] for one toward whom you have no obligation."[101] This sense of kindness and generosity beyond the call of duty goes to the heart of Ruth. The narrative exemplifies what *ḥesed* looks like and also advances the view that *ḥesed*, when cultivated, is contagious and transformative. In Ruth, *ḥesed* has a domino effect, moving the story from death and despair to the renewal of life and hope.

The term *ḥesed* appears only three times in the book (1:8; 2:20, and 3:10), but its meaning is woven into the book's entire fabric. When still in Moab, Naomi is the widow, the poor, and the stranger. In refusing to abandon Naomi, Ruth embodies *ḥesed* (1:8; 1:16–17). Ruth's loyalty to her mother-in-law inspires wealthy Boaz, who extends generosity toward Ruth, stretching himself beyond the call of duty (2:8–12). The domino effect continues: Naomi, enlivened by Ruth's success with Boaz, regains hope and takes responsibility for Ruth's welfare (3:1–4). At the threshing floor, Ruth draws Boaz toward his better self by urging him to undertake the role of redeemer (3:9–10). As a result, Boaz extends the circle of *ḥesed* into the public arena (4:1–10), linking redemption of the land to the redeemer's responsibility for the widows and their deceased husbands. Then, going even further beyond the redeemer's call of duty, he marries Ruth, taking the fullest responsibility for her. The circle of *ḥesed* reaches its fullness when the entire community blesses their union (4:11–12).

Ḥesed in Ruth is not so much a case of good people doing good things, but rather an example of how ordinary people with mixed motives become extraordinary through the cultivation of *ḥesed*. Indeed, neither Naomi nor Boaz begin as exemplary figures. Naomi seems ambivalent about Ruth (see, e.g., comments at 1:21 and "annoyed" at 2:22); and Boaz offers some charity at first, but takes no responsibility for Ruth. It is Ruth's well-placed acts of *ḥesed* that nurture their potential to go further. If the book was written (as many scholars suppose) to counter the exclusionary laws against Moabites (Deut. 23:4 and Ezra-Nehemiah; see "Conversion" and "Intermarriage," above), then the *ḥesed* exemplified in Ruth generates a "conspiracy of goodness,"[102] which finds an honorable way to welcome the stranger. Although *ḥesed* in Ruth is explicitly ascribed to human beings, the text suggests that those who act with *ḥesed* mirror the ways of God, serving as agents of God's *ḥesed* through their deeds of kindness.

The Theology of the Book of Ruth

As Rachel Adler observes, *ḥesed* and blessings are gifts that even the destitute can bestow.[103] The theology of Ruth illustrates the power of blessings and *ḥesed* to transform futility into fertility and despair into hope. However, because God is such a pervasive presence in the blessings that people bestow on each other here, it is easy to overlook the fact that God acts only once in the book, and only at the end (4:13). Until that point, God is known only through hearsay (1:6) or is invoked in speeches when people bless or bemoan their fate (1:20–21). This pattern has its own theological significance (see below).

With one exception, God is construed as a purveyor of *ḥesed* and a bestower of abundance. The exception is Naomi's complaint that God's hand is against her (1:13, 20–21). Elsewhere in the book, however, the numerous references to God portray God as a source of well-being who rewards good deeds (1:8–9; 2:12). People thank God for good fortune (Naomi in 2:19–20; the women in 4:14) and bless each other in God's name (as Boaz blesses Ruth for her *ḥesed* in 3:10), or they invoke God's name in oaths of commitment (Ruth in 1:17 and Boaz in 3:13).

Boaz marries Ruth, and then "the LORD let her conceive, and she bore a son" (4:13). The expression *va-yitten lah herayon,* "let her conceive," literally God "gave her pregnancy," is unique. Although God plays a role in several important birth narratives elsewhere in the Bible, God's role is never depicted quite this directly. The case of Sarah is more typical: "The LORD took note of Sarah as He had promised, and the LORD did for Sarah as He had spoken. Sarah conceived and bore a son" (Gen. 21:1–2). The unique phrasing in Ruth credits God with more than the usual role in conception, as if to signal divine approval.

This single reference to God's action at the end of the book throws into sharper relief the vital roles played by human beings in transforming famine and despair into abundance and hope. Although Naomi hears a rumor in Moab that God has given Israel sustenance (1:6), as the story unfolds we learn that the abundance she receives comes to her through human generosity: Ruth brings food to Naomi after gleaning in the field (2:17–18), and when Boaz offers a gift of grain (3:17). This narrative pattern typifies this book: what one person wishes for another comes to fruition principally through the actions of the well-wisher. Thus, although people frequently invoke God's intercession, it is they who actually intercede in setting things right. As Frymer-Kensky observes, "the characters in Book of Ruth themselves act to fulfill the blessing that they bestow on one another in God's name."[104]

Other examples of this are even more readily discernible: Naomi wishes that God would help her daughters-in-law find security, or a home (*menuḥah*), with a new husband (1:9). Yet it is Naomi herself who acts to make such security or a home (*manoaḥ*) possible for Ruth by urging her to approach Boaz at night (3:1–4). Similarly, when Boaz meets Ruth, he invokes God's blessings on her as a reward for what she has done for her mother-in-law (2:12); at that point he expresses the hope that she will find shelter under God's wings. And it is such words that Ruth later pronounces to Boaz when she asks him to take her under his wings (see "robe" in 3:9). Indeed, Boaz rewards Ruth when he first meets her and ultimately provides shelter for her through marriage.

The protagonists' references to God's *ḥesed* (1:8; 2:20) or care (4:14) in the book are then an activating agent in and of themselves. Alicia Ostriker writes: "God's kindness, invoked by human beings, is also enacted by them. To put it another way, the kindness of human beings reveals the kindness of a God."[105] Or, as Hubbard has it: God "acts through human agents . . . when people act with *ḥesed*, God is acting in them."[106]

Although other biblical books explicitly enjoin Israel to emulate God (e.g., Lev. 19:2), Ruth seems to say more: it is almost as if human actions and words bring God into the world. God-centered people prompt God to show up, as it were. This bold theological view is made explicit in Pesikta de-Rav Kahana, which daringly represents Boaz's actions as a role model for God. It has God exclaim: "Boaz comforts! Will I not comfort?!"[107] At the very least, God expects people to do their part in "repairing the world": "Boaz did his [part], and Ruth did hers, and Naomi did hers; [then] the Holy One said: 'I too will do mine.'"[108]

The book seems to teach that the capacities and actions initially projected upon God by the book's protagonists, in turn, empower people to emulate God. It helps them sustain one another through their blessings and wisdom, enabling them to act in God's stead. Human happiness and success are essentially the consequence of such personal actions in response to presumed divine providence. And it is only when people have taken care of one another that God intervenes.

Yet when we consider some of the book's ambiguities, we discern an even more complex theology at play. For in a book so elegantly and carefully crafted, it is indeed surprising that so many striking ambiguities remain, often occurring at key moments in the narrative. The most glaring ones are in 3:9, when Ruth either proposes marriage or simply asks for Boaz's protection; and in 4:5, when Boaz either expects the unnamed redeemer to take Ruth or announces his own intention to do so. Other ambiguities concern the role of God in the unfolding events. For example, to what extent is God responsible for the deaths of Elimelech and his sons? Do the famine and the deaths of these men signal sin and punishment (as the Rabbinic sages conclude)? If so, why doesn't the book explicitly state this theological point?

What about the meeting between Boaz and Ruth? Is the phrase *va-yikker mikreha* ("as luck would have it") in 2:3 a hint of God's providence, as is the case with a related term in Gen. 24:12? Or is it simply an indication of coincidence, as is true with the related term in 1 Sam. 6:9? As noted later in the commentary on this verse, biblical sources support either position (see comment at 2:3). Ruth's narrator leaves these questions unanswered.

As Hayyim Angel shows, these textual ambiguities render the book and its protagonists more complex and evocative.[109] Such complexity shows that the book is not simply an idealized representation of an idyllic world. Furthermore, as Angel also points out, midrashic interpretations of Ruth, by ramifying the different possibilities suggested by these ambiguities, make ambiguities even more visible. Ruth's distinctive narrative technique has profound implications; its textual ambiguities hold significant theological import. With God's role in the narrative as ambiguous, the text (with one exception in 4:13) provides the interpreter no authoritative confirmation of divine intercession. Affirming God's presence is a hermeneutical stance rather than a given fact.

Such a narrative technique, coupled with granting God active agency only at the end, expresses a profound and audacious theology. Elsewhere in biblical narrative, the narrator regularly vouches for God's presence in the unfolding human drama. Virtually every "God said," beginning with Gen. 1:3, is such an attestation, as are the countless situations in which God acts. The exceptions are found in Esther, where God is never even mentioned; and in Ezra-Nehemiah, which, like Ruth, restricts God's direct appearances in the text (Ezra 1:1,5; 7:6). But Ruth goes one step further than Ezra-Nehemiah in hiding God's face in the text. Whereas in the latter, God operates behind the scenes, such explicit confirmation is absent in Ruth until the very end.[110]

The central question one may ask is: What are we to believe or do in a world where God's presence is not self-evident? If we view Ruth against the historical backdrop of Judges, this question becomes even more pointed: What are we to do in a world pervaded by chaos and violence? In answer to these questions, Ruth delineates a theology of *ḥesed*—generosity that goes beyond the call of duty. Human *ḥesed,* when rightly cultivated "for the sake of heaven" (in its later Rabbinic formulation), serves as a real power for good even when—perhaps especially when—God's presence is not otherwise discernible.

In Ruth, it is human beings who bring God into the world, depending upon how they choose to interpret the texts of their lives. So, too, readers are invited to make interpretive choices when responding to the book or to the moral ambiguities in their own lives. Ruth's narrator would have readers weigh in on the side of *ḥesed.*

Redemption in the Bible

Redemption in the Bible refers to the obligation to rehabilitate destitute relatives in their time of need. It also pertains to restoring property or persons to their original or better condition. The subject of redemption is more prominent in Ruth than in any other biblical book. Writing about Ruth, Ostriker observes that in Ruth, the term redemption "signifies responsibility and accountability; . . . and there is obviously both a practical and a spiritual dimension to the term. The root *g-ʾ-l* (redeem) occurs twenty-one times in the story, always referring to human beings as redeemers, but no reader would fail to connect the term with the familiar epithet for God, *goʾel Yisraʾel*, the redeemer of Israel."[111]

God as redeemer looms large in the Bible. Referring to the forthcoming exodus from Egypt, God instructs Moses to tell the Israelites that "I will free you from the labors of the Egyptians and deliver you from their bondage. I will redeem you with an outstretched arm and through extraordinary chastisements" (Exod. 6:6). God as Israel's redeemer secures Israel's well-being and safety and avenges its abuse at the hands of the enemy: "Thus said the LORD, Your Redeemer, the Holy One of Israel: For your sake I send to Babylon; I will bring down all her bars" (Isa. 43:14). But God also redeems worthy individuals from oppression. According to Ps. 72:13–14, God "cares about the poor and the needy; He brings the needy deliverance. He redeems them from fraud and lawlessness." Therefore, says the Psalmist elsewhere, "'Praise the LORD, for He is good; His steadfast love is eternal!' Thus let the redeemed of the LORD say, those He redeemed from adversity" (107:1–2). In Gen. 48:16, Jacob sums up what redeeming persons might mean when he invokes "The Angel who has redeemed me from all harm" to bless his grandchildren. Redemption thus couples rescue from dire circumstances with bestowing blessing.

Biblical laws require that Israelites act as redeemers for relatives in four situations:

1. Redemption of land (Lev. 25:25–34). When circumstances force one to give up land, relatives must regain the land for the family if they are able. Thus Leviticus instructs: "If your kinsman is in straits and has to sell part of his holding, his nearest redeemer shall come and redeem what his kinsman has sold" (25:25). If no redeemer is available, the land reverts to its original owner in the jubilee year (25:28).[112]

2. Redemption of persons from slavery (see esp. Lev. 25:47–50). Israelites are obliged to restore to freedom fellow Israelites sold into slavery. In this context, Leviticus lists the kinship chain of those expected to help: "One of his kinsmen shall redeem him, or his uncle or his uncle's son shall redeem him, or anyone of his family who is of his own flesh shall redeem him" (25:48–49). The term "family" (*mishpaḥah*) here refers to the clan, a larger kinship unit than modern Hebrew usage implies. The basic point seems to be that whoever can undertake the task, should, with responsibility falling first on the nearest relative. Redemption, then, is not restricted only to the nearest kin. (One notes that the sons are not listed, presumably because they are accounted for with the needy head of the household.)

3. Redemption of objects dedicated to the sanctuary (Lev. 27:9–28). Here *ga'al*, "to redeem," something means to restore an object to its original owner, although the unredeemed state is not a degraded one. Here also it describes the act of reappropriation—as the term is meant in Leviticus 25.

4. Avenging the blood of a murdered relative (Num. 35). The assigned avenger is called "blood-avenger" (*go'el ha-dam*; see, e.g., 35:19).

The overriding notion of redemption in these four categories of redemption laws is responsibility for a needy relative. This expectation is confirmed in biblical narratives when land or persons are forfeited, even if the term "redeem" does not appear. In 2 Kings 4:1, a widow cries out because her children are about to become slaves to cover her husband's debts. In Neh. 5:1–5, the people complain that their fields and their children are being seized to cover their debts. The term "redemption" is not mentioned in either case, but the expectation of help is nonetheless assumed.

Redemption of land is integral to one other narrative: Jeremiah 32. Here Jeremiah relates how his cousin requested that Jeremiah acquire from him the family land because he, Jeremiah, had "the duty of redemption" (Jer. 32:8). The story is set in the time when Jerusalem was already under Babylonians siege, and the cousin may want to liquidate assets so he can leave the city.[113] Jeremiah ceremoniously complies (Jer. 32:7–12). The root *k-n-h*, "acquire," is used throughout this episode and likewise in Ruth 4:4 and 4:10.

The common denominator regarding redemption, the responsibility of relatives to protect more vulnerable members of the (extended) family, takes many forms. As Shlomo Bahar observes, the protection can have physical, economic, or spiritual dimensions.[114] This broader sense of the redeemer as a helper in times of distress, coupled with responsibility for restoring family property, best explains the meaning of the term in Ruth.

Redemption in Ruth Forms of the Hebrew root *g-ʾ-l,* "redeem," appear in Ruth proportionately more often than elsewhere in the Bible: twenty-one times in Ruth's four chapters, compared to twenty-one times in the twenty-seven chapters of Leviticus and twenty-five times in the sixty-six chapters of Isaiah.

Naomi first identifies Boaz as "one of our redeeming kinsmen" (2:20). Ruth refers to this role when she approaches Boaz at midnight with a request for support based on his role as "a redeeming kinsman" (*go'el*; 3:9), and Boaz responds by declaring "I will act as a redeemer for you" (3:13). The last mention of a redeemer comes from the women of Bethlehem, who identify Ruth's son as Naomi's redeemer and offer what can be regarded as a definition of the redeemer's role within this book. The child (say the women) is a God-granted redeemer who renews her life and will sustain Naomi in her old age (4:17). As Ostriker observes (see above), the reader cannot fail to connect such references to the redeemer in Ruth with God's own acts on behalf of the vulnerable (2:20; 3:10; 4:17).

Boaz undertakes the role of redeemer in public by first framing it in terms of redeeming land. He announces that Naomi is selling (or has sold) a portion of the family land and invites a closer, unnamed relative to step up to this role and take responsibility for the land (4:3–4).

In Ruth 4, the status of this land is not altogether clear (see "Inheritance" above). Boaz describes it as belonging to Elimelech, but now Naomi is the seller. Did she inherit it when Elimelech died? Or when their sons died ten years later? Does Ruth, as Mahlon's widow, also own the land? The narrator does not resolve these ambiguities, focusing instead on the interaction: the unnamed relative first agrees to redeem the land. But the land is not all that Boaz has in mind; he also introduces responsibility for the widow(s), and for the deceased husband(s), whose memory is to be preserved (4:5–6).[115]

After the unnamed relative declines to redeem, Boaz announces his marriage to Ruth. Such an extension of the notion of redemption to include marriage exceeds expectations and provides utmost security for an otherwise marginalized person, by integrating her fully into the household in the most respectable fashion. Although marriage is not elsewhere demanded in the Bible in conjunction with redemption, marriage as a metaphor for God's redemptive actions on Israel's behalf is integral to some prophetic writings, expressed, for example, in Isa. 54:5, where God is husband and redeemer. For readers of the Bible, these associations play in the background, alluding to the larger significance of the redemption of the land and the redemption of Ruth. The blessings that the community bestows on the union of Boaz and Ruth, together with the genealogy at the end, show how redemption—in the sense of restoration to well-being—expands to embrace the nation as a whole.

Pre-modern Rabbinic Interpretations

> R. Zeira said: This [Ruth] scroll tells us nothing of ritual purity or defilement, of prohibition or permission. For what purpose was it written? To teach you how great is the reward of those who dispense *ḥesed.* (Ruth R. 2.15)

The *ḥesed* that permeates the Book of Ruth also serves as a leitmotif of pre-modern Rabbinic interpretations of the book. The sages perceive God's loving presence throughout the book. With rare exception, they view Naomi, Boaz, and especially Ruth as exemplars above reproach, motivated by the noblest principles, imbued with generosity and lovingkindness.

Ruth is a model of loyalty, piety, *ḥesed,* and modesty, a veritable "woman of valor," an *ʾeshet ḥayil*, as depicted in Prov. 31:10–31. The Rabbis consider her virtues and her decision to become a proselyte all the more praiseworthy, given her Moabite origin. According to the Midrash, she and Naomi arrive in Bethlehem the very day that Boaz's wife dies. Ruth is said to be forty years old when she marries Boaz (Ruth R. 6.1), but she lives a long life according to the sages. (The Talmud [B. BB 91a] reads 1 Kings 2:19 not as a reference to Bathsheba, King Solomon's mother, but as a veiled reference to "'the mother of royalty'—this is Ruth." If this were the case, Ruth would have lived to see her great-great-grandson.)

Naomi, likewise, is generous and righteous as Ruth's mentor in spiritual and practical matters. The sages sympathize greatly with Naomi's dire predicament, her loss, and her suffering; they also credit her with converting Ruth. In addition, she receives praise for helping to make possible the birth of Israel's King David, whose royal line will culminate in the Messiah.

In Rabbinic sources, Boaz (identified as Ibzan of Judg. 12 in B. BB 91a) is a learned and pious man. His judgment is so respected that his saluting the workers in God's name (Ruth 2:4) is approved by the earthly and heavenly courts (B. Mak. 23b). According to Rabbinic sources, he is eighty when he marries Ruth, and his advanced age may account for his reluctance to court Ruth until she reaches out to him. When she does, he undertakes responsibility for her with alacrity and blesses her, prophetically bestowing upon her the gift of grain, which symbolizes the pious descendants who will issue from her, including David, Daniel, and the Messiah (B. Sanh. 93a).

Rabbinic literature about Ruth is virtually inexhaustible. Despite R. Zeira's claim that Ruth is meant primarily to teach us about *ḥesed*, the Rabbis derive many important legal and theological teachings from the book, most obviously the criteria and process of conversion. The summary below offers only representative examples of how traditional sources handle six topics that are prominent in these sources:

1. The deaths of men in Ruth
2. The names and genealogies
3. The Jewish status of Ruth as a convert
4. The meeting between Ruth and Boaz on the threshing floor
5. Why and how Boaz marries Ruth
6. The relation and relevance to King David

The first entries in the section below focus on what the Targum, the Talmud, and Ruth Rabbah say about these matters; the second group of entries includes additional interpretations from later commentators and Rabbinic collections on Ruth.

The Book of Ruth in the Targum, the Talmud, and in Ruth Rabbah[116]

THE DEATHS OF MEN IN RUTH

The unexplained deaths of Elimelech, Mahlon, and Chilion in the first verses of Ruth become a touchstone of complex theologies and debates in Rabbinic literature. Presuming a justifiable cause for these deaths, Rabbinic sages impute various sins to Elimelech and his sons. They conclude that Elimelech must have been a leading figure in Bethlehem, and his migration to Moab during the famine demoralized others who regarded him as a role model. The sages also claim that he possessed sufficient resources to assist the people of his town but was stingy and deserted them in the time of their need (Ruth R. 1.6), leaving the land when it was still possible to survive (B. BB 91a) and forcing his family to leave as well.

As for the sons, the sources disagree about whether their wives, Ruth and Orpah, had converted prior to their marriage. According to the Targum on Ruth 1:4, the sons died because they transgressed God's word by marrying Moabite women. This is also the conclusion of R. Meir in Ruth R. 2.9, who adds that the marriages took place prior to the halakhah (legal ruling) that made such marriages permissible (see "The Jewish Status of Ruth as a Convert," below). Other sources suppose a conversion of the wives prior to marriage and blame the deaths on the sons' decision to remain in Moab instead of returning to the Land of Israel.

THE NAMES AND GENEALOGIES

The names in the book prompt Rabbinic interest as sources of theological and ethical meanings. Word associations serve to uncover explanations for otherwise thorny problems, such as the inexplicable death of Elimelech and Naomi's sons. Elimelech's and Naomi's names are the most self-evident. Elimelech means "My God is king." Yet in Ruth R. 2.5, Rabbi Meir criticizes Elimelech, reading his name as a shameful boast: "to me—[*elai* instead of *eli*]—will come royalty." Naomi's name, related to the word "pleasant," prompts the sages to explain that her actions were pleasing (Ruth R. 2.5).

The sons' unusual names provoke a range of interpretations. One son is named Mahlon, from *ḥ-l-l,* "to profane," because they both profaned their bodies; the other is named Chilion, from *k-l-h,* "to destroy," for they deserved destruction. Another interpretation is that their names forecast their fates: Mahlon and Chilion were "wiped out and disappeared from the world" (B. BB 91a; Ruth R. 2.5). Mahlon is also said to derive from *maḥalah* or *ḥalah,* words that refer to illness. The Rabbis identify the sons also with Joash and Saraph in 1 Chron. 4:22, who both married Moabites and whose names mean despair (*ye'ush*) and burning (*seraph,* burnt) (B. BB 91b), for they despaired of the Land of Israel and burnt (i.e., destroyed) the Torah (by marrying Moabites).

According to the Rabbis, Orpah is derived from *oreph,* meaning the back of the neck, for she turned her back on Naomi (Ruth R. 2.9). She is identified as the ancestor of Goliath, whom David—great-grandson of Ruth—later slays (B. Sot. 42b).[117]

The name of Ruth is more complicated because it lacks an obvious etymology. Some sources connect Ruth's name with *revayah,* the Hebrew term for saturation (B. Ber. 7b). "Why was she named Ruth?" ask the Rabbis. "Because from her came David, who satiated (*ravvah* or *rivvah,* from *r-w-t*) the Holy One with songs and praises" (B. BB 14b). Elsewhere Ruth's name is said to reflect the fact that she considered well (*ra'atah,* lit. "saw") the words of her mother-in-law (Ruth R. 2.9).

Boaz's name is taken to refer to strength (*'oz*). Some Rabbis suppose that Elimelech's nearer kin, called So-and-So in 4:1, was named Tov (good), based on 3:13: *'im yig'aleikh tov,* which NJPS, like most translations, renders as "if he will act as a redeemer, good [*tov*]!" (Ruth R. 6.3). The Rabbis claim that Naomi's and Boaz's fathers were brothers (B. BB 91a) and that Boaz was a nephew of Elimelech. As for Ruth, she and Orpah were sisters, descendants from Eglon the king of Moab, mentioned in Joshua 10 and Judges 3 (see the Targum of Ruth 1:4 and B. Sanh. 105b).

The mention of six measures of barley in Ruth 3:15 is interpreted by the sages as symbolizing six righteous descendants for Ruth: Daniel and his three friends, and most importantly, David and the Messiah (see Targum of 3:15). Ruth R. 7.2 includes kings Hezekiah and Josiah and counts the three friends of Daniel as one, also ascribing six virtues to each of the six descendants.

THE JEWISH STATUS OF RUTH AS A CONVERT

The Rabbinic sages regard Ruth as a righteous proselyte, but debate the when and how of her conversion. Most Rabbinic sources take Ruth's declaration of loyalty to be a response to Naomi's specific instructions, and as part of her conversion (for details, see "Intermarriage" and "Conversion," above and the commentary on 1:16–17).

What most concerns the Rabbis about Ruth's conversion is her status as a Moabite. They are keen to establish that this status does not exclude her from becoming a legitimate Israelite. According to Rabbinic interpretation, Deut. 23:4 excludes from the congregation only Moabite *men*, not Moabite *women*. For if Ruth's status as an Israelite is questionable, so is the legitimacy of her descendant David as a king of Israel.

The issue comes up, for example, in B. Yev. 76b–77a, when the Edomite Doeg says, "Instead of inquiring whether [David] is fit to be king or not, inquire instead whether he is permitted to enter the assembly or not!" What is the reason? "Because he descended from Ruth the Moabite." The Rabbinic sage Raba then reports the tradition that the *bet din* (court of law) of the prophet Samuel decreed that Deut. 23:4 solely excludes a Moabite man (*mo'avi*), not a Moabite woman (*mo'avit*). And Raba confirms the authority of Samuel's ruling, clarifying that the prohibition in Deut. 23:4 condemns Moabites because they did not come with provisions when they met the Israelites who approached Moab from the wilderness (Deut. 23:5). Since Moabite women were not expected to meet the Israelites, the condemnation does not apply to them, and they are not excluded from the community of Israel. Ruth Rabbah 7.10 and other sources make clear that the sages considered this interpretation of Deut. 23:5 as late: the earlier biblical sense of Deut. 23:4 (excluding both Moabite women and men) was altered to allow Moabite women to join the community. The sages, therefore, refer to the new teaching as a renewed or reinstated (*nitḥaddeshah,* "made new") halakhah (Ruth R. 4.1). According to the Rabbis, not everyone in Ruth's time was aware of this new halakhah.

B. Yevamot 48b claims that Ruth converted when young, but other sources debate this claim. Ruth Rabbah 2.9 maintains that Mahlon and Chilion did not convert their wives prior to marriage. However, Rabbinic sources concur that whatever Ruth's actions vis-à-vis conversion prior to her marriage with Mahlon, she undergoes a legitimate and binding conversion when she later vows loyalty to Naomi (Ruth 1:16–17). According to Ruth R., Ruth insists that it would be a sin to reject her wish to become a Jew (Ruth R. 2.22). The Targum, in particular, repeatedly mentions Ruth's conversion (1:16; 2:6, 11; 3:10).

THE MEETING BETWEEN RUTH AND BOAZ ON THE THRESHING FLOOR

In Ruth 3:1–5, Naomi tells Ruth to wash and dress up, then to visit Boaz at night at the threshing floor, approach him alone (after he eats and drinks), and lie at his feet. The Rabbis ponder: How could Naomi propose the secretive, nighttime encounter between Boaz and Ruth on the threshing floor? What did Ruth actually do? And what exactly transpired between Boaz and Ruth when they spent the night together (3:6–14)? There is a consensus that Naomi's instructions to Ruth transgress the accepted norms. But the sages emphasize the purity of the goal and the piety of the protagonists, which render the instructions excusable and even laudable.

Some introduce modesty into Naomi's instructions that Ruth groom herself before approaching Boaz (3:1–4). Thus, Ruth R. 5.12 has Naomi refer to cleansing from idolatry (not adorning oneself to attract a man); however, the Targum (3:3), in contrast, mentions perfumes and donning jewelry. The Targum and other sources (e.g., Ruth R. 6.1) insist that Boaz responded to the tempting presence of a woman at his feet at midnight with the utmost restraint: he struggled mightily with his *yetzer hara* (evil inclination), just as Joseph did when tempted by Potiphar's wife (Gen. 39:7–13); and like Paltiel (2 Sam. 3:13–16), who (according to the sages) placed a knife between himself and his wife Michal because he regarded her as still married to David. Ruth Rabbah 6.4 compares Boaz also with David, who restrained himself from killing his adversary, Saul.

The sages in Ruth Rabbah only briefly refer to Ruth's request in 3:9 but offer a very long digression on Boaz's instructions that Ruth "stay the night" (3:13). These include anecdotes in which reality and appearance clash (Ruth R. 7.4). The section concludes by reiterating that Boaz successfully resisted temptation, a topic mentioned elsewhere as well (Ruth R. 4.4; 4.6; 7.1).

WHY AND HOW BOAZ MARRIES RUTH

Ambiguities in the biblical account of the marriage between Boaz and Ruth result from uncertainty about what Ruth specifically asks of Boaz on the threshing floor (3:9), and, even more, from Boaz's statement in 4:5. These ambiguities offer Rabbinic sages ample opportunities to fill in the gaps.

The Targum disambiguates Ruth's request at the threshing floor and says that she boldly asks Boaz to marry her: "Let your name be called over your maidservant, by taking me to wife, inasmuch as you are a redeemer" (3:9). In response, Boaz acknowledges her status as a proselyte and praises her for seeking out a levir (3:9). In rendering the account at the city gate, the Targum has Boaz state explicitly that the redeemer must undertake the role of a levir and marry Ruth when acquiring the land (*ḥayav... leyabama*), using the technical term for levirate union, *y-b-m* (4:5). Ruth Rabbah also supposes a marriage proposal but contrasts Ruth's decency and modesty with the crude demand of Potiphar's wife, who tries to seduce Joseph in Gen. 39:7 (Ruth R. 6.1). (For the extensive dialogue between Ruth and Boaz that the Rabbis develop, see the commentary on Ruth 3:8–9.)

Ruth Rabbah and other sources consider the entire proceedings that lead to the marriage to be guided by God's providence. Thus, commenting on 4:1, Ruth R. 7.7 states in the name of two illustrious rabbis, R. Eliezer and R. Joshua, that "Boaz did his [part], and Ruth did hers, and Naomi did hers; [then] the Holy One said, 'I too will do mine!'" (Ruth R. 7.7). Such providence accounts for the fortuitous appearance of the kin whom Boaz is seeking to challenge. In addition, such divine providence lends authority to the legal proceedings that follow.

Ruth Rabbah also takes advantage of the ambiguity of the verb "acquire," which appears in the Hebrew text in two forms, *kerey* (*kanita,* "you acquire[d]") and *ketiv* (*kaniti,* "I acquired[d]"). On the one hand, reading "you acquire(d)," it maintains that Boaz announces that the redeemer has to marry Ruth, and that the man refuses because of her Moabite status (7.7 and 7.10). But, on the other hand, it uses the written form, "I acquire(d)" as Boaz's hint to the other man that Ruth is designated for Boaz, a hint that the other man honors and consequently clears the path for Boaz (Ruth R. 7.10; see commentary at 4:5).

THE RELATION AND RELEVANCE TO KING DAVID

David plays an important role in Rabbinic interpretations of Ruth: as a king in his own time, as a composer of Psalms, and as the forerunner of the Messiah. Ruth herself is celebrated as "mother of royalty," and the story is interpreted as proof of David's legitimacy (see B. Yev. 76b and Ruth R. 8.1).

Later Jewish Interpretations

Similar concerns and opinions continue in subsequent Jewish writing about the Book of Ruth. What follows are some additional or different perspectives in later Jewish sources.

MIDRASH RUTH ZUTA (probably tenth century). This short midrash, which follows the biblical book closely with relatively few digressions, highlights its focus on comforting the poor. Ruth Zuta begins by connecting Ruth to Shavuot and states that the Torah was given only to, or through, those who are poor and suffering. Elaborating on Naomi's complaint about returning empty from Moab (1:20), it has Naomi speak at length about the fate of the impoverished pious person. Similarly, Boaz reassures Ruth that "you see yourself as poor, but one will come from you who will dedicate a hundred thousand gold talents in one day" (Ruth Z. 2.2 on Ruth 2:13).

The midrash adds telling details to the unadorned portraits of the biblical characters. Ruth is cast as a most pious proselyte, and the midrash emphasizes God's special love for the proselyte (Ruth Z. 1.30 on Ruth 1:12). Ruth's pledge to Naomi (Ruth 1:16–17), depicted here, as in other midrashic sources, as a series of responses to Naomi's instructions, reveals Ruth's respect for Israel's sexual mores. Her reverence and devotion are repeatedly extolled. Midrash Zuta affirms Ruth's origin as a king's daughter (perhaps to underscore her sacrifice in accepting poverty). The midrash associates the name of Ruth's first husband, Mahlon, with *m-ḥ-l,* "to absolve," an indication that he was indeed worthy of Ruth (Ruth Z. 1.7). As for Naomi, Ruth Zuta highlights some ambivalence: "Why did Naomi urge them to return? So as not to be ashamed on their account, for they were recognizable by their clothing" (Ruth Z. 1:24–25 on Ruth 1:8).

Orpah does not fare well in this midrash. In contrast to her fortunate sister-in-law, she is violated once she leaves Naomi (Ruth Z. 1.34). Boaz dies on his wedding night (Ruth Z. on Ruth 4:13), apparently to account for why Naomi, not Boaz, raises his son (as Ruth 4:14 implies).

SALMON BEN YEROḤAM AND YEFET BEN ALI (tenth century). An extensive commentary on Ruth, attributed by some to Salmon and by others to his younger contemporary Yefet ben Ali,[118] reflects a distinctive approach that is characteristic of the Karaites. Karaites are Jews, especially prominent in the eighth to eleventh centuries, who do not accept the Rabbinic "oral Torah" but rely primarily on the Hebrew Bible as the source of legal ruling. They interpret the Bible by focusing on the straightforward or plain (*peshat*) meaning of the text, with an eye to its historical setting.

This Ruth commentary explicitly opposes a number of Rabbinic interpretations of the biblical book. But like some Rabbinic sources, it concludes that the story of Ruth teaches us how much God cherishes those of humble beginning, including male and female converts. It also praises the value of righteousness and wisdom above nobility of pedigree, most likely as an extension of the Karaites' conflict with the competing Rabbinic authorities.[119]

The commentator is an astute grammarian. His analysis of the verb *teʿagenah* ("debar" in 1:13), for example, adds several possible meanings of this troublesome term: including Rabbinic interpretations. He suggests that the word could also be rendered as "grieving women," or as a reference to "tying oneself" (e.g., Naomi could be saying "would you tie yourselves to my sons?"). The commentator, however, castigates Rabbinic interpretation of levirate marriage. Writing further on 1:13, he continues: "Know that the rabbinates, the ignoramuses, think that this is evidence for us that the duty of levirate marriage applies to two actual brothers, since it is said, 'Have I yet sons in my womb?' But this is wrong, for even the Sages allow levirate marriage only when the brothers were alive at the same time, and not in the cases of the brother who 'was not in his world,' and here . . . it is a rhetorical language."[120] Furthermore, the commentator, in discussing 4:10, uses several pages to argue that levirate marriage *excludes* (!) actual biological brothers (born to the same father).

RASHI (R. Shlomo Yitzḥaki; 1040–1105). Rashi, the most influential of the medieval commentators, distills Rabbinic traditions but adds his own distinct perspective. Presupposing that Naomi converts Ruth, he cites in his commentary (to Ruth 1:16–17) the midrash in which Ruth's pledge responds to Naomi's instructions. Yet Rashi does not place as much emphasis on Ruth's conversion as do the Rabbinic sages. Significantly, he departs from Rabbinic traditions in how he understands the marriage of Boaz and Ruth. For him, their union is not a case of levirate marriage or even redemption. Rather, Boaz marries Ruth because she asks him to when she requests that he redeem the family land (see at 3:9). According to Rashi, Ruth also explains to Boaz that their marriage will perpetuate her deceased husband's name because when people see her on Mahlon's land, they will say: "There goes Mahlon's wife." Boaz agrees to marry her. But Ruth is still not satisfied. In response to Boaz's promise to be her champion, she retorts (according to Rashi on 3:13): "You dismiss me with words!" Boaz then confirms his commitment with an oath.

R. ABRAHAM IBN EZRA (ca. 1092–1167). Among the most laconic of the medieval commentators and noted for his grammatical precision, Ibn Ezra nonetheless reproduces a number of midrashim on Ruth, such as homilies on the names of Mahlon and Chilion (1:2). He considers it inconceivable that Naomi's sons would have married their Moabite wives unless the women had first converted. Ibn Ezra distinguishes between redemption and levirate marriage (see his comment on 2:20) and supposes that Naomi's goal in sending Ruth to the threshing floor is to obtain a husband for her (3:1). As for Ruth's intent during that incident, he understands her words "Spread your robe over your handmaid" (3:9) as only intimating to Boaz (not explicitly stating) that he take her as his wife.

BARTENURA (R. Ovadia ben Abraham, ca. 1450–1509). R. Ovadiah, commonly called Bartenura (after the name of his birthplace), interprets the entire Book of Ruth in light of a messianic subtext. Bartenura's long commentary presents the book as an allegory about the relationship between God and Israel. Living as he did during the traumatic expulsion of the Jews from Spain (1492), a time of fervent messianic longing, Bartenura portrays Ruth as giving hope to the Jewish exiles and explaining their destiny among the nations. Although not entirely consistent in how he correlates the characters in Ruth allegorically, Bartenura follows midrashic tradition in interpolating within the Ruth narrative certain verses from the vast repertoire of Jewish texts. In his hands, these intertextual links validate his allegory, thereby "proving" that redemption is near but cautioning against human efforts to bring it about.

In Bartenura's allegorical reading, everything in Ruth is a coded teaching about the messianic age and the redemption of Israel. Boaz is a manifestation of God as "might" (*beʿoz*), who will ultimately bring redemption. However, until that redemption comes, whatever blessings Israel experiences are mediated through the other nations (this is how he interprets the marriage with Moabite women in Ruth 1:4). Naomi symbolizes Israel, living among the nations and influenced by them. Ruth the Moabite likewise symbolizes Israel in its present exile, oppressed among the nations, all the while anticipating these other nations' transformation. The bread that Ruth receives from Boaz while still a foreigner (2:14) suffices to slake her hunger, but it is bitter, dipped in vinegar, because she is still in exile, *galut*. Soon, however, she will taste the sweet milk and honey of her new homeland.

Bartenura depicts the drama at the threshing floor as the unfolding love story between God and Israel (Ruth 3:9–14). As Israel (Ruth) and God (Boaz) lie together, talking intimately like husband and wife, God promises to redeem Israel, delighted that she prefers his help to that of human heroes (the biblical judges). During this lovers' conversation, God describes for his beloved two types of redemption: one generated by Israel's merit; the other initiated by God for God's own sake. The first type of redemption corresponds to the negotiations between the unnamed redeemer and Boaz (Ruth 4). Such human acts, which Bartenura equates with the ill-fated second-century rebellion of Bar Kochba (spelled here Ben Kosiba, a name that implies deception or disappointment), are costly and ineffectual. In the biblical story of Ruth, the nearer relative of Elimelech renounces his role, protesting, "I cannot redeem it . . . lest I impair my estate" (4:6). This estate (in Bartenura) is Israel herself. Boaz, in contrast, represents the divinely orchestrated redemption, which though requiring greater patience, promises greater reward: the complete redemption of Israel. Boaz's acquisition of Elimelech's inheritance (4:10) represents God's full reclamation of Israel, the promise of redemption from exile and from the control of the nations. Until such future time, Israel is better off following the example of Ruth (in Ruth 1:16–17), pledging herself faithfully to God.

ZOHAR ḤADASH (1597). This kabbalistic collection, comprised of sayings assembled by R. Avraham Ha-Levi Berukhim, includes a specific short commentary on Ruth. Much of its homiletic material does not pertain directly to the story of Ruth; but when it does, it is generally focused on David and his lineage. Indeed, here R. Yossi bar Kosma and R. Eliezer ben Joseph claim that the scroll was written expressly to establish David's lineage (on Ruth 1:4). Zohar Ḥadash is kinder to Elimelech than other sources, explaining that Elimelech left the Land of Israel because he wanted to distance himself from his wicked generation. Yet though "Elimelech did not sin," R. Joshua declares that he nonetheless "departed from the community; the community's merit, therefore, did not protect him; when the people of Bethlehem were remembered by God, he was not included in their redemption" (61a). Mahlon is also treated more sympathetically. Zohar Ḥadash derives Mahlon's name from the root *m-ḥ-l,* as if it meant "to forgive or absolve from wrong deeds," because he helped his father, Elimelech (61a). Boaz is named after the Temple's pillar of the same name, which he resembles, being one of the pillars of the world (66a).

According to this midrash, Ruth acquires her name only when she joins the family of Mahlon. Ruth herself is compared to a turtledove, fit (*kasher*) for the altar, hence able to join the people Israel. On account of her merits, states Zohar Ḥadash, it was established that Deut. 23:4 excludes only Ammonite and Moabite males. The rabbis in Zohar Hadash disagree as to whether Ruth was converted by Mahlon, or only later, by Naomi. The discussion concludes with the view that though Mahlon did convert Ruth for the sake of marriage, the conversion was rather superficial; it is only with Naomi that Ruth genuinely and fully attaches (*dabhka*) herself to her mother-in-law and to the Torah (62a and 64a).[121]

R. MOSHE ALSHEIKH (also Alshech, Alshekh, Alshich; 1508–1593).[122] This prolific commentator adds a number of distinct interpretations to the story of Ruth. He comments that according to some sources, Naomi's husband and sons (Ruth 1:1–4) died because they did not pray for the welfare of others. Alsheikh highlights the various problems caused by Ruth's Moabite status: Naomi is ashamed to contact Boaz because she has brought a forbidden Moabite to Judah (2:1). Boaz's assistant insults Ruth, implying that Moabite women are indecent and forbidden to Israelites (2:6–7), which is why Boaz tries to comfort her (2:8). Boaz goes to the city gate to inquire whether marriage with a Moabite is permitted in this case (4:1). Alsheikh also makes the controversial nature of the union between Boaz and Ruth more transparent; he adds to the blessings bestowed upon Boaz and Ruth in the biblical account—"May the LORD make the woman who is coming into your house like Rachel and Leah" (4:11)—the following words: "even though she is a Moabite." For Alsheikh, Ruth's final words in 3:17, reporting to Naomi that Boaz has given Naomi a gift of grain, are meant to reassure Naomi that Ruth's marriage to Boaz will not distance the two women, for Boaz cares about Naomi's welfare.

Contemporary Readings

For centuries the Book of Ruth has been admired principally for its charm. Ruth's impassioned pledge ("Wherever you go, I will go . . .") has been repeated in countless wedding and conversion ceremonies. When the book is read on Shavuot, its spiritual messages are emphasized. Because Shavuot first and foremost celebrates the giving of the Torah at Sinai, Ruth is thereby inextricably linked with this foundational moment in Jewish history, bestowing even greater religious significance to its messages (see "Ruth and Shavuot," above). In the wake of the contemporary women's movement, new dimensions of the Ruth narrative have come to the fore. First, Ruth has been claimed as an important source for understanding women's lives in the past and for empowering women in the present.

Judith A. Kates and Gail Twersky Reimer aptly characterize Ruth's appeal to contemporary readers interested in women's concerns:

> So many experiences, qualities, dilemmas, and traditional issues of concern to women surface in this text. Its central figures are women, its central story (or stories) is relationship. It tells the story of marriage and childbirth, of widowhood and childlessness from within women's experience... It focuses on the experience of being "other"—the other as foreigner and the other as woman. It addresses the problems of women's powerlessness and vulnerability in a man's world and illustrates the power generated when women mobilize their resources.[123]

But what began primarily as a feminist reevaluation of Ruth soon expanded into a broader appreciation of the book. Interpreters have widened their inquiry, focusing on new cultural, intellectual, and practical arenas of concern to women and men alike, such as questions of identity, community, and ethics. The book came to be recognized as a spiritual source for contemporary women and men and as a sophisticated contribution to understanding the dynamics of class, gender, and ethnicity, both in the past and the present. Whereas earlier studies emphasized the book's harmonious portrait of biblical life, contemporary writings point to the challenges the book poses to biblical norms and stereotypes, and see it as a model of change and hope.

Surveying the Landscape Although contemporary readers have access to several excellent scholarly commentaries on Ruth in English, only a few (typically slim ones) present a singularly Jewish perspective on the book. The most widely used non-Jewish commentaries include Edward Campbell's *Ruth: A New Translation with Introduction and Commentary*, Jack M. Sasson's *Ruth: A New Translation with a Philological Commentary and a Formalist-Folklorist Interpretation*, Robert Hubbard Jr.'s *The Book of Ruth,* and Frederic Bush's *Ruth/Esther.* The last work stands out as the most thorough. Bush, professor emeritus in Old Testament at Fuller Theological Seminary, investigates linguistic issues in depth (such as assessing whether the Hebrew in Ruth is late or standard) and engages the gamut of European and American scholarship. This commentary, like other academic ones from a previous generation, concentrates largely on understanding the book in its ancient context.

Newer commentaries emphasize the book's provocative and innovative aspects. André LaCocque's commentary emphasizes several levels of subversiveness in Ruth. He views the book as operating primarily on two fronts: challenging the Israelite judicial system and welcoming the foreigner despite opposition.[124] In addition, LaCocque explicitly examines Ruth's impact on both Jewish and Christian communities.

Tod Linafelt, in his *Ruth* commentary, argues that uncertainties are integral to Ruth's art and intent. He exposes purposive ambiguities of grammar, syntax, and the like, claiming they are meant to highlight complexities in the narrative. The characters are "far from exemplifying simple godliness"; they are "a mass of conflicting desires and vested interests, each of them existing within a social structure that limits a person in some ways . . . yet each struggling . . . to transcend or subvert those bounds."[125]

Feminist Interpretations Feminist approaches to Ruth can be traced back to the nineteenth century, especially in the work of Elizabeth Cady Stanton,[126] perhaps also to Grace Aguilar, the Jewish writer and poet. Aguilar's monumental work, *The Women of Israel,* appeared in 1845 and took up the cause of women to combat both Christian anti-Semitism and restrictions on women within Jewish tradition.[127] However, feminist interpretations of the Bible truly came to the fore in the field of biblical studies with the publication of Phyllis Trible's ground-breaking work in the 1970s. Trible, who pioneered the field of feminist biblical scholarship, titles her influential chapter on Ruth as "A Human Comedy,"[128] evoking thereby Dante's epic, *The Divine Comedy.* Her title casts Ruth as the story of yet another momentous journey, but this time the journey made by women in a man's world. Trible shows how the women in this story work out their salvation within culture—even against culture—as they also transform it.[129]

Another rich source of feminist interpretation can be found in the two volumes on Ruth in *The Feminist Companion to the Bible* series, edited by Athalya Brenner.[130] These explore an array of issues about Ruth as an ancient text and as a source for contemporary thinking about new issues. Several essays examine the possibility of women's authorship of the book and its implications. Others, like Carol Meyers, use social scientific lenses, including archaeology and ethnography. Meyers situates the Book of Ruth in its social matrix in ancient Israel to discern what can be established about the lives of women in that world. She highlights the networking of women evident in the text and in the material remains, disclosing a culture where vital activities required multiple hands and cooperation among women, and a society in which women had significant roles in ritual, as well as in socioeconomic spheres.[131] Brenner writes on "Ruth as a Foreign Worker and the Politics of Exogamy," while Laura Donaldson offers "The Sign of Orpah: Reading Ruth through Native Eyes," and Irmtraud Fischer considers whether Ruth can be read as a "feminist" commentary on the Torah itself.[132]

Whereas most interpreters of Ruth celebrate its affirmation of female bonding, D. M. Fewell and D. N. Gunn introduce a discordant note. In one essay, they portray Naomi as self-centered and self-absorbed, unable or unwilling to respond to Ruth.[133] They identify several silences as evidence of Naomi's resentment of, or resistance to, Ruth's presence: first, her silence after Ruth's pledge in 1:16–17; second, her silence about Ruth upon arriving in Bethlehem; third her silence about the existence of her wealthy relative, Boaz; and finally, Naomi's silence after the women praise Ruth in 4:15. In a later response to a colleague's critique, they soften their claim, adding that Naomi's responses are not necessarily negative: vulnerable women often must safeguard their self-interest.[134] Fewell and Gunn think more highly of Boaz's actions, for though he manipulates the patriarchal system to his own advantage under the cloak of respectability, his acts of *ḥesed,* exemplified in his offering of grain to Ruth, redeem him.[135]

Esther Fuchs takes the critique of Ruth even further. Far from celebrating female bonding, she argues, the book has a patriarchal agenda. After all, Ruth leaves her mother's home to follow the mother of her dead husband, thereby prioritizing a woman's commitment to a man's family, even beyond the grave.[136]

Subsequent interpretations of Ruth have typically engaged these critiques, providing readers with a more nuanced assessment of the book's messages. In fact, the mixed motives that characterize protagonists in this biblical text are precisely what makes the story so vital, enabling it to acknowledge human limitations and at the same time illustrate ways to expand human potential, especially in the direction of generosity.

Modern Jewish Interpretations In the modern period, Jewish discourse about Ruth depended heavily at first on Rabbinic approaches to the text, providing a synthesis of Jewish exegesis with an eye to challenges that Jews faced in the modern world. In his slender commentary, the nineteenth-century Ukrainian rabbinic scholar Malbim (R. Meir Loeb ben Jeḥiel Michael Weisser; 1809–1879) emphasizes the piety of the protagonists, the book's harmonious worldview, and its significance in establishing the Davidic dynasty.[137] J. J. Stoltki's "Ruth" in *The Five Megilloth,*[138] like others in the Soncino series that originated in the United Kingdom, transmits Rabbinic traditions but also incorporates non-Jewish scholarship. For Slotki, Ruth is "a placid oasis," an escape from the tumult and strife of Judges; however, this "was where real world history was made. Not in the arena of battle, but in the peaceful homes of simple country folk—there nature built Israel's character and fashioned his heroes."[139] Highlighting the virtuous nature of the protagonists is especially important to Slotki. He marshals non-Jewish sources to underscore it, as in his comment on 3:5 (where Ruth consents to Naomi's daring plan). Here, Slotki cites the view of the Christian Hebraist Nowack as stating that "Ruth's conduct must not be judged by modern standards, but by those of the times in which she lived. She is fulfilling a duty of love and piety towards the dead by approaching Boaz. . . ."[140]

Yehoshua Bachrach represents a more contemporary approach in the manner with which he handles ambiguities in the text. Restating a rich variety of Rabbinic interpretations in his book *Mother of Royalty: An Exposition of the Book of Ruth in Light of the Sources,* Bachrach combines them to highlight complexities of situations and characters. Like the older Rabbinic sources, he emphasizes the important reconciliation between the line of Abraham and Lot (Moab) that Ruth effectuates when she "returns" to Judah (see comment at 1:22): "From the cursed valley of Sodom rises the image of Ruth and revives and refurbishes the affection between the ancients, extending back to the time when the original ancestor accompanied Abraham. . . ."[141] But Bachrach departs from earlier Jewish commentators in his treatment of ambiguities. Writing about Naomi, who urges her Moabite daughters-in-law to leave her, he sympathetically notes both Naomi's affection and her ambivalence:[142] On the one hand (he writes), "how fervently Naomi desired them to stay with her"; they were, after all, a heartwarming reminder of her sons and of the life they shared. But, as ardently she did not want them to accompany her, because they were a reminder of all that had gone wrong, and because they were Moabites. As for the homecoming, Bachrach highlights the desolation of Naomi and Ruth at home (2:1–2): Did people shun them out of resentment for their earlier departure? Out of discomfort with Moabite Ruth? Or was it not shunning but simply indifference?[143]

Reading Ruth: Contemporary Women Reclaim a Sacred Story This exemplary anthology features diverse interpretations by scholars in a number of fields, as well as readings by artists, intellectuals, and poets. It effectively illustrates the power of Ruth to revitalize dimensions in Jewish life.[144] Kates's essay[145] highlights the multilayered nature of the story. She elaborates on the meaning of *ḥesed* in Ruth and how it unfolds, first embodied in the acts of women. But she also points to the broader reach of the book's message: "The deepening of the speaking voices initiate a mode of narration that constantly invites us to perceive, in this apparently personal, mundane story of food and family connections, large realms of spiritual significance." Kates explains that this spiritual significance is intimately tied to pragmatic, socio-economic realities: The book's central characters call attention to those for whose benefit the Torah advocates: the poor, the widow, and the orphan.

Ruth Sohn creates a modern feminist commentary and midrash after the manner of the great medieval commentator Rashi, filtering her reading through a contemporary woman's eyes.[146] Gail Twersky Reimer's "Her Mother's House" challenges the popular tendency to see Ruth as above all longing for a child. Reimer argues that the book's uniqueness (and one of its chief feminist contributions) is to present a story in which maternity is not the predominant goal of one of the main women protagonists. In choosing to join Naomi, Ruth decisively rejects the typical female destiny (marriage and maternity). Instead, Ruth favors her relationship with another woman, a relationship in which marriage and maternity are at best incidental. Rebecca Alpert, noting how the Book of Ruth challenges us to rethink notions of sexual orientation, points out that the story of Ruth and Naomi has proven to be "a model for the powerful love that is possible between women," and "resonates with lesbian women in search of role models."[147]

In her study of Naomi's Kafkaesque experience of loss and the toll it takes on her relationship with Ruth, Avivah Zornberg plumbs the tension beneath the shimmering surface of the text.[148] She skillfully interweaves midrashic traditions with contemporary sensibilities, ethics, and Freud.

Other Contemporary Interpretations Reviewing different interpretations of Ruth (including structuralist analysis by Harold Fisch and poststructuralist analysis by Mieke Bal), Edward L. Greenstein explores the results of different reading strategies. He shows that, depending on one's theoretical frame of reference, the book can be read as a political work about patriarchy or a story about rebirth of land and family; yet one may also find here "moral or theological lessons about the virtues of personal kindness" or "a tale that sublimates universal human insecurities about fertility and order. . . . Or one may adduce the Ruth narrative to demonstrate the benefits that may accrue to a society from the collaboration of independent, assertive women."[149]

Rachel Adler's "Ruth: Of *Ḥesed* and Cutting Corners" is a concise yet multilayered reading of the narrative. She traces the ebb and flow of reciprocity fueled by attention to *ḥesed* and blessings (the two things even the destitute can bestow), as an ethics of relationship. In addition, Adler highlights "the cutting of legal corners," first by Naomi and Ruth and subsequently also by Boaz. Such "cutting corners" (an allusion to not cutting the corners of the field in Lev. 19:9 and leaving it for gleaners) "undermines even while it appears to uphold, the patriarchal power to extend or withhold the *kanaf*" (with *kanaf* as the wing, representing a sheltering protection). The concluding lesson, Adler points out, falls on the teaching of *ḥesed,* "without which law has no power to redeem."[150]

Laurie Zoloth-Dorfman uses the Book of Ruth to construct an ethics of encounter, influenced by the philosopher Emmanuel Levinas and responsive to Jewish halakhah (legal rulings). She identifies seven elements in Ruth as basic components for an ethics that not only comports with Jewish tradition but also contributes to public discourse about issues such as public health and the allocation of scarce resources. Among these elements are the following: (1) the recognition that there is no escape from collective scarcity; (2) that to "assume responsibility, even if one is powerless, is the just course for every citizen"; and (3) that to "have a face to face encounter makes generations and redemption possible."[151] Philosopher Claire Katz also interweaves insights from Ruth with those of Levinas's philosophy of the face of the Other; she likewise considers how the Book of Ruth contributes to ethical thinking.[152]

In *Democracy and the Foreigner,* Bonnie Honig dedicates an entire chapter to the Book of Ruth.[153] She considers Ruth a "foreign-founder" text, a paradigm in which the arrival of a foreigner effects significant changes in a society. Honig compares Ruth to Moses, another "foreign founder," noting that Ruth rises "from the shadows of Moses' unknown grave in Moab."[154] She is a founder in that "Ruth the Moabite is a vehicle of a regime change from the rule of judges to the rule by kings,"[155] but also a founder in the sense that she (re)-founds a "people."

In her book *The Murmuring Deep*, Zornberg writes further about Ruth.[156] She takes her cue from Robert Cover's influential study of law and narrative,[157] tracing the ways law and *ḥesed* intersect in Ruth. Zornberg explains that in Ruth, "law" specifically refers to the law of exclusion (Deut. 23:4, the directive to exclude Moabites from the Israelite congregation), even if it is not explicitly stated as such. Ruth's "stickiness," her clinging to Naomi ("But Ruth clung to her," 1:14), challenges the law. But the Book of Ruth is set in a world where law has broken down. In such a world, works of *ḥesed*—of lovingkindness—nurture life, sustain connections, and fulfill needs.

Susan Schept draws upon Ruth as a biblical resource for the ethics of care, a notion inspired by the work of Carol Gilligan.[158] Examining how the "other" plays a role in

Israel's history and specifically how the Bible presents the other, David Perlstein studies Ruth with other key biblical non-Israelites such as Jethro, Jael, and Cyrus to expound on the roles of "the other" in the Bible.[159] Mira Morgenstern considers Ruth as a critique of Judean society, claiming that its narrative holds lessons about moral responsibility that sustain the quest for both selfhood and communal engagement in a religious context.[160]

As this selective review illustrates, *Megillat Ruth*—speaks and is heard in a variety of voices, somewhat like the revelation at Sinai, which a midrash claims was heard differently by each Israelite. The Rabbis, who directed that the book be read on Shavuot (see "Ruth and Shavuot" above), already connected Ruth with the giving of the Torah at Sinai. However, Ruth also contrasts with the great revelation at Sinai. Instead of the fire and the blaring of the horn at Sinai, the messages of Ruth, like the revelation granted to the prophet Elijah, come as the ***kol demamah dakkah***, the "still small voice" or the "soft murmuring sound" (1 Kings 19:12). This soft yet powerful revelatory voice of Ruth continues to resonate anew with those attentive to the book's richly varied meanings.[161]

Notes to the Introduction

1. Technically speaking, the Hebrew title of this book should be rendered as either *Megillath Ruth* or *Megillat Rut*, since the Hebrew letter *t* is without a dagesh (a dot in it), and thus a soft *t*, often written and pronounced as "th." However, it has become the convention in the English-speaking world to use Ruth for the name of protagonist and for the name of the book, and to omit the "*h*" in *Megillat*.

2. The Introduction to "Ruth," *The Five Scrolls with Twelve Commentaries* [Hebrew] (Jerusalem: Fridman Lewin-Epstein, 1977).

3. Jack M. Sasson, *Ruth: A New Translation with a Philological Commentary and a Formalist-Folklorist Interpretation,* 2d ed. (Sheffield: *JSOT*, 1989; originally: Baltimore: The John Hopkins University Press, 1979), Baltimore: The John Hopkins University Press, 1979), 225–26.

4. S. D. Goitein, "Women as Creators of Biblical Genres," *Prooftexts* 8, no. 1 (1988): 1–33 [Hebrew original in *Studies in Miqra,* 1948, 252].

5. Edward F. Campbell, *Ruth: A New Translation with Introduction and Commentary,* AB, 7 (Garden City, NY: Doubleday, 1975), 22–23. Campbell's suggestion is particularly interesting given that, as R. Bauckham notes, Campbell's commentary does not as a rule show awareness of feminist issues ("The Book of Ruth and the Possibility of a Feminist Hermeneutical Canon," *Biblical Interpretation* 5, no. 1 (1997): 29–45, 30n2. See also Robert L. Hubbard Jr., *The Book of Ruth,* The New International Commentary of the Old Testament (Grand Rapids, MI: Eerdmans, 1988), 24; Adrien J. Bledstein, "Female Companionships" in *A Feminist Companion to Ruth,* ed. Athalya Brenner (Sheffield: Sheffield Academic, 1993), 116–33; Fokkelien van Dijk-Hemmes, "Ruth: A Product of Women's Culture?" in *A Feminist Companion to Ruth,* 134–39.

6. Mishael Caspi, with Rachel Havrelock, *Women on the Biblical Road* (Lanham, MD: University Press of America 1996), 53–101, 196–216.

7. R. Bauckham, "The Book of Ruth and the Possibility of Feminist Canonical Hermeneutic," 32.

8. Qumran yielded fragments from four manuscripts of Ruth; 2Q Ruth[a] (2:13–4, 1st century C.E.); 2Q Ruth[b] (3:13–18, 1st century B.C.E); 4Q Ruth[a] (from Ruth 1); and 4Q Ruth[b].

9. Hubbard, *The Book of Ruth,* 23. The supposition that the Davidic or Solomonic court in the 10th century B.C.E. was sufficiently developed to contain royal or archival material is greatly vitiated by recent scholarship about the historical David. Evidence indicates that Jerusalem in the 10th century B.C.E. was not well developed and did not have substantial royal or administrative structures. For details, see, e.g., Israel Finkelstein and Neil Asher Silverman, *David and Solomon* (New York: Free Press, 2006). The existence of archives at that point is unlikely.

10. Campbell, *Ruth,* 23–28.

11. Frederic W. Bush, *Ruth/Esther,* Word Biblical Commentary 9 (Waco, TX: Word Books, 1996), 30.

12. See Ziony Zevit, "Dating Ruth: Legal, Linguistic and Historical Observations," *ZAW* 117, no. 4 (2005): 574–600.

13. For a good summary, see Robert Gordis, "Love, Marriage and Business in the Book of Ruth," in *A Light Unto My Path,* ed. H. Bream, R. Heim, and C. Moore (Philadelphia: Temple University Press, 1974), 244–46.

14. For the criteria of Late biblical Hebrew, see, e.g., Robert Polzin, *Late Biblical Hebrew* (Missoula, MT: Scholars, 1976).

15. Bush, *Ruth/Esther,* 19–30.

16. A. Bendavid, in passing, places Ruth linguistically with Joshua through 2 Kings. (See his *Biblical Hebrew and Mishnaic Hebrew,* vol. 1 [Tel Aviv: Dvir, 1967], 60). Bendavid places Jonah among the later books (60–61). Bendavid published his book in 1967, some 30 years before Bush's systematic analysis of the language of Ruth. Bush (although not responding specifically to Bendavid) identifies in Ruth the kinds of examples that Bendavid uses to place Jonah in the postexilic period, such as Aramaisms and new vocabulary. See also Zevit's support for the later date for Ruth.

17. Hubbard, *The Book of Ruth,* 33.

18. Bush, *Ruth/Esther,* 19; E. Davies, "Inheritance Rights and the Hebrew Levirate Marriage, II," *VT* 31 (1981): 257–68.

19. Hubbard, *The Book of Ruth,* 36–38.

20. See Yair Zakovitch, *Ruth: Introduction and Commentary* [Hebrew], Mikra Leyisra'el: A Bible Commentary for Israel (Tel Aviv: Am Oved, 1990), 19.

21. Hubbard, *The Book of Ruth,* 37–42.

22. Hubbard, in a critique of a late date for Ruth, systematically addresses these points. He concludes that each can be challenged and used to support an early date as well (30–35). His linguistic arguments are weakened by Bush's careful analysis, which is later than Hubbard's. Zevit's work further responds to Hubbard and concludes that the legal evidence points to a development in which Ruth is late.

23. See, e.g., Tamara Cohn Eskenazi, *Ezra-Nehemiah: A New Translation and Commentary,* AB (forthcoming); and "The Missions of Ezra and Nehemiah," in O. Lipschits and M. Oeming, eds., *Judah and the Judeans in the Persian Period* (Winona Lake, IN: Eisenbrauns, 2006), 509–29.

24. Campbell, followed by Hubbard, proposes a more specific term, "a Hebrew short story," exemplified also by Gen. 24, 38, and the Joseph story in Gen. 37–50. But Susan Niditch cogently argues that the characteristics typify great literature in general and cannot be limited to the Hebrew Bible. See Campbell, *Ruth,* 4–10, 18–23; Hubbard, *Book of Ruth,* 47–48; and Niditch, "Legends of Wise Heroes and Heroines, II: Ruth," in *The Hebrew Bible and Its Modern Interpreters,* ed. D. Knight and G. Tucker (Philadelphia: Fortress, 1985), 451–56.

25. W. Humphries, "Novella," in *Saga, Legend, Tale, Novella, Fable,* ed. G. Coats. *JSOT*Supp 62 (Sheffield: *JSOT*, 1985), 84; emphasis in the original.

26. Humphries, "Novella," 84; emphasis in the original.

27. Bush, *Ruth/Esther,* 42.

28 E. Wurtheim, *Die Fünf Megilloth.* HAT 18, 2nd ed. (Tubingen: Mohr/Siebeck, 1969), 3–6.

29. Phyllis Trible, *God and the Rhetoric of Sexuality,* Overtures to Biblical Theology (Philadelphia: Fortress, 1978), 166–99.

30. J. William Whedbee, *The Bible and The Comic Vision* (Cambridge: Cambridge University Press, 1998).

31. A. H. Friedlander, ed., *The Five Scrolls: Hebrew Texts, English Translations, Introductions, and New Liturgies* (New York: CCAR Press, 1984) begins with Eccles. but then follows with Esther, Songs, Ruth, and Lam. This sequence follows the calendar with autumn as the beginning of the year.

32. The same order is also reflected in the slightly older but incompletely preserved Aleppo Codex (10th century C.E.). Although incomplete, the extant pages from its section of *Kethuvim* includes a few pages from Ruth (after Prov.), indicating the same sequence as the Leningrad Codex.

33. The mother's house is mentioned again in the Bible only in Songs 3:4 and 8:2.

34. Harold Fisch, "Ruth and the Structure of Covenant History," *VT* 32, no. 4 (October 1982): 427.

35. Fisch identifies 8 common themes in the 3 stories, namely: descent, disaster, the *agunah* theme/abandonment, redemption, the bed trick, celebration, Levirate union, and the issue (430–31).

36. Ibid., 433.

37. Ibid., 435, 436.

38. Ibid., 436.

39. Ibid., 435.

40. See Zakovitch, *Ruth,* 18–20. I thank David E. S. Stein for his correct observation that Deut. 23:4–7 does not explicitly refer to marriage (in a private communication).

41. Ezra 6:21 could be read as referring to a loophole in this exclusionary policy. The verse refers to "all who joined them in separating themselves from the uncleanliness of the nations of the lands to worship the LORD God of Israel." It is thus plausible that intermarriage was to be outlawed only when foreign spouses fail to make such commitments to Israel's God.

42. Birthplace ceases to be a reliable marker of identity once the province of Yehud (Judah) includes foreigners who settled there for decades in the wake of the Temple's destruction in 586 B.C.E., and when people who call themselves Jews are born in the Diaspora or exile.

43. See David Perlman, *God's Others: Non-Israelites' Encounters With God in the Hebrew Bible* (New York and Bloomington, IN: iUniverse, 2010).

44. Tamar of Gen. 38 (Judah's daughter-in-law; see also Ruth 4:12) represents a special case. Many commentators take for granted that Tamar is Canaanite because Judah, who secures her as a wife for his son(s), is already

married to a Canaanite (Gen. 38:2) and lives in a Canaanite region (for the fuller story of Tamar and Judah and its relation to Ruth, see "Levirate Marriage" and "Ruth's Relationship to Other Biblical Books" in this book's introduction). The line of Judah from the start is a product of an intermarriage. Intriguingly, however, Genesis leaves Tamar's ethnic identity veiled.

45. Shavuot is mentioned in the Bible in Exod. 34:22 and Deut. 16:10. The day is also called *Yom Ha-bikkurim*, "day of the first fruits," in Num. 28:26. In early Jewish Hellenistic sources, Shavuot is called Pentecost, "the fiftieth," a term also used in subsequent Christian sources.

46. Lekach Tov (11th commentary compiled by R. Toviah ben Eliezer).

47. R. Yehudah Aryeh Leib Alter (1847–1905).

48. Shavuot. 4:23; see Arthur Green, *The Language of Truth: The Torah Commentary of the Sefat Emet, Rabbi Yehudah Leb Alter of Ger* (Philadelphia: Jewish Publication Society, 1998), 403–404.

49. Fivel Meltzer, "Ruth," in *The Five Scrolls* [Hebrew] (Jerusalem: Mosad Ha-Rav Kook, 1973), 21.

50. For a discussion, see L. G. Perdue, J. Blenkinsopp, J. J. Collins, and C. Meyers, eds., *Families in Ancient Israel* (Louisville, KY: Westminster/John Knox, 1997); and Carol Meyers "Women in Ancient Israel—An Overview," in *The Torah: A Women's Commentary,* ed. T. C. Eskenazi and A. Weiss (New York: URJ Press, 2008), xli–xliii; as well as "In the Household and Beyond," *Studia Theologia* 63 (2009): 19–41.

51. The terminology and actual size of the different groups change over time, but the relative size remains.

52. In the Bible, *banim* often refers to males and females collectively.

53. For a detailed exploration of women's roles in ancient Israel, see Carol Meyers, *Discovering Eve* (Oxford: Oxford University Press, 1988).

54. See B. Levine, "The Inalienable Right to the Land of Israel," *The JPS Torah Commentary: Leviticus* (Philadelphia: Jewish Publication Society, 1989), 270–74.

55. "Women and the Inheritance of Land in Early Israel," in *Women in the Biblical Tradition,* ed. G. J. Brooke (Lewiston, NY: Edwin Mellen, 1992), 45–47.

56. See Zevit, "Dating Ruth," 587; for the debate about the authenticity of the memorandum, see 587n.15.

57. Bezalel Porten, ed., and Ada Yardeni, trans., *Textbook of Aramaic Documents from Ancient Egypt* [newly copied, edited, and translated into Hebrew and English], vol. 1: Letters; and vol. 2: Contracts (Jerusalem: The Hebrew University, Dept. of History of the Jewish People, 1986).

58. Zevit, "Dating Ruth," 591.

59. Osgood, "Women and Inheritance," 51.

60. For ancient Near Eastern practices, see Laws of Lipit-Ishtar 21–32, in J.B. Pritchard, *Ancient Near Eastern Texts Relating to the Old Testament* (Princeton: Princeton University Press, 1955), 160; M. Roth, *Law Collections from Mesopotamia and Asia Minor,* SBL Writings from the Ancient World Series (Atlanta: Scholars, 1997) 30–32; and the Laws of Eshnunna 17–18; 29–30 in Pritchard, *Ancient Near Eastern Texts*, 162; and Roth, *Law Collections,* 61 and 63; and the discussion in Timothy M. Willis, *The Elders of the City,* SBL Monograph Series 55 (Atlanta: Society of Biblical Literature, 2001), 243–50.

61. See, for example, the marriage document of Ananiah and Tamut, in Kraeling 2, E.G. Kraeling, *The Brooklyn Museum Aramaic Papyri: New Documents of the Fifth Century* B.C. *from the Jewish Colony at Elephantine* (New Haven: Yale University Press, 1953); see also B. Porten, with J. J. Farber, C. J. Martin, and G. Vittman, eds., *The Elephantine Papyri in English* (Leiden: Brill, 1996); and B. Porten, *Archives from Elephantine* (Berkeley and Los Angeles: University of California Press, 1968).

62. Kraeling 2.10–11. Similarly, should Tamut die first, her husband gains control over their possessions (Kraeling 2.12–13). See Kraeling, *The Brooklyn Museum Aramaic Papyri,* 143.

63. Cited from J. J. Collins, "Marriage, Divorce and Family in Second Temple Judaism," in *Families in Ancient Israel,* 111–12. See also Y. Yadin, J. C. Greenfield, and A. Yardeni, "Babatha Ketuba" in *IEJ* 44 (1994): 75–108.

64. See Dvora E. Weisberg, *Levirate Marriage and the Family in Ancient Judaism* (Waltham, MA: Brandeis University Press, 2009), esp. 1–22.

65. Ibid., 17.

66. Timothy M. Willis has reached different conclusions from those of Weisberg. According to Willis, a widow has a great deal of flexibility in determining which relative will father the child (*The Elders of the City*, 236). His references for this come largely from tribal arrangements in Africa. As he indicates, however, Middle-Eastern laws are more restrictive as to who can act as "replacement" (248–49). This conforms to the law in Deut. 25. Willis also supposes that Ruth 3–4 pertains to levirate marriage. However, Ruth, Naomi, Boaz, and the narrator never refer to Boaz as a levir. They only refer to him as a redeemer (see, e.g., 2:20, 3:9, and 3:12). If levirate marriage was the issue in Ruth 3–4, and if the widow could choose, then the entire negotiation with the other redeemer would be pointless.

67. See Pritchard, *Ancient Near Eastern Texts,* 196; Roth, *Law Collections,* 236.

68. Willis, *Elders of the City,* 244–45.

69. Pritchard, *Ancient Near Eastern Texts,* 190; Roth, *Law Collections,* 164.

70. Willis, *Elders of the City*, 247.

71. Rabbinic sources deal extensively with such complexities and developments. See Weisberg, *Levirate Marriage.*

72. Concern with the boundary between incest and levirate union is apparent also in Mesopotamian sources. See Willis, *The Elders of the City,* 244.

73. Weisberg, *Levirate Marriage,* xxv; emphasis added.

74. See, e.g., the Targum. Modern interpreters include Campbell, *Ruth*, 132–39; Hubbard, *Book of Ruth*, 51–52 and 187; K. Nielsen, *Ruth: A Commentary*, Old Testament Library (Louisville, KY: Westminster/John Knox, 1997), 73; Willis, *Elders of the City;* Zakovitch, *Ruth*, 93.

75. See, e.g., Yossi Prager, who writes: "... as Boaz explains to Peloni Almoni, the *ge'ula* of the land carries the further obligation for the *go'el* to marry Ruth. This second halakhah, although reminiscent of the laws of *yibbum* contained in *Deuteronomy* (25), has no source in Jewish law, written or oral" ("Megillat Ruth: A Unique Story of Torat Ḥesed," *Tradition: A Journal of Orthodox Jewish Thought* 34, no. 4 [2001]:15).

76. Bush, *Ruth/Esther*, 166–67.

77. As Bush points out, "the passages in the OT legal corpora dealing with redemption never touch upon the levirate obligation; nor do the passages dealing with the levirate ever call the one responsible for this obligation a 'redeemer'" (Bush, *Ruth/Esther*, 167).

78. See Willis, *Elders of the City*, 252.

79. Zevit, "Dating Ruth," 580–82. Zevit oddly adds: "The sandal ceremony in Deuteronomy is exactly the same as in Ruth" (580). But as noted above, only the mention of a sandal connects Ruth with the ritual in Deut. 25:5–10, and in Ruth this represents any kind of transaction, a detail that distances the ritual further from the levirate situation.

80. Robert Gordis, "Love, Marriage and Business," 246–52.

81. R. G. Beattie, "The Book of Ruth as Evidence for Israelite Legal Practice," *VT* 24 (1974): 251–67; Gordis, "Love, Marriage and Business, 246–52; Jack Sasson, "The Issue of G'ullah in Ruth," *JSOT* 5 (1978): 52–64; Bush, *Ruth/Esther*, 225.

82. Bush, *Ruth/Esther*, 225.

83. Avivah Gottlieb Zornberg, "The Concealed Alternative," in *Reading Ruth*, ed. Judith A. Kates and Gail Twersky Reimer (New York: Ballantine Books, 1994), 74.

84. Shaye J. D. Cohen, *The Beginning of Jewishness* (Berkeley and Los Angeles: University of California Press, 1999), 260. Cohen writes: "A general prohibition of intermarriage between Jews and non-Jews does not appear anywhere in the Tanakh," 260.

85. It is supposed that children were counted matrilineally only when the marriage was matrilocal, i.e., when the husband joined the family of the wife, as in Lev. 24:10 and 1 Chron. 2:17 (see, ibid., 266).

86. Scholars debate the question of whether the women are foreign or whether they represent an indigenous Israelite and Judahite population whose customs differ from those of the repatriating Jews from Babylonia. The conclusion of such debates, however, does not change the relevant issue here, namely, that if and when a woman is deemed foreign, then she is to be excluded. See Eskenazi, "The Missions of Ezra and Nehemiah."

87. For a detailed exegesis of the issues in Ezra 9–10 and Neh. 13, see Michael Fishbane, *Biblical Interpretation in Ancient Israel* (Oxford: Clarendon, 1985), 114–34.

88. The one possible hint that such a lineage was not unproblematic is Jacob's adoption of these two sons of Joseph and Asenath as his own (Gen. 48:5–6).

89. Cohen, *The Beginning of Jewishness.*

90. Ibid., 121.

91. Ibid., 122.

92. The verb is subject to different interpretations and does not signal genuine conversion. See Adele Berlin, *The JPS Bible Commentary: Esther* (Philadelphia: Jewish Publication Society, 2001), 80–81. The date of the Book of Esther is uncertain; Berlin dates it between 400 and 300 B.C.E. (ibid., xli).

93. "'Your People, My People': An Exploration of Ethnicity in Ruth," *JSOT* 33, no. 3 (2009): 293–313.

94. Ibid., 295.

95. Cohen, *The Beginning of Jewishness*, 246.

96. See Eccles. R., 8.10.1; and PdRE, 35 and 37.

97. Cohen, *The Beginning of Jewishness*, 248.

98. PdRK, Nachamu 16.1. English translation, trans. William G. Braude and Israel J. Kapstein (Philadelphia: Jewish Publication Society, 1975 and 2002), 385.

99. See especially Yehoshua Bachrach's poignant treatment in *Mother of Royalty* (Jerusalem: Feldheim, 1973, 1980 ed.).

100. R. Moses ben Maimon, known as Rambam (1135–1204; Spain and Egypt).

101. *The Guide for the Perplexed*, III: 54.

102. P. P. Haillie's phrase for the activities of Christian villagers in France during the German occupation when they saved thousands of Jews. See *Lest Innocent Blood Be Shed* (New York: Harper and Row, 1979).

103. Rachel Adler, *Engendering Judaism* (Philadelphia: Jewish Publication Society, 1998), 148–56.

104. Tikva Frymer-Kensky, "Royal Origins: Ruth on the Royal Way," *Reading the Women of the Bible* (New York: Schocken, 2002), 243.

105. Alicia Ostriker, "Ruth and the Love of the Land," *Biblical Interpretation* 10, no. 4 (2002): 343–359.

106. Hubbard, *The Book of Ruth*, 72.

107. PdRK, Nachamu 16.1.

108. An insight expressed more explicitly in Ruth R. 7.7 and Lekach Tov on Ruth 4:1.

109. "A Midrashic View of Ruth: Amidst the Sea of Ambiguities," *Jewish Bible Quarterly*, 33/2 (2005), 91–99.

110. In Ezra 7:6, the narrator confirms at least one of the protagonists' claims about God.

111. Ostriker, "The Book of Ruth and the Love of the Land," 343–59.

112. Property in cities and levitical property are handled differently: "If a man sells a dwelling house in a walled city, it may be redeemed until a year has elapsed since its sale; the redemption period shall be a year. If it is not redeemed before a full year has elapsed, the house in the walled city shall pass to the purchaser beyond reclaim throughout the ages; it shall not be released in the jubilee" (25:29–30).

113. This anecdote sheds light on what one would have expected Elimelech to have done before leaving for Moab. Indeed, some commentators suppose that he did make various provisions. But the narrative says nothing about the subject and whatever arrangements might have been made, they are not, finally, mentioned in Ruth 4.

114. Shlomo Bahar, "What is the Difference between חלץ (ḥalaṣ) and שלף (šalap)? The Purpose of Recalling the 'Form of Attestation' in the Scroll of Ruth (4:7)" [Hebrew] *Shnaton: An Annual for Bible and Ancient Near East Studies* 20 (2010): 75.

115. For details about Boaz's problematic announcement, see commentary at 4:5 and 4:10.

116. The sources for this section include the following: *The Explicated Midrash Rabba: Ruth Rabbah and Esther Rabbah* [Hebrew] (Jerusalem: Institute of the Explicated Midrash, 1983 edition); *Mikra'ot Gedolot: The Five Scrolls* [Hebrew] (Jerusalem: Hamaor Institute, 2001 edition); *The Five Scrolls with Twelve Commentaries* [Hebrew] (Jerusalem: Fridman Lewin-Epstein, 1976).

117. B. Sot. 42b imputes all sorts of sexual improprieties to Orpah in the aftermath of her departure. But the four tears that she shed, according to Rabbinic traditions, also merited that four mighty warriors would issue from her. (See also Ruth R. 2.20–21).

118. See the discussion about authorship in Beattie, *Jewish Exegesis*, 24–27; Beattie retains the traditional ascription of the commentary to Salmon, whereas A. Nemoy contests it. I follow Beattie in retaining Salmon's name without claiming that the ascription is historically secure. The translation follows Beattie, who relies on the English translation by I. D. Markon (see Beattie, 24).

119. Beattie, *Jewish Exegesis,* 47–48.

120. Ibid., 57.

121. The references are based on the 1701 edition of Mosheh ben Avraham Mendes Koitinyo and published in Amsterdam in 1701. The source for information about Zohar Hadash: *Encyclopadia Judaica,* vol. 21:659.

122. For Alsheikh, see *The Five Scrolls with Twelve Commentaries.*

123. Kates and Reimer, *Reading Ruth*, xviii–xix.

124 André LaCocque, *Ruth: A Continental Commentary* (Minneapolis: Fortress, 2004), 153–54.

125. Tod Linafelt and Timothy K. Beal, *Ruth and Esther,* Berit Olam: Studies in Hebrew Narrative and Poetry (Collegeville, MN: Liturgical, 1999), xiv–xv.

126. Elizabeth Cady Stanton, "The Book of Ruth," *The Woman's Bible* (New York: European Publishing House, 1892), 47–43.

127. Grace Aguilar, *The Women of Israel or Characters and Sketches from the Holy Scriptures and Jewish History* (London: George Routledge and Sons, 1945); see her "Naomi" (228–45), which is about the Book of Ruth.

128. Phyllis Trible, "A Human Comedy," in *God and the Rhetoric of Sexuality,* Overtures to Biblical Theology (Philadelphia: Fortress, 1978), 168–99.

129. Trible, "A Human Comedy," 196.

130. Athalya Brenner, ed., *A Feminist Companion to Ruth* (Sheffield: Sheffield Academic, 1993) and *A Feminist Companion to Ruth and Esther,* 2nd series (Sheffield: Sheffield Academic, 1999).

131. Carol Meyers, " 'Women of the Neighborhood' (Ruth 4:17)" in *A Feminist Companion to Ruth and Esther,* 110–27; also "Returning Home: Ruth 1:8 and the Gendering of the Book of Ruth," in *A Feminist Companion to Ruth,* 85–114.

132. Irmtraud Fischer, "The Book of Ruth: A 'Feminist' Commentary on the Torah?" in *A Feminist Companion to Ruth and Esther,* 24–49.

133. D. N. Fewell and D. M. Gunn, "A Son is Born to Naomi!" *JSOT* 40 (1988): 99–108.

134. D. N. Fewell and D. M. Gunn, "Is Coxon a Scold? On Responding to the Book of Ruth," *JSOT* 45 (1989): 39–43.

135. D. N. Fewell and D. M. Gunn, "Boaz, Pillar of Society: Measures of Worth in the Book of Ruth," *JSOT* 45 (1989): 45–59.

136. Esther Fuchs, "The Literary Presentation of Mothers and Sexual Politics in the Hebrew Bible," *Feminist Perspectives on Biblical Scholarship,* ed. Adela Y. Collins (Missoula, MT: Scholars Press and the Society of Biblical Literature, 1985), 117–36.

137. Although written in the 19th century, Malbim's commentary was not translated into English until 1999.

138. A. Cohen, ed. *The Five Megilloth* (London: Soncino, 1952), 35–65.

139. J. J. Slotki, "Ruth," in *The Five Megilloth*, 37.

140. Ibid., 57.

141. Ibid., 51.

142. Ibid., 33–36.

143. Ibid., 62–65.

144. Kates and Reimer, *Reading Ruth*.

145. Ibid., "Women at the Center: Ruth and Shavuot," pp. 187–98.

146. Ibid., "Verse by Verse: A Modern Commentary," 14–27 For an earlier midrash by a woman, see Grace Goldin, *Come Under the Wings: A Midrash on Ruth* (Philadelphia: Jewish Publication Society, 1958).

147. Kates and Reimer, *Reading Ruth,* "Finding Our Past: A Lesbian Interpretation of the Book of Ruth," 91–96.

148. Ibid., "The Concealed Alternative," 65–81.

149. E. L. Greenstein, "Reading Strategies and the Story of Ruth," in A. Bach, *Women in the Hebrew Bible: A Reader* (New York and London: Routledge, 1999), 211–31.

150. Adler, *Engendering Judaism,* 156.

151. Laurie Zoloth-Dorfman, "An Ethics of Encounter: Public Choices and Private Acts" in *Contemporary Jewish Ethics and Morality: A Reader,* ed. E. N. Dorff and L. E. Newman (Oxford: Oxford University Press, 1995), 219–45.

152. Claire Katz, "Ruth: Love and the Ethics of Fecundity" in *Levinas, Judaism, and the Feminine* (Bloomington: Indiana University Press, 2003), 78–96. See also Tamara Cohn Eskenazi, "Re-Reading the Bible with Levinas," in *Responsibility, God and Society,* ed. J. de Tavernier, J. Selling, J. Verstraeten, and P. Schotsmanns (Leuven: Peeters, 2008), 69–82.

153. Bonnie Honig, *Democracy and the Foreigner* (Princeton, NJ: Princeton University Press, 2001), 41–72.

154. Ibid., 59.

155. Ibid., 41.

156. Avivah Gottlieb Zornberg, *The Murmuring Deep: Reflections on the Biblical Unconscious* (New York: Schocken, 2009), 344–79.

157. Robert Cover, *Narrative, Violence, and the Law* (Ann Arbor: University of Michigan Press, 1992).

158. Susan Schept, "*Ḥesed*: Feminist Ethics in Jewish Tradition," *Conservative Judaism* 57, no. 1 (2004): 21–29.

159. Perlstein, *God's Others* (New York and Bloomington, IN: iUniverse, 2010).

160. Mira Morgenstern, "Ruth and the Sense of Self: Midrash and Difference," *Judaism* 48, no. 2 (1999): 131–45.

161. See 1 Kings 19:9–13, where we read that when Elijah encountered God at Horeb (another name for Sinai), God was not in the fire or in the earthquake but rather came forth as a *kol demamah dakkah.* This is translated by NJPS as "a soft murmuring sound" but as "a still small voice" in older translations. On Ruth as a "still small voice," see esp. biblical scholar Ellen F. Davis, " 'All that you say, I will do': A Sermon on the Book of Ruth," *Scrolls of Love: Ruth and Song of Songs,* ed. Peter S. Hawkins and Lesleigh Cushing Stahlberg (New York: Fordham University Press, 2006), 3–8.

THE COMMENTARY TO RUTH

1 In the days when the chieftains ruled, there was a famine in the land; and a man of Bethlehem in Judah, with his wife and two sons, went to reside in the

א וַיְהִ֗י בִּימֵי֙ שְׁפֹ֣ט הַשֹּׁפְטִ֔ים וַיְהִ֥י רָעָ֖ב
בָּאָ֑רֶץ וַיֵּ֨לֶךְ אִ֜ישׁ מִבֵּ֧ית לֶ֣חֶם יְהוּדָ֗ה לָגוּר֙

CHAPTER 1

Departure and Return: The Journey from Loss to Redemption Begins

The Book of Ruth begins inauspiciously, with famine and death. Famine drives a man to leave home (Bethlehem) and homeland (Judah) and go to Moab with his wife, Naomi, and their two sons. After the three men die, their widows prepare to return to Bethlehem.

The first chapter introduces the protagonists and the challenges they face. At its center stands the dialogue between Naomi and her two Moabite daughters-in-law, Ruth and Orpah, at the crossroad (in more ways than one) between life in Moab and life in Bethlehem. Its hallmark is Ruth's pledge of complete devotion to Naomi, her people, and her God: "Wherever you go, I will go . . ." (1:16). Ruth's attachment to Naomi is all the more striking against the background of the tension in the Bible between Israel and Moab (see, e.g., the exclusion of Moabites in Deut. 23:4–9). The chapter concludes when aged Naomi returns to her hometown with her Moabite daughter-in-law in tow.

OUTLINE OF CHAPTER 1

I. Prologue: The departure from Bethlehem (1–7)
II. The turning point on the road to Bethlehem (8–18)
III. The return to Bethlehem (19–22)

PROLOGUE: THE DEPARTURE FROM BETHLEHEM (1:1–7)

Elimelech leaves his home in Bethlehem to escape famine and moves to Moab with Naomi and their two sons. Within the span of a few verses, death claims the lives of all three men—leaving three widows: Naomi and her two Moabite daughters-in-law, Orpah and Ruth. The Prologue ends when the prospect of food prompts Naomi to return to Bethlehem.

Yet the narration conveys more than heart-rending misfortune. The opening lines hark back to other journeys in search of food. The very vocabulary of the Prologue echoes patriarchal and matriarchal stories in Genesis, in which famine drives Abram and Sarai (Gen. 12:10) as well as Isaac and Rebekah (Gen. 26:1) to leave the land. Such echoes of Genesis, which continue throughout Ruth (see, especially, the comment at 4:11–12), inform the reader that this is a story about ancestors.

The prologue provides the setting and introduces the protagonists, as well as the problems that the book seeks to solve. The setting is the time of the chieftains, a period in Israel's history that the Book of Judges describes as unstable. The protagonists are widows, and the problem is lack of food and progeny. The journey from Bethlehem has led to death. Would a return restore life?

1:1. In the days when the chieftains ruled Literally "when the judges (*shofetim*) judged." The NJPS translators explain in a footnote to this verse that "chieftains" is a more precise English designation for the leaders who arose in the period before the Israelite monarchy (1200–1000 B.C.E.). The Book of Judges portrays this period as consisting of cycles of religious apostasy and punishment. But when Israel repents, then God appoints temporary military leaders (*shofetim*), like Deborah and Gideon, to rescue the Israelite tribes from oppression. The period ends with a disastrous intra-Israelite tribal war triggered by rape. The narrator ominously frames the concluding decline and mayhem with the statement that "there was no king in Israel" (Judg. 17:6; 18:1; 19:1; 21:25) and (as recorded in the last line of the book) "everyone did as he pleased" (21:25).The commentator Malbim situates Ruth at this final period of disintegration, whereas other Rabbinic sources place it earlier, at the time of Ibzan (Judg. 12:8–10; B. BB 91a).

The chaos described in Judges throws into sharp relief the extraordinary kindness that pervades the Book of Ruth. This kindness—*ḥesed*—functions as a key agent for the transformation that occurs in the course of the book's narrative. It ultimately leads to Ruth's descendant David (with whom this book ends)—Israel's most famous king (see 4:17 and 22). Ruth, then, is a bridge between the anarchy of the Book of Judges and the emergence of the monarchy in the Book of Samuel.

there was a famine in the land Famine (Hebrew *ra'av*) is an important theme in biblical literature. An identical sentence introduces ancestral stories about Abram and Sarai (Gen. 12:10) as well as Isaac and Rebekah (26:1). Jacob and his sons also journey at times of famine (Genesis 41–47). Famine in these ancestors' stories functions simply to set in motion human events of interest; yet other biblical texts, such as Deut. 11:13–17, attribute famine to divine retribution. The Targum to Ruth applies this perspective to Ruth and provides a list of ten famines that have occurred since the Creation, all brought to reprove or punish people, even though the Bible does not always say so. This interpretation of biblical famines also becomes pervasive in the Midrash, which speculates as to which specific sins prompted the famine mentioned in the Book of Ruth (see Ruth R. 1.4; Rashi).

man Hebrew *'ish* in this verse (and the next) refers to the head of a household. In the minds of the ancient audience, the use of *'ish* in this context would have evoked questions of land ownership, a subject that turns out to be important in this story (see 4:1–10).[1]

Bethlehem The Canaanite etymology of this name may be "house of (the god) Laḥmu," but to a Hebrew speaker, the active meaning is "house of *leḥem,*" with *leḥem* meaning "food" (Arabic: "meat")—although it is usually translated as "bread." Ironically, then, famine prompts this household to leave "the house of bread." The town of Bethlehem is located six miles south of Jerusalem. The Bible identifies Bethlehem as David's place of origin (1 Sam. 17:12). As a locale, it also evokes several other biblical scenes. Genesis 35:19 and 48:7 establish Rachel's burial place in relation to it. In Judg. 12:8–10, it is the town of the chieftain Ibzan, whom later Jewish sources identify as Boaz (see below, 2:1). In Judges 19–21, a particularly fateful journey begins in Bethlehem and ends with rape and murder, then intertribal war, which concludes the Book of Judges. All these associations hover in the background of Ruth.

to reside Hebrew *lagur,* "to sojourn," that is, reside temporarily. As in the ancestral stories in Genesis, those who leave Israel because of famine do not intend to settle abroad permanently. Abram and Sarai sojourn in Egypt during a famine (Gen. 12:10); when Isaac and Rebekah goes to Gerar, God says, "Reside (*gur*) in this land" (Gen. 26:3); Joseph's brothers tell him, "We have come to sojourn in this land" (Gen. 47:4). Likewise, Israel's central creed (recited at the Passover seder) recalls, "My father . . . went to Egypt and sojourned there . . ." (Deut. 26:5). Certain later Rabbinic texts condemn Elimelech's decision to leave Bethlehem as a dereliction of duty to the community (e.g., Ruth R. 1.4);

country of Moab. 2 The man's name was Elimelech,
his wife's name was Naomi, and his two sons were

בִּשְׂדֵי מוֹאָב הוּא וְאִשְׁתּוֹ וּשְׁנֵי בָנָיו׃
2 וְשֵׁם הָאִישׁ אֱלִימֶלֶךְ וְשֵׁם אִשְׁתּוֹ נָעֳמִי

however, the narrator in Ruth does not disparage the choice to temporarily leave a famine-stricken town. (See also comment at v. 3.)

country Literally "fields," in contrast to 1:6, 2:6, and 4:3, which use the singular noun ("field"). There seems to be no substantive difference between the two forms in this book.

Moab This name refers to an agricultural area in the southern part of modern Jordan. Bethlehem is about fifty miles from the northern part of Moab;[2] Moab includes the plains (Numbers 22), part of the rift valley across the Jordan from Jericho. As one proceeds southward, one rises to the flat tableland, 3300–3700 feet above the Dead Sea. The abrupt rise from the Dead Sea forms a rain barrier, so that the plateau becomes a windy pastureland with a 16-inch yearly rainfall. The Moab referred to in the Bible usually means the area north of the Arnon river (see Num. 21:20, 22:1, and 28:69; the area south of the Arnon has less rainfall). Moses' final speeches take place on the steppes of Moab (Deut. 1:5 and 34:1).

Culturally and linguistically, Moabites and Israelites shared a great deal (see the discussion of the Moabite Mesha inscription in "The Status of the Moabites" in the introduction), although each worshiped a different deity (Chemosh for Moab, YHWH for Israel), which is probably why Deuteronomy is so concerned about limiting contact between the two groups (23:4). The two nations, Israel and Moab, emerged at roughly the same time, both subject to frequent encroachment by neighboring states. According to Gen. 19:30–37, the Moabites descend from Abraham's nephew Lot. Specifically, they descend from an incestuous encounter between Lot and his older daughter. According to 2 Kings 3:4–5 (and the Mesha Stone from Moab), Moab, which had been subjugated by Israel for a time, rebelled in the ninth century B.C.E. Deuteronomy 2:9 notes that God gave the Moabites their land, and verses 2:28–29 imply that the Moabites provided the escaping Israelites with water and food. However, Deut. 23:5 accuses the Moabites of refusing to provide water and food after Israel fled Egypt (a view repeated in Neh. 13:1–3). It therefore prohibits Moabites from being "admitted into the congregation of the LORD" (Deut. 23:4). Ezra 9–10 and Neh. 13:23–27 perpetuate the opposition to the Moabites by forbidding marriages with Moabite women (among others).[3] This background of tension between the two ethnic groups is essential to understanding Ruth's relationship to the Judahite community of Bethlehem (see "Moabite women" at v. 4 below, as well as "The Status of the Moabites" in the introduction).

2. ***Elimelech*** Most names in Ruth convey meaning. "Elimelech" means "My God is king." (In some manuscripts of the Septuagint—a pre-Christian Greek translation of the Bible—the name appears as Abimelech, a more common biblical name.)[4] Elimelech appears in the Bible only in Ruth but is attested in extra-biblical records such as the Amarna letters from the fourteenth century B.C.E.

Naomi This name comes from the Hebrew root *n-ʿ-m*, meaning "pleasant." The name Naomi is an old one, appearing already in Ugaritic (an ancient language related to, but older than, Hebrew) as Nu-ʿu-ma-ya; in Ugaritic texts, the element *nʿm,* "pleasant," also appears both as an epithet of gods and of the heroes Aqhat and Keret.

named Mahlon and Chilion—Ephrathites of Bethlehem in Judah. They came to the country of Moab
and remained there.
3 Elimelech, Naomi's husband, died; and she was

וְשֵׁ֣ם שְׁנֵֽי־בָנָ֣יו ׀ מַחְל֤וֹן וְכִלְיוֹן֙ אֶפְרָתִ֔ים
מִבֵּ֥ית לֶ֖חֶם יְהוּדָ֑ה וַיָּבֹ֥אוּ שְׂדֵי־מוֹאָ֖ב
וַיִּֽהְיוּ־שָֽׁם׃
3 וַיָּ֥מָת אֱלִימֶ֖לֶךְ אִ֣ישׁ נָעֳמִ֑י וַתִּשָּׁאֵ֥ר הִ֖יא

Mahlon One meaning of this name is related to illness (from the Hebrew root *ḥ-l-h,* as in Exod. 15:26). In postbiblical Hebrew, the verbal root ***m-ḥ-l*** (also possible for Mahlon) means "to forgive," and in a few cases, the verb form refers to petitioning God for help, as Moses does in Exod. 32:11. Rabbinic sources develop these multiple possibilities (B. BB 91a; Ruth R. 2:5; see "Pre-modern Rabbinic Interpretations" in the introduction). A similar name appears as a woman's (and place) name, Mahlah, in Num. 27:1 and elsewhere, suggesting that illness may not be the only connotation of Mahlon. This name appears only in Ruth.

Chilion This name, derived from either ***k-l-y*** or ***k-l-h,*** indicates an end. It can have a positive connotation in the sense of completion as in "The heaven and the earth were finished" (Gen. 2:1), but can also mean "annihilation" as in Ezek. 11:13. The name appears only in Ruth, but a related one, Ki-li-ya-nu, appears in Ugarit.[5] Rabbinic sources explore the name further (see comment at "Mahlon" above and "Pre-modern Rabbinic Interpretations" in the introduction).

Ephrathites of Bethlehem in Judah Certain biblical texts indicate that the Judahite clan that settled Bethlehem is known also as Ephrath or Ephrathah (Mic. 5:1; see also below, 4:11). In the genealogy of the Judah tribe, Ephrat is the wife of Caleb (1 Chron. 2:19,50) and the mother of a major line of descendants ("Hur, the first-born of Ephrathah, the father of Bethlehem," 1 Chron. 4:4). According to Ibn Ezra, the place is named after her. Similarly, Ephrath points to the place where Rachel (who is mentioned in Ruth 4:11) is buried (Gen. 35:19). By referring to Ephrathites here, the narrator situates the action of the book in the penumbra of female presences.

More overtly, this name may allude to Ruth's descendant David (see 4:22), who in the Book of Samuel is "the son of a certain Ephrathite of Bethlehem in Judah" (1 Sam. 17:12). Furthermore, Bethlehem is where David is first anointed (1 Sam. 16:4). The role of Ephrath(ah) in Israel's consciousness is so great that Micah proclaims "Bethlehem of Ephrath" as the place of origin for the future Davidic ruler (Mic. 5:1). In ancient Israel, a place name is often synonymous with its resident clan. When referring to a locale, the name Ephrath(ah) often appears together with Bethlehem. Apparently the two areas overlapped: Ephrath(ah) was either part of the town or it was the larger district of which the town was a part. The Targum renders "Ephrathites" as ***rabbanin,*** that is, great scholars, and Rashi understands the term to mean "important," epithets that account for the honor granted Elimelech's family (according to Rabbinic sources) by Moab's king.

3. Elimelech, Naomi's husband, died The author gives no reason for his death. In particular, nothing suggests divine punishment; but later Jewish traditions accuse Elimelech of having deserted his people (Ruth R. 1.5). By now identifying Elimelech in relation to Naomi, as "Naomi's husband," the narrator signals a shift in focus, foregrounding Naomi as a key protagonist; others are identified in relation to her. It is from this verse that the Rabbis derive the insight that a person's death most strongly affects the spouse (*'ein 'ish meit ela le-'ishto,* "a person dies primarily to his wife" (B. Sanh. 22b).

left with her two sons. [4]They married Moabite women, one named Orpah and the other Ruth, and

וּשְׁנֵ֥י בָנֶֽיהָ׃ 4 וַיִּשְׂא֣וּ לָהֶ֗ם נָשִׁים֙ מֹאֲבִיּ֔וֹת
שֵׁ֤ם הָֽאַחַת֙ עָרְפָּ֔ה וְשֵׁ֥ם הַשֵּׁנִ֖ית ר֑וּת

4. married Hebrew *va-yis'u, from n-s-'*, literally "carried, lifted up." The term also connotes "taking away" or "treating favorably" (as when Abraham lifts his eyes in Gen. 22:4, and when God's favor is invoked in the Priestly Blessing, Num. 6:26). This is an idiom for marriage in late biblical Hebrew, found in Ezra (10:44) and Chronicles (2 Chron. 11:21; 13:21; 24:3), books written in the postexilic period. In the postbiblical tradition, it becomes the standard word for marriage. Earlier texts that refer to marriage use the verb *l-k-ḥ,* which literally means "to take" (Isaac "took Rebekah" in Gen. 24:69; priests "may not marry [*lo yikḥu*] a woman defiled" in Lev. 21:7; see further comment at 4:13).[6]

Moabite women Structurally, a marriage with a Moabite woman stands at the center of the Prologue. Moabite status may also be the focal point of the dilemma that must be faced when Ruth the Moabite comes to Judah. It is not uncommon in the Bible for Israelites who live outside the land to marry local women: Joseph marries Asenath the Egyptian, and Moses marries Zipporah the Midianite. Neither man, however, returns to the land of Canaan with his foreign wife.

Marriage with Moabites is a particularly thorny problem, given the injunction in Deut. 23:4–7 to exclude Moabites permanently from the community. Significantly, the narrator of Ruth says nothing negative about this marriage. However, the earliest interpreters of the book criticized this marriage. The Targum to Ruth "translates" the verse by adding: "they transgressed the decree of the Word of the Lord and took unto themselves foreign wives from the daughters of Moab."[7]

Some rabbinic Jewish interpreters, notably Ibn Ezra and Radak, suggest that the men had converted the women first. Others exonerate the men from a seeming violation of Deut. 23:4–7 by interpreting the prohibition against Moabites as referring only to Moabite males—not females. (See "Intermarriage" and "Conversion" and "The Status of the Moabites" in the introduction; and below comment at 4:5–10.)

Orpah Interpreters associate this name with the noun *oreph,* back of the neck, for Orpah is the one who eventually turns her back on Naomi and goes back to her parents (albeit at Naomi's insistence). Frymer-Kensky connects the name also with the word *'rp,* a common word in Ugaritic for "cloud," which is also found in Ps. 68:5 in the divine epithet, "the rider of the clouds."[8]

Ruth The etymology of this name, which appears only in this book, is difficult. The Moabite Mesha inscription uses the form *ryt*, "satiation" (1.12: for a description of the Moabite Mesha inscription, see "The Status of the Moabites," in the introduction). In Hebrew, the name may derive from the root *r-w-h*, "overflowing with moisture," as in the "watered garden" in Isa. 58:1 (so, too, B. BB 14b, which refers to saturation with blessings).[9] Thus, the two wives' names are linked together by the element of water: Orpah is the cloud above that passes without bringing rain; Ruth is the moisture below that brings the desiccated family back to life. The Targum adds here that Ruth was the daughter of the Moabite king Eglon, mentioned in Judg. 3:12–22.

about ten years This may be another allusion to the Abraham story, for Abraham and Sarah were in Canaan for ten years before Sarah gave Hagar to Abraham to serve as a surrogate to birth a child (Gen. 16:3). The parallel alludes to the fact that the two couples

they lived there about ten years. 5 Then those two—
Mahlon and Chilion—also died; so the woman was
left without her two sons and without her husband.
6 She started out with her daughters-in-law to
return from the country of Moab; for in the country
of Moab she had heard that the LORD had taken note

וַיֵּ֥שְׁבוּ שָׁ֖ם כְּעֶ֥שֶׂר שָׁנִֽים׃ 5 וַיָּמ֥וּתוּ גַם־
שְׁנֵיהֶ֖ם מַחְל֣וֹן וְכִלְי֑וֹן וַתִּשָּׁאֵר֙ הָֽאִשָּׁ֔ה
מִשְּׁנֵ֥י יְלָדֶ֖יהָ וּמֵאִישָֽׁהּ׃
6 וַתָּ֤קָם הִיא֙ וְכַלֹּתֶ֔יהָ וַתָּ֖שָׁב מִשְּׂדֵ֣י מוֹאָ֑ב
כִּ֤י שָֽׁמְעָה֙ בִּשְׂדֵ֣ה מוֹאָ֔ב כִּֽי־פָקַ֤ד יְהוָה֙

are childless—something the text does not otherwise mention. (The text does not provide reasons for the childlessness.)

5. Then those two—Mahlon and Chilion—also died Like the death of their father, the sons' deaths are noted without any reference to punishment. The Targum attributes their premature death to their marrying Moabite women, but the story's plain sense does not connect the two events.

the woman was left without her two sons The Hebrew is somewhat unusual syntactically (lit. "She was left *from* her two sons"), creating a poignant contrast with verse 3: there she was left with her sons; now she is left without them. The narrator underscores the contrast by mentioning the sons here before the husband, which also emphasizes the mother's sorrows, for her husband died a decade ago, whereas the sons' deaths are the fresh sorrows. Naomi is all that remains of the family that departed Judah. Now other individuals are described in relation to her ("Naomi's husband" and "her two sons" in 1:3 and "her daughters-in-law" in 1:6).

her...sons Hebrew *yeladeha,* "her children," "the ones she gave birth to." With few exceptions (such as 1 Kings 12:10), the noun *yeled* usually designates a young child, not a grown man. Using the term here calls attention to Naomi's role as their mother. It also emphasizes the theme of giving birth, which plays a prominent role later in the story (4:16) when Naomi is given the new child (*yeled*), born to her daughter-in-law Ruth. The last reference will in some sense mend the genealogical chain that breaks in the present verse.

6. She started out with her daughters-in-law Literally "she rose up, she and her daughters-in-law." In accord with ancient Israelite traditions, Naomi has now become the head of the household. (Other biblical women in a similar position include Hagar after her expulsion in Gen. 21:21 and several widows with minor children, e.g., 1 Kings 17:11.) The men's death makes Naomi a chief protagonist—in charge of her own destiny and responsible for that of others. The family that plans to return after the famine has radically changed: the three men are dead; the bereft three widows wend their way back.

daughters-in-law Hebrew *kalotehah.* As in modern Hebrew, *kalah* in the Bible can refer to a bride (e.g., Isa. 49:18); but it often appears in relation to in-laws (e.g., Gen. 38:16, which refers to Tamar, the daughter-in-law of Judah, as *kalato*). Similarly, its masculine counterpart, *ḥatan,* means both "son-in-law" (as David becomes in relation to Saul when David marries Saul's daughter Michal, 1 Sam. 18:22), as well as "groom" (Isa. 61:10).

for...she had heard The narrator does not tell the reader how Naomi heard, leaving the impression that it was a rumor that spread naturally. The Targum to Ruth has an angel inform her. The Targum also claims that the famine ends because of the merit and the petitionary prayer of the judge Ibzan (Judg. 12:8), whom the Rabbis identify with Boaz.

the LORD had taken note of His people and given them food This is one of only two times in the book that God actually intervenes in human affairs (the other is 4:13).

of His people and given them food. [7] Accompanied by
her two daughters-in-law, she left the place where she
had been living; and they set out on the road back to
the land of Judah.

אֶת־עַמּ֔וֹ לָתֵ֥ת לָהֶ֖ם לָֽחֶם׃ 7 וַתֵּצֵ֗א מִן־
הַמָּקוֹם֙ אֲשֶׁ֣ר הָֽיְתָה־שָׁ֔מָּה וּשְׁתֵּ֥י כַלֹּתֶ֖יהָ
עִמָּ֑הּ וַתֵּלַ֣כְנָה בַדֶּ֔רֶךְ לָשׁ֖וּב אֶל־אֶ֥רֶץ
יְהוּדָֽה׃

Elsewhere God appears in name only in the blessings and oaths that people offer. Even here, the narrator does not claim that God has ended the famine, but only that this is what Naomi has heard. On the role of God in the book, see "The Theology of the Book of Ruth" in the introduction.

taken note Hebrew *pakad,* the classic term for divine remembrance (as when God recalls Sarah and she becomes pregnant in Gen. 21:1). It can refer to a reckoning for sins or other misdeeds (as in the Decalogue, Exod. 20:5), or to describe God's decision to help (as when God takes note of Israel's suffering in Exod. 4:31). *P-k-d* can also refer to taking stock and noticing someone missing, like David's absence from Saul's feast (1 Sam. 20:6).

7. As is usual when mentioning the head of a household, Hebrew syntax places Naomi first, stating that she led the way, and her two daughters-in-law accompanied her. This pattern mirrors verses 1–2 implicitly, contrasting the original departure of the head of a Judahite household together with his family (two men and a woman). Such symmetry underscores the degree of transformation this family has undergone.

she left the place Noting that this information seems redundant, Rashi explains that it serves to teach that the departure of a righteous person is noteworthy.

back Hebrew *lashuv,* "to return." Technically, only Naomi is "returning," whereas the other women are actually leaving their homeland. Yet, the narrator paints all three as setting out to return, showing their unity of purpose. Further instances of this verbal root *sh-w-v* play a major role in the following scenes, making it a *leitwort,* a leading or theme word, in this chapter. In biblical texts, such repeated words highlight central themes.

THE TURNING POINT ON THE ROAD TO BETHLEHEM (1:8–18)

While en route, the three widows come to a crossroads in their lives when Naomi insists that her two daughters-in-law return home to Moab. Although both younger women resist Naomi's urging, Orpah at the end complies, but Ruth refuses. The scene culminates when Ruth vows to remain with Naomi forever, and the two women continue their journey to Bethlehem.

Why does Naomi want the Moabite women to return home? Her own words indicate high esteem for the women and emphasize her concern for their welfare. She seeks to repay the benevolence (*ḥesed*) that they have shown her, and she seeks God's help on their behalf. There is no need to doubt this motive. Frymer-Kensky emphasizes Naomi's wish to release the younger women from any obligations toward her, and also to free herself from any connection to her sons' wives. Most Rabbinic texts and subsequent interpreters concur that Naomi is generous, even self-sacrificing, when she sends her daughters-in-law away. Yet, more may be at play here. As the story unfolds, certain statements—and Naomi's treatment of Ruth when they arrive in Bethlehem—cast a shadow on this altruistic picture. The Rabbinic source Midrash Ruth Zuta on this passage, for example, suggests that Naomi is ashamed to bring the women with her. Similarly, some modern commentators[10] argue that

8 But Naomi said to her two daughters-in-law,
"Turn back, each of you to her mother's house. May
the LORD deal kindly with you, as you have dealt with

8 וַתֹּאמֶר נָעֳמִי לִשְׁתֵּי כַלֹּתֶיהָ לֵכְנָה
שֹּׁבְנָה אִשָּׁה לְבֵית אִמָּהּ יעשה יַעַשׂ יְהוָה
עִמָּכֶם חֶסֶד כַּאֲשֶׁר עֲשִׂיתֶם עִם־הַמֵּתִים

conspicuous silences in the narrative imply that Naomi is resentful, maybe even embarrassed by the prospect of coming home with Moabite daughters-in-law (see further comment at 1:18, 1:22, 2:1, 3:17, and 4:14; see also "Contemporary Readings" in the introduction).

Most likely, the author understands that a person in Naomi's position would be propelled by mixed motives and therefore depicts Naomi in this manner. Such realism contributes to the book's power in that it shows that even good people can have mixed motives—a more illuminating and useful scenario than an idyll that strips out ordinary human emotions and conflicts.

The Targum and most Rabbinic literature (Ruth R. 2.22; Rashi) read the exchanges on the road primarily in terms of religious conversion. The sages consider Naomi's words and Ruth's commitment as steps in the process of conversion. Naomi's three-fold attempt to dissuade the younger women from joining her ("Turn back" in 1:8, 11, and 12) becomes in Rabbinic texts a model for how to approach would-be converts: one must try to discourage a proselyte three times (Ruth R. 2:17). In the Book of Ruth itself, however, Ruth continues to be designated as a Moabite even after her famous address to Naomi (see "Intermarriage" and "Conversion" in the introduction and the comment at 1:22).

OUTLINE

I. The first dialogue: Naomi urges Orpah and Ruth to return home (1:8–10)
II. The second dialogue: Turning point for Orpah and Ruth (1:11–14)
III. The third dialogue: Ruth's point of no return (1:15–18)

THE FIRST DIALOGUE: NAOMI URGES ORPAH AND RUTH TO RETURN HOME (1:8–10)

The widows have come to a turning point, an unspecified place en route between Moab and Judah. Naomi's short first speech traces the typical journey of a woman, first to the house of her mother and then to the house of her husband. Because she views marriage as the best reward a woman can receive for her good deeds and for economic and physical security, she urges the two women to return to their mothers' houses for what she hopes will be a temporary stay; she calls upon God to help them find new husbands.

8. Naomi said Naomi's first words in the book show concern for her daughters-in-law. This is significant; as literary critics note, a character's first words in the Bible can reveal important aspects of the character's perspective.[11]

Turn back Hebrew *shovenah.* The verb *sh-w-v,* "return," is a key word in this first chapter. The women will indeed turn their lives around, but the question is: in which direction? Naomi pressures them to return to their previous lives in Moab.

her mother's house Hebrew *beit 'immah.* This term appears only in two other places in the Bible, both similarly connected to a strong female persona: Rebekah runs to her "mother's house" to report the arrival of Abraham's servant (Gen. 24:28); and the woman in the Song of Songs speaks of taking her beloved to her "mother's house" for safety or pleasure (Songs. 3:4 and 8:2). In Song of Songs, the term alludes to an amorous setting; for Naomi, the term relates to matrimonial hopes. Elsewhere in the Bible, a widow is expected to return to her father's house: Judah sends Tamar to her father's house to wait until his youngest son matures (Gen. 38:11). A priest's daughter is to return to her father's house when widowed or divorced (Lev. 22:13). Apparently, for this reason, the Septuagint here reads "your father's house."[12]

The household, usually called the *beit 'av,* "father's house," was the basic unit of Israelite life. Physically, it consisted of a cluster of dwellings for living and economic production (see "The Family" and "Marriage" in the introduction). The "mother's house" may have been designated as one of these units; however, more likely the term refers here not to a physical dwelling but rather to a conceptual unit: the mother's jurisdiction. As Meyers notes, *beit 'em* may be a technical term and a "social equivalence to the far more common" *beit 'av.*[13] The mention of the mother's house is one of several elements in Ruth that represents a female perspective.[14] Naomi, then, is not sending the young women to live under their father's tutelage but wants them to prepare for new lives with new husbands in new households.

May the Lord[15] In this first of many blessings in the book, Naomi expresses trust in God's benevolence toward those who merit it. Naomi repeatedly sees the hand of God in human affairs. In 1:20–21 she interprets her plight as God's doing. Here she hopes that her daughters-in-law will be rewarded for what they have done, even though she herself cannot offer reward. As Adler observes (commenting on the Book of Ruth), blessings are one of two things that even the destitute can bestow (the other is *ḥesed*).[16] Naomi, then, does her best to give the younger women what she can.

deal kindly Hebrew *ya'as . . . ḥesed,* literally "may[17] [YHWH] do *ḥesed.*" *Ḥesed,* often also translated as "lovingkindness," refers in Ruth to acts of benevolence that one does out of kindness, not out of any contractual obligation. *Ḥesed,* "a benevolent act," is an important concept in the Book of Ruth, and it reappears at critical junctures (2:20; 3:10). Here *ḥesed* is grounded in the perception of (or hope for) a just universe, where a good deed is rewarded. A similar view is found elsewhere in the Bible, sometimes attached to the concept of retribution. Psalm 62 declares "*Ḥesed* is yours, oh my Lord, for you repay each person according to his deeds" (Ps. 62:13). God's actions toward Israel in events of deliverance such as the Exodus are the paradigm of *ḥesed* (e.g., Exod. 15:13). Yet the idea of *ḥesed* also connotes legal obligations in ancient Near Eastern and certain biblical texts, tied to an expectation of reciprocity and mutual aid grounded in covenantal relationship (as in 2 Sam. 9:1).[18] Legal obligations play a role in how Ruth R. 2.14 interprets Naomi's words: the *ḥesed* is the relinquishing of the ***ketubah*** that obligates Naomi or the estate to provide for them. Rabbinic sources elaborate on the notion of *ḥesed*. According to an often cited statement by R. Zeira, the main purpose of the Book of Ruth is to teach about *ḥesed* (Ruth R. 2.15). See further *"Ḥesed"* in the introduction.

with you Naomi, who has previously addressed the women with the special feminine plural suffix, here uses the masculine plural suffix *-em.* Although many commentators have speculated about the reason for this grammatical oddity, it is most likely insignificant.[19]

as you have dealt with the dead and with me! Naomi is referring to Orpah's and Ruth's (otherwise unspecified) kindness toward their husbands, her two sons. Naomi now wishes to reciprocate and acknowledge their prior kindness to her as well. In this story, the Moabite women are the first to show kindness. A circle of kindness continues to expand as the story unfolds.

with the dead Rabbinic texts elaborate: the women granted posthumous kindness to the dead by caring for their shrouds (Ruth R. 2.14; Malbim). Generosity toward

the dead and with me! 9 May the LORD grant that each
of you find security in the house of a husband!" And
she kissed them farewell. They broke into weeping
10 and said to her, "No, we will return with you to
your people."

וְעִמָּדִי׃ 9 יִתֵּן יְהוָה לָכֶם וּמְצֶאןָ מְנוּחָה
אִשָּׁה בֵּית אִישָׁהּ וַתִּשַּׁק לָהֶן וַתִּשֶּׂאנָה
קוֹלָן וַתִּבְכֶּינָה׃ 10 וַתֹּאמַרְנָה־לָּהּ כִּי־אִתָּךְ
נָשׁוּב לְעַמֵּךְ׃

the dead is kindness without any possibility of recompense, what the Rabbis call *ḥesed shel emet,* genuine or true *ḥesed.* Rabbinic elaboration here aptly exemplifies the nature of *ḥesed* in Ruth as wholly without expectation of reward.

9. May the LORD grant that each of you find security in the house of a husband! Naomi invokes Israel's God for the second time, as one who will help the younger women gain security. In 3:1–5, she herself takes steps to implement that wish. A similar trajectory is enacted by Boaz, who invokes God's blessing for reward (2:12) and then acts to make that reward possible (see comment at 2:14; 3:9). For the book's early readers, Boaz's marriage announcement in 4:10 is the culmination of such reward.

security in the house of a husband The word *menuḥah,* translated here as "security," like the related term *manoaḥ* (which Naomi uses in 3:1), is more precisely translated as "rest" or "repose." But the translation effectively captures Naomi's sense that a woman's "security" is achieved by marriage, which brings with it rest and repose. Elsewhere, Solomon blesses God for giving rest, *menuḥah,* to his people (1 Kings 8:56; see also 1 Chron. 22:9).[20] Naomi articulates a social reality typical of ancient Near Eastern cultures, portrayed in biblical as well as Mesopotamian texts that illustrate how a woman's security usually depended upon having a husband and a home. The medieval exegete Ibn Ezra, commenting on the related term *manoaḥ* in 3:1, explains that a woman can find rest only when married. Yet the figure of Ruth and the book as a whole both confirm and subvert this presumption: In this story it is a woman, Ruth, who serves as the catalyst for the security that comes to Naomi, even if it is through the protection of the man whom Ruth enlists and the son whom she bears (see comment at 4:15, where the women exclaim that Ruth is "better . . . than seven sons").

And she kissed them farewell. They broke into weeping This scene is suffused with pathos. The Hebrew states simply that she kissed them; the NJPS translators add the word "farewell." In the Bible, tearful kissing marks both reunion (as when Jacob and Esau meet in Gen. 33:4 or Joseph and his brothers reunite in Gen. 45:15) and separation (as when Laban kisses his sons and daughters in Gen. 32:1).

They broke into weeping Literally "and lifted their voices and wept." The fragment from Qumran (4QRuth[a]) has a masculine ending for "voices" (*kolam*) instead of the feminine MT (*kolan*).

10. No Hebrew *ki.* The daughters-in-law refuse to heed Naomi's exhortation. *Ki,* usually meaning "because" or "but," can carry the meaning as here,[21] in the sense of "(but) surely!"

we will return with you to your people Literally "it is with *you* that we *return* to *your* people." The wording of their statement underscores their commitment specifically to Naomi. The syntax, as well as the sentence's frame of reference, emphatically situates Naomi at the center of their concern. Loyalty to her propels their decision. David Stein also detects in this wording some recognition of Naomi's authority, which prompts him to

11 וַתֹּ֤אמֶר נָעֳמִי֙ שֹׁ֣בְנָה בְנֹתַ֔י לָ֥מָּה תֵלַ֖כְנָה
עִמִּ֑י הַֽעֽוֹד־לִ֤י בָנִים֙ בְּֽמֵעַ֔י וְהָי֥וּ לָכֶ֖ם

11 But Naomi replied, "Turn back, my daughters!
Why should you go with me? Have I any more sons

render the phrase as: "Rather, it is under your jurisdiction [as head of the household] that we will return. . . ."[22]

return The use of *shuv* ("return") for the second time in this short exchange reiterates the central theme of this section.

THE SECOND DIALOGUE: THE TURNING POINT FOR ORPAH AND RUTH (1:11–14)

In her first speech, Naomi urges each daughter-in-law to return to her mother's house and expresses the wish that God help each of them find a new husband. Now she goes a step further, explaining that she herself cannot provide husbands for them and that therefore they need to leave her. Her four references to marriage in this short speech attest to Naomi's focus. Frymer-Kensky considers Naomi's insistence to reflect genuine concern for the younger women's future: Naomi formally releases the women from any binding attachment to her or her family. In the end, Orpah agrees to leave, but Ruth responds by reattaching herself, in effect "adopting" Naomi.

Frymer-Kensky emphasizes that Naomi's speech is grounded in ancient Israel's social system, in the experience of widows and in the biblical institution of the levirate marriage (see comment below at v. 11 and "Levirate Marriage" in the introduction). Although Naomi alludes to the institution of levirate marriage, her main argument is that she is too old to (re)produce sons for these women to wed. She can no longer provide what they need. Therefore, the women should go back to a world where they can remarry. Her plea reveals her concern with the welfare of her daughters-in-law and a strong sense of obligation toward them. Yet what Naomi does not say also discloses a great deal. Significantly, she does not think they can find spouses in Judah, possibly because they are Moabites. Most important, she does not mention the possibility that a levir (i.e., a brother qualified or obligated to provide a widow with a son) may be available in Judah. She gives no indication that this obligation might or could fall to more distant male relatives (some of whom are still alive in Bethlehem). This omission has important implications for understanding the negotiations about marriage in Chapter 4.

Some contemporary commentators criticize Naomi, blaming her for refusing to continue caring for her daughters-in-law or argue that she perceives them as a burden.[23] But as Frymer-Kensky observes, in this ancient society it is adult sons and daughters-in-law who care for aging parents or for a widow left alone, not the other way around. Rather than releasing herself from obligations to these women, Naomi is releasing them from obligations to her. Yet the author's presentation allows for mixed motives in the portrait of Naomi and thereby adds depth to the book's characterization (see at v. 13; see also Naomi's complaint about her bitter fate in 1:11).

11. Turn back Hebrew *Shovenah,* derived from the root *sh-w-v*—a key term in this section—is the first word in Naomi's second speech, in which she urges the younger women (again) to return to their lives in Moab (compare v. 8).

my daughters! Calling them "my daughters" expresses Naomi's kinship bond with them and conveys her maternal solicitude. This is the term used also by an older person to a younger female.

לַאֲנָשִֽׁים׃ 12 שֹׁבְנָה בְנֹתַי֙ לֵ֫כְןָ כִּי זָקַנְתִּי
מִהְיוֹת לְאִישׁ כִּי אָמַ֙רְתִּי֙ יֶשׁ־לִי תִקְוָה
גַּם הָיִיתִי הַלַּ֙יְלָה֙ לְאִישׁ וְגַם יָלַדְתִּי בָנִֽים׃

in my body who might be husbands for you?
12 Turn back, my daughters, for I am too old to be
married. Even if I thought there was hope for me,
even if I were married tonight and I also bore sons,

Why should you go with me? Have I any more sons in my body who might be husbands for you? These rhetorical questions reveal Naomi's conviction that only the desire to find a husband should motivate women in Orpah's and Ruth's position. However, the Book of Ruth then proceeds to undermine the attitude that Naomi articulates here. In a sense, the rest of the narrative "answers" Naomi's questions, at least in terms of Ruth: at the end of the book, the women of Bethlehem proclaim Ruth's love for Naomi. This would seem a sufficient and effective motive for Ruth's choices and actions (see 4:15).

Have I any more sons in my body who might be husbands for you? Naomi's argument alludes to the biblical institute of the levirate marriage. Since Naomi is no longer capable of becoming pregnant, she cannot provide men for her daughters-in-law to marry. Various forms of levirate arrangement appear in the Bible and in other cultures, ancient and modern. By this means, a childless widow and a man's brother provide a posthumous heir to maintain the deceased man's name and lineage. At the same time, moreover, the birth of a child strengthens the widowed mother's social and economic position. The later Hebrew name for this arrangement, *yibbum*, is based on biblical references that use the root *y-b-m* when discussing this practice in Gen. 38:6–11 and Deut. 25:5–10 (see comment at 4:5 and "Levirate Marriage" in the introduction).[24]

Naomi's rhetorical statements imply that the responsibility of levirate marriage can (in theory) fall upon brothers by the same mother (even if by a different father). However, the laws of the Torah (Deut. 25:5–10) and the story about a levir (Genesis 38) refer only to brothers who are sons from the same father. Regardless, Naomi rejects this possibility in this particular case (on the ground that she is too old) and hence urges them to look elsewhere.[25]

12. Turn back, my daughters Naomi repeats her exhortation that the younger women return to their families in Moab (compare vv. 8 and 11). The repetition emphasizes Naomi's persistence and her sense of urgency. The expected return of childless widows to their fathers' homes is supported by Gen. 38:11 when Judah sends his daughter-in-law Tamar to her father's home (see also Lev. 22:13). However, recall that Naomi speaks of the mother's house (1:8).

I am too old to be married Although Naomi does not explicitly say that she is too old to conceive children, this implication is clear, for only if she were to give birth to more sons might she be able to help her widowed daughters-in-law by providing new husbands for them.

for... Even if... even if... Naomi follows her rhetorical questions with a retort: "I am too old to marry." She then presents to the women a concatenation of hypothetical cases: even were she to marry that very day, and even if she were to give birth to more sons, would her daughters-in-law be willing to wait, remaining bound to them, all the while forbidden to marry anyone else? Naomi develops this improbable scenario, only to reject it as a viable solution to the problem that preoccupies her.

hope Hebrew *tikvah*. Naomi is referring here to the biblical ideal of a fulfilling future: a life with children. Frymer-Kensky points out that the word *tikvah,* normally

13 should you wait for them to grow up? Should you on their account debar yourselves from marriage?

13 הֲלָהֵ֣ן ׀ תְּשַׂבֵּ֗רְנָה עַ֚ד אֲשֶׁ֣ר יִגְדָּ֔לוּ הֲלָהֵן֙
תֵּעָגֵ֔נָה לְבִלְתִּ֖י הֱי֣וֹת לְאִ֑ישׁ אַ֣ל בְּנֹתַ֗י

translated as "hope," is related to a Hebrew word meaning "thread," as in *tikvat ḥut ha-shani,* the cord of scarlet thread that the prostitute Rahab hangs outside her window as a signal to Joshua to spare her family (Josh. 2:18). The imagery in this idiom suggests that our life is spun out like a cord, and hope arises from the strength of that cord, representing the prospect of a viable future. Indeed, *tikvah,* used in this sense, appears four times elsewhere in the Bible in parallel with Hebrew *'aḥarit* "future" (Jer. 29:11; 31:17; Prov. 23:18; 24:14). In the two passages cited in Proverbs, the phrases "to have a future" and "not to have your hope/cord cut" (Heb. *karet*) are rhetorically equivalent. So, too, a tree is said to be especially full of *tikvah,* for even if it is cut down, new shoots grow from the stump (Job 14:7). Similarly, God says to Mother Rachel: "There is *tikvah* in your future, for your sons will return to their domain" (Jer. 31:17); and God shows Ezekiel a vision in which the Israelites say, "Our bones are dry, our *tikvah* is lost, we are cut off" (Ezek. 37:11).

13. should you wait for them to grow up? Should you on their account debar yourselves from marriage? Naomi's rhetorical questions continue to allude to levirate marriage. They evoke the story of Judah and Tamar (who are mentioned later, in Ruth 4:12), in which Judah tells his widowed daughter-in-law Tamar to wait at her father's house until Judah's youngest son is old enough to impregnate her (Gen. 38:11). When referring to the hypothetical sons she might bear, Naomi uses an unusual dual ending, *lahen,* meaning "them" and "their." This construction is usually a feminine form, but here it refers to male antecedents, "sons." Much scholarly debate revolves around this oddity; some suggest that Naomi is using an archaic form or an Aramaism.[26]

should you wait Naomi's speech contains two unusual terms that may have had specific legal connotations in ancient Israel. The verb *s-b-r* "wait" appears a few times in late (postexilic) biblical contexts. It is similar to the Aramaic *sbr,* and it may have been a technical term for waiting until something (favorable) occurs. When followed by a noun, it means "to wait with anticipation for something," as in "I wait for your salvation" (Ps. 119:166). Usually it refers to waiting for God (as in Ps. 104:27; 145:15) but can be secular as here and in Esther 9:1.

debar Hebrew *tei'ageinah*, the second unusual word, is a *hapax legomenon*, that is, a word that appears only once in the Hebrew Bible.[27] The Masoretic vocalization links the verb with a term connected to a Hebrew root that means "to bake [a cake of bread]" (so too Ibn Ezra), which in Rabbinic Hebrew came to mean "to draw a circle." The NJPS "debar" conforms to the meaning indicated by such Masoretic vocalization. It suggests something like "draw a circle around yourselves" so as to prevent yourselves from marrying. In the Mishnah, a related term, *'ogen,* means "anchor," as in "whoever sells a boat, sells it with mast, sail, and anchor" (M. BB 5.1; see also B. BB 73a). From Mishnaic times, the feminine passive participle *'agunah,* "the anchored one," has been a technical term for a woman who cannot legally remarry. (This situation might arise either because she does not possess a written decree of divorce, has not found a witness to attest to her husband's death, or because she is a childless widow who has not been released from the levirate obligation.) Given that Naomi is speaking about marriage, it is conceivable that she is using it here as a technical term, suggesting that the concept of the "anchored wife" already existed in biblical times. Rashi, however, argues against a connection with *'agunah.* He points out that to make such a connection, a dot (*dagesh*) would have been placed in the letter *nun:*

Oh no, my daughters! My lot is far more bitter than yours, for the hand of the LORD has struck out against me."

כִּֽי־מַר־לִ֤י מְאֹד֙ מִכֶּ֔ם כִּֽי־יָצְאָ֥ה בִ֖י יַד־יְהוָֽה׃

tei'agennah rather than *tei'ageinah*. Radak, however, ties it to yet another root, *'-g-h*, meaning "delay."[28]

Oh no Literally, "Do not!" Naomi doesn't wait for the women to answer but immediately enjoins them not to do this. She urges them to leave because, she claims, God has turned against her.

my daughters As in v.11, Naomi underscores her maternal concern for them.

My lot is far more bitter than yours Hebrew *mar li me'od mi-kem*. Naomi concludes her second speech with an anguished cry about her own condition. However, it is not clear whether she is claiming to be more bitter than her daughters-in-law or bitter on their account. NJPS follows the usual interpretation, according to which Naomi claims that she suffers the most. Yet the Hebrew can also be read to mean: "it is bitter for me *because of* you,"[29] and even, "it grieveth me much for your sakes," which is how the KJV translates it. Frymer-Kensky points out that there are no occurrences of *mar* with the preposition *mi-* meaning "because of you," but there is also no occurrence of *mar* with any other preposition, no other way of saying "bitter because of" other than by saying "bitter that" (*ki*) with a verbal clause. She concludes that such silence cannot prove that the *mi-* does mean "because of you." Ruth Rabbah 2:18 considers all these meanings possible (including "it is on account of you that 'the hand of the LORD'..."). The Targum, however, removes the ambiguity by having Naomi state explicitly that "I am more embittered than you." Which of these meanings is intended? Perhaps the narrator intends a double message. Such a reading bestows upon Naomi a complex set of responses, a trait that appears elsewhere in the book (see comment at 2:1–2 and 2:22). The commentator Alsheikh adds a different nuance: "I cannot bear your sorrow. You did nothing wrong. The sin is mine and you might be punished on my account."

bitter Hebrew *mar.* In the Bible, one becomes *mar* because of loss. This could be a loss of property (1 Sam. 22:2), of loved ones (as at funerals, Ezek. 27:30–31; Amos 8:10), and above all, of children—for example, being childless (1 Sam. 1:10), the loss of children who have been carried off by marauders (1 Sam. 30:6), or having one's child die (2 Kings 4:27; Zech. 12:10). (See further comment at v. 20.) Naomi's bitterness is that of a widow who has also lost her children, a fate shared by many women in Israel's history, due to wars and sieges, as well as to a high rate of child mortality. Here, all three women have lost their husbands; but only Naomi has lost her sons as well, a fate even more bitter than theirs.

hand of the LORD Naomi consistently sees God acting in people's lives, as she does already when expressing the hope that God will secure a husband for each young widow (1:8–9). The same conviction is at work here, which is why she sees her own desperate situation as a result of God's "hand" at work. The "hand of the LORD" appears in both narrative and poetic texts to express God's direct role in human affairs, usually for good (Ezra 7:28), but sometimes for ill (Exod. 9:3).[30] Ibn Ezra explains that the "hand" here is metaphoric. *Iggeret Shemuel* has Naomi reassure Orpah and Ruth with this statement that she is not blaming them: "Do not think that my bitterness is because of you. Definitely not!"[31] Naomi sounds like Job, who attributes his own life's tragedies to God's

14 They broke into weeping again, and Orpah kissed her mother-in-law farewell. But Ruth clung to her.

14 וַתִּשֶּׂנָה* קוֹלָן וַתִּבְכֶּינָה עוֹד וַתִּשַּׁק
עָרְפָּה לַחֲמוֹתָהּ וְרוּת דָּבְקָה בָּהּ׃

v. 14. חסר א׳

direct, personal intercession and uses similar language of embitterment (Job 27:2). Some interpretations (e.g., *Iggeret Shemuel*), detect in Naomi's words a veiled sense of guilt, as if she suspects that she somehow deserves divine punishment. However, the similarities to Job (see comment at 1:20), who is by all accounts innocent and whose suffering is undeserved, suggest otherwise. Rather, Naomi ascribes to God both the good and the bad. (The comparison with Job becomes more pronounced in 1:20–21.)

has struck out Literally, "went out against." Naomi's statement is the only biblical occurrence in which "the hand of the LORD" is used with the verb *y-tz-'* (lit. "go out"); in its other occurrences, the hand of God either "is" against animals or people, or is said to "touch" someone.

14. They broke into weeping again Once more the women respond with tears. They are overcome with emotion and say nothing. The narrator speaks for them, describing laconically what is a pivotal turning point in the story of the three women: two go "back" to Judah; one goes "back" to Moab.

Orpah kissed her...farewell The context implies that this is a farewell kiss (as in v. 9) and that Orpah then leaves. There is no hint of condemnation by the narrator. Orpah has been portrayed as devoted to her mother-in-law. Indeed, her devotion is manifested again here when she obeys Naomi's instructions by departing. Nothing further is told of her. Later Rabbinic midrashim evaluate Orpah's actions differently. They describe violent consequences as a result of her departure from Naomi: after leaving, she is repeatedly brutalized and raped (Ruth R. 2.20). According to another Rabbinic tradition, the legacies of Ruth and Orpah remain at odds for some time to come. Years later, Ruth's great-grandson David meets Goliath, who in this midrashic retelling is Orpah's great-grandson (Ruth R. 2.20; Ruth Z. 12.34). But Rashi, who frequently incorporates the midrashic material on the Book of Ruth in his writings, omits mention of these traditions.

But Ruth In the Hebrew, Ruth's name is preceded by *vav,* which can be read either as conjunctive ("and") or contrastive ("but"). The comparison with Orpah suggests that here the syntax is disjunctive and contrastive, hence the translation. This is the "turning point" in Ruth's life as she turns her back on Moab and her life there, linking her life's course with Naomi instead.

clung to her Hebrew *dabhekah bah;* more precisely, "stuck to her." The verb, from the root *d-b-k,* usually carries the sense of permanent bonding, as with adhesive. The term is used in the Bible for covenantal devotion and cleaving to God or a person; it is the major term for spiritual cleaving to God in Rabbinic literature and in later mystical writing. In the Bible, this verb first refers to the archetypal union of man and woman: "Hence a man leaves his father and mother and clings [*d-b-k*] to his wife, so that they become one flesh" (Gen. 2:24). Likewise it describes the attachment of Shechem to Dinah (Gen. 34:3). In Deuteronomy it is used to depict Israel's hoped-for attachment to God (4:4; 10:20; 11:22; 13:5; 30:20; see also Josh. 22:5 and 23:8), as part of the covenantal ritual. Many of these instances express an exclusive, single-minded attachment, which most likely applies here as well. In the Psalms *d-b-k* often refers to attachment to God but also to other forms of attachment. In a famous passage, the Psalmist declares, "let my tongue stick [*d-b-k*] to my palate if I cease to think of you, if I do not keep Jerusalem in memory even at my happiest hour" (Ps. 137:6). The verb appears again several times in the Book of Ruth in less intimate settings, as when Boaz directs Ruth to "cling" to his handmaids (2:9, translated there as "stay close") and later when Ruth repeats his instructions (albeit with a difference; 2:21).

THE THIRD DIALOGUE: RUTH'S POINT OF NO RETURN (1:15–18)

The turning point on the road to Bethlehem is also a point of no return. Despite Naomi's three exhortations, Ruth refuses to return to her earlier life or leave as did Orpah. Instead, Ruth commits herself permanently to Naomi, "sticking" to her (see previous comment) and being ready to share her fate. Ruth vows lifelong commitment to Naomi, Naomi's people, and Naomi's God (1:16). Her impassioned declaration—the most quoted passage from the book—has found its way into wedding and conversion ceremonies in which persons bind themselves wholly to one another or to Judaism. What is Ruth's motive for this unilateral and permanent commitment? Neither Ruth nor the narrator offers an explanation. The reader is left to surmise the motive from the language used and the actions that follow. The women of the town best express a possible motive when they speak to Naomi about Ruth as "your daughter-in-law, who loves you" (4:15), who secured Naomi's future sustenance. Aspects of this love can be culled from Ruth's final words, in which Ruth speaks of not coming to Naomi "empty" (a response, as it were, to Naomi's claim of emptiness; see comments at 1:21 and 3:17). Ruth's declaration omits any mention of progeny or a desire for a husband (see comment at 3:9 for the discussion). At no point does she speak of loyalty to her dead husband. Her first words express her commitment to Naomi and Naomi's well-being—as will her last words (3:17).

In its biblical context, Ruth's pledge echoes formulaic language for a covenant or a treaty in the Bible and the ancient Near East. It evokes divine utterances such as "They shall be My people, and I will be their God" (Jer. 32:38; also 31:33). It also recalls words uttered by King Jehoshaphat of Judah when speaking to Israelite kings who invited him to join forces (1 Kings 22:4 and 2 Kings 3:7); the similarity is even greater in 2 Chron. 18:3, which is a parallel account to 2 Kings 3:7.[32] Mark Smith compares Ruth's pledge with Hittite and Ugaritic treaties, as well as the above cited references to 1 and 2 Kings, to highlight the similarities in language and concepts. Smith disagrees with Campbell's conclusion that Ruth "brings the lofty concept of covenant into vital contact with day-to-day life, not at the royal court or in the temple, but right here in the narrow compass of village life."[33] Instead, Smith considers covenant language to exist at all levels of society, with royal treaties capitalizing on familiar metaphorical constructions.[34]

The closest and most revealing analogy to Ruth's vow (1:16–17) is that of another foreigner in the Bible who swears loyalty to a Judahite of Bethlehem, namely Ittai the Gittite. When King David flees Jerusalem after his son usurps the throne, Ittai comes to join and support him. David, sounding much like Naomi, attempts to deter Ittai, saying: "Why should you too go with us? Go back [*shuv*] and stay with the new king, for you are a foreigner and you are also an exile from your country. You came only yesterday; should I make you wander about with us today, when I myself must go wherever I can? Go back [*shuv*], and take your kinsmen with you, in true faithfulness [*ḥesed*]" (2 Sam. 15:19–20). Like Naomi, David also uses the key word *shuv,* "return" or "go back," in his urging. But like Ruth, Ittai refuses to turn back. Instead he vows to link his fate with David's: "As the LORD lives and as my lord the king lives, wherever my lord the king may be, there your servant will be, whether for death or for life!" (15:21). In both these instances, a foreigner

15 So she said, "See, your sister-in-law has returned to her people and her gods. Go follow your sister-in-

15 וַתֹּאמֶר הִנֵּה שָׁבָה יְבִמְתֵּךְ אֶל־עַמָּהּ וְאֶל־אֱלֹהֶיהָ שׁוּבִי אַחֲרֵי יְבִמְתֵּךְ׃

leaves the comfort of home and joins a wandering Judean. The comparison suggests an altruistic motive for both. Each places the welfare of the other person ahead of self-interest.

Two important differences highlight the distinctiveness of Ruth's gesture in contrast to Ittai's: first, as a widow, Ruth goes to Judah with only the impoverished Naomi as a familiar companion, whereas Ittai is accompanied by his men and presumably his wealth. More importantly, Ittai has made a commitment to a king, even if this is a king on the run. There is a prospect of some reward when the wheel of fortune turns. In contrast, Ruth has linked herself to a person of no standing, who seems to be going back to nothing and (according to Naomi in Ruth 1:21) with nothing, having to fend for herself alone.

Most Rabbinic traditions understand that Ruth's vow signifies her conversion. The Rabbinic sages also provide a motive for it: Naomi's piety was so impressive that Ruth longed to follow her and learn from her. The Targum explains Ruth's reason for following with Naomi: "for I desire to become a proselyte. . . ." The Targum then presents each part of Ruth's declaration as a point-by-point response to a specific teaching by Naomi (see below for details), a tradition evident in several sources (e.g., Ruth R. 2.20; B. Yev. 47b; also Rashi on 1:16–17, where the same process unfolds but Naomi's statements differ). These additions amplify the extent to which Ruth commits herself to Israel's traditions. But none of this appears in the text. Rather, the plain sense implies that what propels Ruth is her unwillingness to abandon Naomi (see comment at 1:16). Her love for Naomi exemplifies the Torah's teaching about loving the stranger (Lev. 19:33–34; Deut. 10:19), for in Moab, Naomi is the stranger.

Ruth's status after her vow is subject to discussion. Although most early Jewish sources consider this dialogue an act of conversion (Targum; Ruth R. 2.22; Ruth Z. 12), Ruth continues to be called a "Moabite," with no hint that her status has changed. Glover, who examines the processes of conversion in Ruth from an ethnological perspective, suggests that Ruth's declaration can only be seen as a step in the process. Ethnographic studies indicate that changing affiliation cannot be enacted unilaterally but requires communal consent, and the Book of Ruth, Glover shows, charts such a process (even if the notion of conversion was not as yet current at the time of Ruth).[35] See comment at 4:11 and "Intermarriage" and "Conversion" in the introduction.

15. your sister-in-law This is the only verse in the Bible where the term *yebhimteikh,* "your sister-in-law," is used (twice) to designate a relationship between women. The only other occurrence of this noun refers to a *man's* sister-in-law (Deut. 25:7 and 9). The root form of this verb, *y-b-m,* explicitly pertains to the act of levirate marriage prescribed in Deut. 25:5–10, delineating a man's obligations to his brother's widow "when brothers dwell together."[36] Here, in Naomi's mouth, the noun highlights Orpah and Ruth as women to whom levirate connection applies: the husband of one (according to levirate rules) would ordinarily be expected to impregnate the childless widow of the other. (This act is not possible in the present circumstances of their double widowhood, but it is an indication of their legal relationship.) In 1:11–13, Naomi bemoans her inability to produce another son to undertake this obligation.

has returned to her people and her gods Naomi could have said that Orpah has returned "to *your* people and *your* gods," but instead Naomi uses the third person, as if law." 16 But Ruth replied, "Do not urge me to leave you, to turn back and not follow you. For wherever you go, I will go; wherever you lodge, I will lodge; your people shall be my people, and your God my

16 וַתֹּ֤אמֶר רוּת֙ אַל־תִּפְגְּעִי־בִ֔י לְעָזְבֵ֖ךְ
לָשׁ֣וּב מֵאַחֲרָ֑יִךְ כִּ֠י אֶל־אֲשֶׁ֨ר תֵּלְכִ֜י אֵלֵ֗ךְ
וּבַאֲשֶׁ֤ר תָּלִ֙ינִי֙ אָלִ֔ין עַמֵּ֣ךְ עַמִּ֔י וֵאלֹהַ֖יִךְ

these Moabite people and deities are no longer Ruth's. Ruth mirrors these exhortations when she declares her loyalty to Naomi's people and God.

gods Or God/god. The Hebrew is a plural noun, *'elohim* (lit. "gods"), which can be construed as either plural or singular. Rhetorical convention and theological perspective influence the contextual sense of *'elohim*. The word is usually translated as "God" when referring to Israel's deity and as "god" or "gods" when applied to other deities. Naomi here refers to Orpah's deity using the same word that Ruth uses to refer to Naomi's deity in 1:16, where the reference is indubitably to one God. The Moabites' national god was Chemosh. Households in biblical times also acknowledged local deities, but it is unlikely that the author would have been referring to this practice when attributing the statement to Naomi.

Go follow Hebrew *shuvi,* literally "go back" or "turn back." The repetition of this exhortation (see comments above at 1:8, 11, and 12), this time in the singular, underscores Naomi's persistent imploring and her readiness to be left alone. It also highlights the role that turning back plays throughout this chapter. This final entreaty ends Naomi's third speech en route. She has done what she can to free her daughters-in-law and herself. Her last speech recapitulates her first words to the women. Rabbinic sages conclude from Naomi's threefold exhortation to Ruth to return (1:11–12, 15) that a proselyte should be turned away three times before being welcomed (Ruth Z. 12.30).

your sister-in-law See the first comment above on "sister-in-law" in this verse.

16–17. Instead of obeying Naomi, Ruth proclaims complete and permanent loyalty to Naomi and vows to stay with her no matter what. Her single, long speech—an impassioned pledge and detailed vow—redefines the destiny of both women. For the context of the pledge and its interpretations, see the introduction to 1:15–18 above.

16. Do not urge me to leave you Some of the force of Ruth's retort is lost in translation. The Hebrew verb, *p-g-'*, here rendered as "urge," can have three related meanings when used with the preposition *be-*. Malbim identifies them as: to strike or strike down (as in 1 Kings 2:25), to meet (as in Josh. 16:7), and to beseech (as in Gen. 23:8). Naomi uses this verb when cautioning Ruth against going to other fields lest she be harmed (2:22, "be annoyed"). By using this verb, Ruth acknowledges the power of Naomi's words but also hints that she herself would be injured should Naomi continue to implore her to leave.

leave you More precisely, "forsake you." The verb "leave" in English focuses on the one who is departing, whereas Ruth's language focuses on the one who will be abandoned—and whom she refuses to abandon. The term carries theological weight when God promises not to forsake Israel (Deut. 31:6, 8) or when used for apostasy (Josh. 24:20).

to turn back and not follow you Literally, "to turn back [*lashuv*] from after you," echoing Naomi's exhortation to Ruth to "return after" (i.e., follow) Orpah in 1:15 and repeating the key word in this section. Ruth does not express a desire to desert her earlier home but rather a refusal to abandon Naomi. In the Targum and a number of midrashic sources, Ruth adds that she wants to convert. In Ruth R. 2.22, Ruth also adds that since she intends to convert, it is best that she be converted by Naomi and not by another, reasoning that inclines Naomi to consent.

wherever you go, I will go . . . and your God my God Ruth pledges to share every aspect of Naomi's life and in the most comprehensive way. The first two parts of this statement acknowledge the nomadic prospects ahead, anticipating an unsettled life. The language seems formulaic, but the specifics are unique to Ruth (see the introduction to 1:15–18). Rabbinic texts like the Targum and midrashim interpret this statement as an act of conversion that conveys upon Ruth the status of proselyte (see the section introduction above and "Intermarriage" and "Conversion" in the introduction).

I will go Ruth's decision evokes that of Abraham, after he is told to "go forth" from his native land (Gen. 12:1; see comment below at 2:11). It also echoes Rebekah's pronouncement when she decides to leave her home, declaring "I will go" (Gen. 24:58). Like these Israelite progenitors, Ruth dares to venture into the unknown. But unlike Abraham, she is not accompanied by family and wealth, nor guided by a promise of greatness. And unlike Rebekah, "she knows full well that there is no protecting husband waiting for her."[37] Through these thematic and verbal links, the two parallel stories from Genesis serve to magnify the singular power of Ruth's *ḥesed* (lovingkindness).[38] Indeed, unlike her predecessors, Ruth has nothing to gain by going with Naomi. She willingly makes herself a stranger in a strange land so as not to abandon Naomi, who herself has been a stranger in Ruth's Moabite homeland.

In Rabbinic sources, each of Ruth's statements is cast as a specific response to Naomi's explanations or instructions (see the section introduction above). In the Targum, at this point, Naomi says: "We are commanded to keep the Sabbaths and holidays, not to walk more than two thousand cubits," to which Ruth responds in kind: "Wherever you go, I go." (The other sources are similar.)

wherever you lodge, I will lodge Hebrew *lin* ("lodge") typically indicates a temporary stay for the night. The use of this word thus anticipates the women's journey ahead. The Targum reads this phrase as Ruth's response to Naomi's explanation that "we are commanded not to spend the night together with non-Jews." In B. Yev. 47b and Rashi, however, this pertains to a meeting between a man and a woman alone.

your people shall be my people Literally, "your people—my people," which suggests a legal formula as in 2 Kings 3:7. Ruth thus articulates a present commitment, not some future action. The Targum reads as follows: "Said Naomi: 'We are commanded to keep six hundred thirteen commandments.' Said Ruth: 'That which your people keep, that I shall keep, as though they had been my people before this.'" Ruth Rabbah, B. Yev. 47b, and Rashi are similar. Alsheikh adds "since [or if] I will be with you day and night, then your people will be my people."

your God my God Ruth affirms her commitment to Israel's God because it is Naomi's God, not because of some independent conviction of her own. Her very next words express this commitment, for she proceeds to make a vow in God's name. The Targum adds that Naomi explains, "We are commanded not to worship idols," to which Ruth replies: "Your God is my God." In declaring "your people—my people" and "your God—my God," Ruth rejects Naomi's earlier exhortation that she, like Orpah, return "to *her* people and *her* gods" (1:15). Through this verbal link, the author underscores that Ruth is indeed standing at a crossroads. Yet whatever transformation takes place at this moment, it is not perceived within the narrative as an altered ethnic or communal identity.

God. 17 Where you die, I will die, and there I will be
buried. Thus and more may the LORD do to me if
anything but death parts me from you." 18 When
[Naomi] saw how determined she was to go with her,

אֱלֹהָי׃ 17 בַּאֲשֶׁר תָּמ֙וּתִי֙ אָמ֔וּת וְשָׁ֖ם
אֶקָּבֵ֑ר כֹּה֩ יַעֲשֶׂ֨ה יְהוָ֥ה לִי֙ וְכֹ֣ה יֹסִ֔יף כִּ֣י
הַמָּ֔וֶת יַפְרִ֖יד בֵּינִ֥י וּבֵינֵֽךְ׃ 18 וַתֵּ֕רֶא כִּֽי־
מִתְאַמֶּ֥צֶת הִ֖יא לָלֶ֣כֶת אִתָּ֑הּ וַתֶּחְדַּ֖ל

Ruth continues to be identified as "the Moabite" even after this pledge, both by the narrator (1:22; 2:2,21) and by Boaz (4:5, 4:10); she too calls herself a foreigner when she first meets him (2:10). What was the social reality in ancient Israel with regard to such identification? Would the text's original audience have understood that Ruth could unilaterally declare herself to be part of Naomi's people? One investigator has concluded, with justification, that such a change in self-identification would not have been recognized without a communal confirmation and other actions.[39] (See "Intermarriage" and "Conversion" in the introduction.)

17. ***Where you die, I will die*** Ruth vows to be at Naomi's side forever. The Targum, B. Yev. 47b, Ruth R. 2.24, and Rashi all interpret this as a response to Naomi's discourse about methods of capital punishment, to which Ruth replies that she would undergo whatever death Naomi is subject to.

Thus and more may the LORD do to me Ruth's oath formula and avowal resemble other biblical oaths (1 Sam. 14:44; 20:13; 2 Sam. 3:9; 1 Kings 2:23). It may seem surprising for a Moabite woman to vow using the name of Israel's God (YHWH), but she has just made a public commitment to this God. Furthermore, she has been part of Mahlon's and Naomi's household for ten years. According to ancient Near Eastern custom, she would have long since adopted the household's patron deity and her husband's as her own, at least for certain purposes. Note that Ittai the Gittite, a non-Judahite, also takes an oath in YHWH's name (2 Sam. 15:21; see the introduction to 1:15–18 above).

if anything but death parts me from you Hebrew *ki ha-mawet yaphrid.* The nuance of *ki* is uncertain; it can mean "if" but also "for" or "indeed." She might be saying that *only* death will separate them; or, conversely, denying that *even* death can do so. Either way, the thrust of her oath is clear: their relationship is to be lifelong.

part...from Hebrew *yaphrid.* The verb often refers to separation of kin, as when Abraham and Lot part company (Gen. 13:9, 11, 14) before the latter becomes the progenitor of the Moabites (including Ruth). Ruth's descendant David uses this term to describe the inseparable bond between Saul and Jonathan in his lament over them (2 Sam. 1:23).

18. ***When [Naomi] saw how determined she was to go with her, she ceased to argue with her*** The dialogues at the crossroad come to an end when Naomi gives up trying to change Ruth's mind and falls silent. Her silence contrasts with David, who responds to Ittai's oath of commitment with an acceptance (2 Sam. 15:22; see introduction to 1:15–18 above). Naomi's silence has been interpreted as that of gratitude, resentment, ambivalence, and more. Trible comments as follows: "A young woman has committed herself to the life of an old woman rather than search for a husband.... One female has chosen another female in a world where life depends upon men. There is no more radical decision in all the memories of Israel. Naomi is silenced by it."[40] Yet some argue that Naomi genuinely wishes to be free of close association with a foreigner. They conclude that Naomi here withdraws emotionally from Ruth.[41] Coxon, however, defends Naomi and, like Trible, interprets the silence as consent, as if no further words are needed.[42] More nuanced inter-

she ceased to argue with her; 19 and the two went on
until they reached Bethlehem.

לְדַבֵּ֥ר אֵלֶֽיהָ׃ 19 וַתֵּלַ֣כְנָה שְׁתֵּיהֶ֔ם עַד־
בֹּאָנָ֖ה בֵּ֣ית לָ֑חֶם

pretations note that the text conveys the understandable ambivalence of a grieving mother. Naomi's inability to acknowledge Ruth's effusive oath of loyalty may convey her utter desolation.[43] When considering ethnological studies about conversion, Naomi's silence can take on a different meaning. If, as Glover maintains, conversion or integration requires communal recognition, then Naomi's silence may be the appropriate response. Ruth's declaration implicated the people and God. Naomi has no authority to speak on their behalf. Thus for the time being, Ruth's declaration must remain unconfirmed. As the story unfolds, the community makes its voice heard (4:11–12). God then indirectly confirms the acceptance of Ruth (4:13). See further "Intermarriage" and "Conversion" in the introduction and comments at 4:11–13.

determined Hebrew *mit'ametzet,* from the root *'-m-tz.* An unusual word in this particular form, it apparently describes exertion (1 Kings 12:18); it also expresses courage or strength, as when Moses encourages Joshua: "Be strong ***and resolute,*** for it is you who shall go with this people" (Deut. 31:7). Salmon ben Yeroḥam's commentary picks up this sense of encouragement and interprets Naomi's response as joyous.

ceased to argue Literally, "ceased to speak to her," presumably saying no more about the topic.

RETURN TO BETHLEHEM (1:19–22)

The journey is over. The narrator does not report how long it took, nor how the women fared along the way (a road between Bethlehem and the nearest spot in Moab, crossing the Jordan, might extend for some fifty miles). Rather, the focus is on what happens when Naomi and Ruth arrive—and on Naomi's bitterness as she returns home, feeling defeated and "empty" (1:20). Forms of the word for "turn back" or "return" (*sh-w-v*) appear three times in this short section (1:21 and twice in 1:22), continuing the overriding emphasis on returning that marks each section of this chapter. A question by the town's women (1:19) draws from Naomi an outcry of bitterness. Naomi rehearses her sense of loss. Her speech is poetic in form. Like Job, and as earlier (1:13), she names God as the cause of her plight. The narrator frames the return by emphasizing that *the two* went (1:19 and 22), which evokes, for Coxon, the same unity of action as is found in the Binding of Isaac story when Abraham and Isaac walk together (Gen. 22:6 and 8). For Fewell and Gunn, this report underscores Naomi's silence concerning Ruth's presence when the women arrive in Bethlehem.

OUTLINE

I. Arrival (1:19a)
II. Naomi's dialogue with the town's women (1:19b–21)
III. Conclusion: the journey back is complete (1:22)

ARRIVAL (1:19a)

19. and the two went on Literally, "and they went, the two of them." Stating "and they went" would have sufficed to include them both. When the narrator emphasizes that the two of them went, it highlights Ruth's presence. Rashi responds to the text's

When they arrived in Bethlehem, the whole city buzzed with excitement over them. The women said, "Can this be Naomi?" 20 "Do not call me Naomi," she

וַיְהִ֗י כְּבֹאָ֙נָה֙ בֵּ֣ית לֶ֔חֶם וַתֵּהֹ֤ם כׇּל־הָעִיר֙
עֲלֵיהֶ֔ן וַתֹּאמַ֖רְנָה הֲזֹ֥את נׇעֳמִֽי׃ 20 וַתֹּ֣אמֶר
אֲלֵיהֶ֔ן אַל־תִּקְרֶ֥אנָה לִ֖י נׇעֳמִ֑י קְרֶ֤אןָ לִי֙

emphasis by citing a midrash (from Ruth R. 3.5) that affirms "how much God loves proselytes [*gerim*]. Because Ruth decided to become a proselyte, Scripture places her on par with Naomi." In citing this midrash, Rashi may be attempting to address Naomi's puzzling silence about Ruth in the verses that follow. Reimer observes that the rabbis gloss the phrase by claiming that in their approach to Bethlehem Naomi and Ruth were "of one heart." "But," she continues, "the absence of the word 'together,' which elsewhere signified 'of one heart,' suggests just the opposite. The two women continue their journey to Bethlehem apart, not together."[44] Ruth R. 3.6 adds that Boaz's wife died that very day, regarding Ruth's arrival as providential.

NAOMI'S DIALOGUE WITH THE TOWN'S WOMEN (1:19b–21)

the whole city Yet it is only the town's women who actually address Naomi.

buzzed with excitement Hebrew *va-teihom,* from the verbal root *h-m-h.* It connotes chaos and confusion (in 1 Sam. 7:10 it describes the confusion of the Philistines); it also evokes a multitude. The appearance of the two women creates a stir.

over them Despite the presence of both Naomi and Ruth, the ensuing dialogue includes only Naomi. Neither the women of the town nor Naomi mention Ruth.

The women So in NJPS, but MT has no subject. As is typical in normal Hebrew syntax, the verb's feminine plural inflection indicates the speakers are the women.

Can this be Naomi? It is not possible to ascertain the tone of this question. The women could be astonished that Naomi has returned, delighted to see her, incredulous that this woman could really be Naomi, given how she's changed—or all of the above. According to the commentator Alsheikh, age and the suffering she endured so changed Naomi as to make her almost unrecognizable.

20. Do not call me Naomi... Call me Mara Naomi acknowledges that she has been completely changed. She rejects her former name because it no longer describes her. "Naomi" comes from *n-ʿ-m,* meaning "pleasant" (see comment at v. 2), whereas "Mara" is the feminine form of *mar,* "bitter" (see comment at 1:13). In changing her name, Naomi aims to show the tragic transformation inflicted upon her. Although Naomi's name change is in essence rhetorical (she remains "Naomi" throughout the rest of the book), this expression of loss shows the meaningfulness of names as markers of identity.

Shaddai This name for Israel's God is relatively uncommon in the Bible, appearing as a name for God only forty-eight times (compared to more than 6,800 instances of the name YHWH), with thirty-one of them in Job and six in Genesis. Since Naomi regularly uses God's more common name, YHWH, her choice here must convey something specific.[45] This term is nearly the same as a word meaning "breasts," when inflected as "my breasts." According to a number of scholars, it might have referred originally to an ancient divinity associated with mountains.[46] If so, the name became absorbed into Israel's religion as another name for Israel's unique God, YHWH. But the etymology

replied. "Call me Mara, for Shaddai has made my lot
very bitter. 21 I went away full, and the LORD has
brought me back empty. How can you call me Naomi,
when the LORD has dealt harshly with me, when
Shaddai has brought misfortune upon me!"

מָרָ֑א* כִּי־הֵמַ֥ר שַׁדַּ֛י לִ֖י מְאֹֽד׃ 21 אֲנִי֙
מְלֵאָ֣ה הָלַ֔כְתִּי וְרֵיקָ֖ם הֱשִׁיבַ֣נִי יְהוָ֑ה לָ֣מָּה
תִקְרֶ֤אנָה לִי֙ נָעֳמִ֔י וַֽיהוָה֙ עָ֣נָה בִ֔י וְשַׁדַּ֖י
הֵ֥רַֽע לִֽי׃

v. 20. א' במקום ה'

may be less significant in Naomi's outcry than the associations that the name invokes. In Gen. 49:25, it is associated with fertility, when Jacob's blessing of Joseph refers to "Shaddai who blesses you" and continues with "blessings of the breast and womb." These associations may be especially appropriate for Naomi who is no longer fertile and who has lost her children.[47]

has made my lot very bitter The Hebrew emphasizes God's role—literally, "for Shaddai has caused much bitterness to me" (that is, "embittered me," *hemar li*). Naomi consistently sees God's hand in all that transpires in her life. So too Job, who cries out regarding "Shaddai, who has embittered [*hemar*] my life!" (Job 27:2). Like Job, Naomi does not suppose that she deserves such treatment.[48] But unlike Job, she does not protest by speaking to God; rather, she complains to other women. Naomi may be describing an emotional state ("Shaddai has made me bitter") or her life situation ("Shaddai has made things bitter for me"), but the difference may not matter since both seem to be at work from her perspective. The term "bitter," *mar,* is used elsewhere in the Bible in opposition to *matok,* sweet, as when Moses turns the bitter waters sweet at Marah (Exod. 18:25); a spirit characterized by *mar* is the opposite of one infused with joy (Prov. 14:10). (See earlier comment at v. 13, where she first speaks of her bitterness.)

21. full...empty In this context, "full" likely means "with a family," specifically with children, and perhaps also with resources in general. Emptiness is not likely to refer to hunger, since Naomi had left Bethlehem at a time of a famine. The Targum makes this point explicit: "I went away full, with my husband and sons, but the Lord has brought me back destitute of them." Naomi is saying in effect, "I came back with nothing and no one." Naomi's sense of emptiness is recalled in Ruth's final words in the book, when Ruth will use the same word to explain Boaz's gift of grain. There, Ruth reports to Naomi that Boaz did not want her to come to Naomi "empty" (3:17). And yet the reader knows that Naomi is not alone. As the narrator emphasizes through a repetition in 1:19 and 1:22, there are two of them now, Naomi and Ruth. But Naomi does not acknowledge Ruth's presence. Naomi's silence here, like the one in 1:18, suggests to some that Naomi is ambivalent or even resentful of Ruth's presence.[49] Others regard the silence in regard to Ruth as a clue to Naomi's self-pity, understandable given the circumstances. Naomi is unable to acknowledge that she is not really alone, that another woman has devoted herself to her well being, and that such devotion can be sustaining.[50] In an important sense, Naomi's perception is consistent with the cultural reality in the ancient world where women without men—without the support of a father, husband, or son—were at a disadvantage. The Book of Ruth exposes this social vulnerability even as it undercuts it. The point is made explicit at the end when the women exclaim (as if in a delayed response to her cry here), that Naomi's daughter-in-law is better than seven sons (4:15; see there).

[22] Thus Naomi returned from the country of Moab; she returned with her daughter-in-law Ruth the Moabite. They arrived in Bethlehem at the beginning of the barley harvest.

22 וַתָּשָׁב נָעֳמִי וְרוּת הַמּוֹאֲבִיָּה כַלָּתָהּ
עִמָּהּ הַשָּׁבָה מִשְּׂדֵי מוֹאָב וְהֵמָּה בָּאוּ
בֵּית לֶחֶם בִּתְחִלַּת קְצִיר שְׂעֹרִים׃

CONCLUSION: THE JOURNEY BACK IS COMPLETE (1:22)

22. Thus Naomi returned . . . she returned with her daughter-in-law Ruth the Moabite The story has now come full circle. It started with a journey out of Bethlehem and concludes with a return to Bethlehem. The word for returning in Hebrew is the same as the one for turning back. This term (*sh-w-v,* here *shavah*) has been a key word all along (as when Naomi urges her daughters-in-law to return to their homes in 1:8, 10, 11, 12, 15). Here it is mentioned twice. The Hebrew syntax is somewhat awkward—literally "Naomi returned, and Ruth the Moabite her daughter-in-law with her, the one returning..." The contextual sense, as rendered by the translation above, emphasizes Naomi's return. But Ruth could be the subject of the second verb.[51] The unusual syntax and the verb's repetition have inspired much Rabbinic reflection on the question: in what sense is Ruth "returning"? Some see an allusion to the notion of repentance (*teshuvah*).[52] Another suggestion is that Ruth has "turned around" a history of conflict between Moab and Israel—a history that begins when Lot departs from Abraham (Genesis 13).[53] In coming to Judah, Ruth effectuates a return (reconciliation) between two communities divided by a history of conflict (see "The Status of the Moabites" in the introduction).

she returned with her daughter-in-law By recording that Naomi has returned with Ruth, the narrator reminds the reader that even though Naomi presents herself as "empty," she is not alone—and will not be alone given Ruth's vow (1:16–17).

Ruth the Moabite It is hardly coincidental that this designation clings to Ruth precisely upon her arrival in Bethlehem. This is the first of six instances in which Ruth is called a Moabite (also 2:2,6,21; 4:5,10) and is so perceived by the residents of Bethlehem (see, e.g., 2:6). Her Moabite status constitutes an obstacle, given the mandated exclusion from the community prescribed in Deut. 23:4 (see comment at vv. 1, 4, 16; "Intermarriage" and "Conversion" and "The Status of the Moabites" in the introduction; and comment below at 3:8–10 and 4:5 and 10).

at the beginning of the barley harvest As the backdrop for the plot, famine has now been replaced with harvest, although it is not yet clear how these two women are to benefit from it. The harvest will become pertinent soon as Ruth goes out to glean. The season is most likely early spring. Biblical sources suggest that Passover coincides with the first ripening of barley.[54] The Gezer calendar, one of the oldest known examples of Paleo-Hebrew script (tenth century B.C.E.) records seasons, with one month for the barley harvest, estimated by scholars to last from the spring equinox in mid-March to mid-April. The Targum narrows the arrival date to the eve of Passover and the beginning of the counting of the Omer.

2 Now Naomi had a kinsman on her husband's side, a man of substance, of the family of Elimelech, whose name was Boaz.

ב וּלְנָעֳמִ֞י מידע מוֹדַ֣ע לְאִישָׁ֗הּ אִ֚ישׁ
גִּבּ֣וֹר חַ֔יִל מִמִּשְׁפַּ֖חַת אֱלִימֶ֑לֶךְ וּשְׁמ֖וֹ
בֹּֽעַז׃

CHAPTER 2

Finding Favor and Food in the Field: When Boaz Meets Ruth

Chapter 2 begins and ends with Naomi and Ruth at home and alone. As it opens, the town's women have vanished from view, leaving the two to fend for themselves (2:1–2). But the central and most detailed scene (2:3–17) depicts a fortuitous meeting between Boaz and Ruth, which presents a solution to the women's hardship. Noticing Ruth as she gleans in his field, Boaz acknowledges her kindness to Naomi. He also displays his own generosity by graciously making it easier for her to obtain food and by extending other privileges to her. At the end of the chapter, Ruth returns to Naomi with abundant food and with good news about her prospects (2:18–23). Was it only chance that led Ruth to Boaz's field? Clearly, no individual has planned the meeting. Naomi herself, who consistently sees God's hand at work in her life, and who has earlier bemoaned her divinely inflicted misfortune, later credits God with this hope-filled change (2:20). But the narrator neither confirms nor contradicts her conclusion.

OUTLINE OF CHAPTER 2

I. Home alone: starting over (1–2)
II. In the Field: finding food and favor (3–17)
III. Home again: (18–23)

HOME ALONE: STARTING OVER (2:1–2)

A brief exchange between Naomi and Ruth plays out against the absence of help from community or family (although we learn here that Naomi's family in Bethlehem includes a rich relative). Ruth determines to find food, and Naomi laconically consents.

2:1. Now Naomi had a kinsman The narrator provides a clue that Naomi has family ties to someone who proves to be of great advantage to her.[55] The comment indicates that Naomi has more resources than meet the eye and more than she has acknowledged. But, in addition, this comment also highlights the two women's isolation: neither the townspeople nor the wealthy relative have come forth to offer help to bitter Naomi.[56] Change in the women's predicament only occurs when Ruth ventures forth alone.

kinsman Hebrew *moda'*, according to the *kerey* (public reading) or *meyuda'*, according to the *ketiv* (written form). A rare term from the root *y-d-'*, "to know," the word is here understood as "someone known," probably a relative, as it is also used in Job 19:14, where it is coupled with "those who are near to me" (see also Prov. 7:4).

on her husband's side . . . of the family of Elimelech We never learn precisely how Boaz is related to Elimelech. Given the vague terminology, he apparently counts as a distant relation (as is confirmed by 3:12). But according to the Rabbinic sages, Boaz is Elimelech's

2 Ruth the Moabite said to Naomi, "I would like
to go to the fields and glean among the ears of grain,

2 וַתֹּאמֶר֩ ר֨וּת הַמּוֹאֲבִיָּ֜ה אֶל־נָעֳמִ֗י
אֵלְכָה־נָּ֤א הַשָּׂדֶה֙ וַאֲלַקֳטָ֣ה בַשִּׁבֳּלִ֔ים אַחַ֕ר

nephew (as well as Naomi's cousin; see B. BB 91a, cited also by Rashi). Speculating such close ties enable the sages to regard him as an ideal potential husband for Ruth.

a man of substance Hebrew *'ish gibor ḥayil.* In biblical narrative about early Israel, the term *gibor ḥayil* applies mostly to military men such as the chieftain Gideon (Judg. 6:11) or to young David before he becomes king of Israel (1 Sam. 16:18). *Gibor,* related to *gebher,* male, usually designates a male hero; *ḥayil* is related to *ḥayal,* "warrior." Used as a collective noun, it means "soldiers" (2 Chron. 17:16–17, 2 Chron. 25:6). The term is also used outside of military contexts. In 1 Chron. 12:29, Zadok is called *gibor ḥayil.* Most likely, this expression in such a late biblical text indicates that Zadok was a person of significance, either in economic or social terms, as is the case in Ruth. The Targum translates the term into Aramaic to mean "strong in *Torah.*" (Compare *Avot de-Rabbi Natan* 2.5, which states that "there are no mighty men other than mighty in *Torah.*") This Rabbinic understanding of *gibor ḥayil*, like its usage in Ruth and Chronicles, reflects the evolution of the term: power is not only, or primarily, vested in military might but also in other qualities like wealth and righteousness. A feminine version of the term is *'eshet ḥayil.* Boaz uses it to describe Ruth in 3:11. In its most familiar setting, Prov. 31:1–31, *'eshet ḥayil*—often translated as a "woman of valor"—refers to a generous and prosperous woman whose virtues Proverbs extols. These examples support the definition of *gibor ḥayil* as referring to economic and social worth in late biblical texts such as Ruth. This understanding is confirmed later in the story when Boaz displays social and economic clout, not military prowess (see comment at 4:1–2).

Boaz The name's meaning is unclear. The Septuagint renders it as *Boos,* which is consistent with an etymology of *bo-'oz,* meaning "there is might" (*'oz*) "in him" (*bo*), an interpretation that certain Rabbinic sources propose.[57] Boaz is also the name of one of the two pillars framing the Great Hall of the Jerusalem Temple (1 Kings 7:21). Perhaps his name is an allusion to the fact that Boaz proves to be a "pillar of society" as the Book of Ruth unfolds (see comment at 4:1–2). By introducing Boaz before he plays a role in the narrative, the narrator sets up an expectation in the reader that these women will be taken care of.

2. ***Ruth the Moabite*** Ruth's Moabite status has not changed since she joined Naomi (see comment at 1:22). The repeated mention of her Moabite identity at this point highlights her status as an outsider entering unfamiliar territory.

I would like to go to the fields Ruth takes the initiative to provide for the two women, since no other resources have materialized.

I would like Hebrew *'elekhah na'* "I would please go" or "let me go."[58] Although Ruth takes the initiative here, as she also did when joining Naomi (1:16–17), she respectfully asks for Naomi's permission. The narrator thus portrays Ruth deferring to Naomi, as befits the relationship of a younger woman to her mother-in-law. Malbim suggests that Ruth did not want her mother-in-law to glean with her because she wanted to shield the once wealthy Naomi from the shame of their reduced circumstances.

glean The Hebrew root *l-k-t* appears twelve times in Chapter 2 (vv. 2, 3, 7, 8, 15 twice, 16, 17 twice, 18, 19, and 23), showing how important this concept is to the author's theme. In the Torah, Israelites are commanded to provide for the poor and the alien by behind someone who may show me kindness." "Yes, daughter, go," she replied; 3 and off she went. She

אֲשֶׁר אֶמְצָא־חֵן בְּעֵינָיו וַתֹּאמֶר לָהּ לְכִי
בִתִּי׃ 3 וַתֵּלֶךְ וַתָּבוֹא וַתְּלַקֵּט בַּשָּׂדֶה אַחֲרֵי

allowing them to gather a portion of each season's produce: "When you reap the harvest of your land, you shall not reap all the way to the edges of your field, or gather the gleanings of your harvest. You shall not pick your vineyard bare, or gather the fallen fruit of your vineyard; you shall leave them for the poor and the stranger: I the LORD am your God." (Lev. 19:9–10; see also Lev. 23:22 and Deut. 24:19). Rabbinic literature develops biblical laws of gleaning extensively to assure equitable access and minimize abuse. It also defines acts of *ḥesed* as generous provisions for gleanings (see, e.g., M. *Pe'ah*).

behind someone who may show me kindness Although gleaning is a right stipulated by law (see Lev. 19:9–10 and 23:22), Ruth nevertheless plans to glean only after she "finds favor in the eyes of" the owner (see next comment). Interpreters have wondered why she takes this stance (see also comment at 2:7 below). Some speculate that the law was not enforced, enabling some landholders to be less scrupulous than others in its observance.[59] Yet Ruth does not tell Naomi that she will seek the field of someone who is law-abiding; rather she hopes to find someone who will look kindly on her. The search for a benefactor may signal Ruth's awareness that even though the law of *leket* (gleaning) was intended to support the vulnerable in society, nonetheless gleaning involved risk. On danger in the field, see further comment at verses 7 and 9.

may show me kindness Hebrew *'emtza ḥen be-'enav,* "that I will find grace [*ḥen*] in his eyes." This formulaic expression is typically used when a speaker wishes to solicit goodwill from someone in power—as when the Egyptians seek Joseph's help (Gen. 47:25), or when Moses seeks to placate God after the Golden Calf episode (Exod. 33:12–13). Most commonly, the beseecher is hoping to be favored, that is, granted special benefits.

Yes, daughter, go Naomi's laconic response uses two words in the Hebrew (*lekhi, biti,* lit. "go, my daughter"). Calling Ruth "my daughter" (see also 1:13) signals acceptance as well as solicitude. Boaz also uses this term when speaking to Ruth (see 2:8). This language need not convey biological kinship but often indicates differences in age or status.[60] Some modern scholars have called attention to certain silences in Naomi's responses to Ruth. They see these as examples of Naomi's ambivalence about Ruth and her attempt to disassociate from Ruth (so, too, in 1:19–21).[61] Here Naomi does not mention her relative Boaz, information that surely would have been of help to Ruth at this juncture. It is surprising that Naomi does not warn Ruth about danger in the field before her daughter-in-law goes out to glean. Only later do we learn that Ruth could have been subject to harm and that Naomi is aware of this (v. 22). With this silence, the narration presents Naomi as only marginally attentive to Ruth's well-being. The message may be either that Naomi is too overwhelmed by her own sorrow, or that she is ambivalent about Ruth's role in her life (as Midrash Ruth Zuta on 1:8 implies). Ruth's Moabite origin may also be a factor. After all, the Torah explicitly excludes Moabites from Israelite society (see Deut. 23:4–7).

IN THE FIELD: FINDING FOOD AND FAVOR (2:3–17)

The narrator lingers at length over this one momentous day. What appears to be happenstance, namely Ruth's going to Boaz's field, changes the course of their lives. The encounter between the deferential Ruth and the chivalrous Boaz takes place in broad daylight in the open field, in view of many (in contrast to their second meeting—at night, without came and gleaned in a field, behind the reapers; and, as luck would have it, it was the piece of land belonging to Boaz, who was of Elimelech's family.

הַקֹּצְרִ֑ים וַיִּ֣קֶר מִקְרֶ֔הָ חֶלְקַ֤ת הַשָּׂדֶה֙ לְבֹ֔עַז
אֲשֶׁ֖ר מִמִּשְׁפַּ֥חַת אֱלִימֶֽלֶךְ׃

witnesses, 3:6–15). Boaz graciously acknowledges Ruth's courage and her commitment to her mother-in-law and extends privileges to her. He takes steps to ensure her safety and comfort and to ease the task of gleaning for her. Yet her basic status does not change. Ruth remains a dependent gleaner and the sole caretaker of his relative, Naomi.

The activities in the field in this section realistically comport with known agricultural practices and are reflected also in ancient iconography. Harvesting entails several kinds of work: reaping the sheaves, gathering them, binding them in portable bundles, and storing them. At a later point comes winnowing (see comment at 3:2). Whereas reaping required tools and often is done by men (but see "they are reaping" at 2:9 below), gathering, bundling, and transport was the work of women. A mural painting from the Deir el-Medina tomb in Egypt (thirteenth–eleventh centuries B.C.E.) depicts an Egyptian couple harvesting crops. Both are seen planting, but the man is consistently ahead, and in subsequent sections is using tools like a plough and sickle, with the woman behind gathering. Murals from fifteenth century B.C.E. Egypt also show groups of male reapers followed by females who gather the crop.[62] As for the agricultural year, the Gezer calendar, an inscription in Paleo-Hebrew from the tenth century B.C.E., describes it as follows: "Two months of planting/Two months are late planting/One month of hoeing/One month of barley harvest/One month of harvest and festival/Two months of grape harvesting/One month of summer fruit."

OUTLINE

I. Boaz discovers Ruth in his field (2:3–7)
II. First dialogue between Boaz and Ruth (2:8–13)
III. Lunch in the field and the beginning of Ruth's reward (2:14–17)

BOAZ DISCOVERS RUTH IN HIS FIELD (2:3–7)

Ruth captures Boaz's attention when she happens to glean in his field. But first she receives the attention of the man who supervises the field, who considers her a hard-working woman. The poet John Keats immortalized the scene when he wrote about "the sad heart of Ruth, when, sick for home, / She stood in tears amid the alien corn" ("Ode to a Nightingale"). And yet nothing in the book suggests that Ruth longs for home. Alien though she is, as her own words attest (2:10), she nonetheless works energetically and earns the respect and welcome of the local landowner.

3. *as luck would have it* Hebrew *va-yikker mikreha*. The root *k-r-h* is uncommon and conveys happenchance, sometimes with theological implication of divine providence. In Gen. 27:20, Jacob, pretending to be Esau, uses this verb to explain to Isaac why he has come back so soon from the hunt: "the LORD your God granted me good fortune," literally "made it happen before me." A close parallel can be found in the prayer of Abraham's servant who is seeking a wife for Isaac. The servant prays to God, "make it happen before me," *hakreh na'* (Gen. 24:12). In these passages and elsewhere, the reader is expected to detect the hand of God at work. But in 1 Sam. 6:9 the term *mikreh* is used in the opposite sense: to exclude God's hidden hand. Thus, the Philistine diviners declare that if the Philistines' wagon goes in one direction, they will know that God is responsible for its

4 Presently Boaz arrived from Bethlehem. He
greeted the reapers, "The LORD be with you!" And
they responded, "The LORD bless you!" 5 Boaz said to
the servant who was in charge of the reapers, "Whose

4 וְהִנֵּה־בֹעַז בָּא מִבֵּית לֶחֶם וַיֹּאמֶר
לַקּוֹצְרִים יְהוָה עִמָּכֶם וַיֹּאמְרוּ לוֹ יְבָרֶכְךָ
יְהוָה׃ 5 וַיֹּאמֶר בֹּעַז לְנַעֲרוֹ הַנִּצָּב עַל־

course. If, however, it goes the other way, then "we shall know that it was not His hand that struck us; it just happened to us by chance [*mikreh*]." Which meaning is intended in Ruth? The narrator does not say. This ambiguity is one of several in Ruth where the reader is left to choose. Traditional interpreters find here, as in Esther, God's hidden presence guiding events.

land belonging to Boaz, who was of Elimelech's family The narrator reminds the reader that Boaz is related to Naomi's husband, and thus also to Ruth's (see comment at 2:1).

4. ***He greeted the reapers, "The LORD be with you!"*** Boaz enters the stage as a godly man of benevolent disposition in that he greets, rather than ignores, his workers. The first words of a biblical character often hold a clue to the person's ethos (see Moses' first words in Exod. 2:13, which are concerned with justice and typify his lifelong pursuit of it). By means of language, Boaz, like other characters in the Book of Ruth, brings God's presence into his interactions with others. Linafelt's observation that blessing the workers with success primarily benefits the master Boaz, not the workers,[63] probably does not represent the narrator's intention.

Persons in the Hebrew Bible freely bless each other using God's name. But postbiblical generations debated whether this was appropriate. Typically, the Targum paraphrases Boaz's words to place God at a remove: "May the *memra* ["Word"] of the LORD be at your assistance." But Mishnah Ber. 9.5 views the practice of invoking God's name as having been permitted during biblical times, using Boaz as its exemplar; and the Babylonian Talmud explains that a greeting in the name of God is one of the "three things the earthly Bet Din [Rabbinical court] decreed and the heavenly Bet Din approved," pointing to Boaz as proof (Ruth R. 4.5; B. Ber. 54a).

The LORD bless you! The reapers' response adds to the portrait of Boaz as a favored and respected gentleman and suggests reciprocity between master and workers. This phrase appears also in Num. 6:24, Jer. 31:23, and Ps. 128:5. These words begin the Priestly Blessing, still pronounced in synagogue worship (usually translated as "May the LORD bless you and protect you! / May the LORD deal kindly and graciously with you! / May the LORD bestow His favor upon you and grant you peace!" (Num. 6:24–26).

5. ***servant*** Hebrew *na'ar,* literally "young man" or even "boy" (as in Jer. 1:6, when Jeremiah resists his prophetic calling by claiming that he is merely a *na'ar*), but often designating a subordinate position. This is the first of thirteen occurrences of this noun in some form in this book. As part of a hierarchy, *na'ar* could also be steward or supervisor as here, in charge of others of lower position. Three seals from the late Israelite monarchy bear the title of *na'ar* of the king, suggesting a high position (see also 2 Sam. 19:18).[64]

in charge of Hebrew *ha-nitzav 'al,* literally "who stands over" or "positioned over," namely a supervisor, in this case the one in charge of the reapers—one of several clues that Boaz's estate is large, with a multilayered workforce.

girl is that?" 6 The servant in charge of the reapers
replied, "She is a Moabite girl who came back with

הַקּוֹצְרִ֖ים לְמִ֖י הַנַּעֲרָ֥ה הַזֹּֽאת׃ 6 וַיַּ֗עַן
הַנַּ֛עַר הַנִּצָּ֥ב עַל־הַקּוֹצְרִ֖ים וַיֹּאמַ֑ר נַעֲרָ֤ה
מוֹאֲבִיָּה֙ הִ֔יא הַשָּׁ֥בָה עִֽם־נָעֳמִ֖י מִשְּׂדֵ֥ה

Whose girl is that? In the biblical world, this question was equivalent to asking: to what household does this person belong? In the ancient world, all persons were reckoned as members of an extended-family household or larger-scale group. The queried servant understands this question in those terms (see next comment). This is the first of three questions as to who Ruth is (see comment at 3:8 and 3:16). Boaz's question helps to link this narrative to other biblical stories. For example, Abraham's servant asks the *na'arah* Rebekah at the well, "Whose daughter are you?" (Gen. 24:16,23). Likewise, this resembles a query that King Saul poses insistently with regard to David, the descendant of Ruth and Boaz: "Whose son is that boy (*na'ar*)?" (1 Sam. 17:55,58).

The narrator does not say why Ruth catches Boaz's eye. Is it the presence of a new person in his field or something in her demeanor that attracts Boaz's attention? Do her clothes or physical features distinguish her visibly from the others? Beauty does not seem to be the cause. Beauty is often used in the Bible to explain attention granted to a woman (e.g., Gen. 24:16). Significantly, nowhere in the book do we read that Ruth was beautiful. The absence of any reference to her beauty implies that attention to Ruth was triggered by something else. Nevertheless, later interpreters typically add that Ruth was beautiful (as Ibn Ezra does in 2:7). Ibn Ezra suggests that Boaz thought she was someone's wife. Some modern interpreters suspect Boaz's motives when he pays attention to "a new girl in town."[65] In contrast, traditional sources extol Ruth's exceptionally modest behavior as the impetus for Boaz's solicitude. The Midrash explains that she was dressed more modestly than the other "girls," and that when gathering sheaves, she lowered her body discreetly, rather than bending over. Other girls may have been flirting, but Ruth abstained (Ruth R. 4.6; B. Shab. 113b). So too Rashi, who (following the Talmud) confronts the issue head on, asking rhetorically: "Is it Boaz's way to ask about girls?!" Rashi explains: "Only that he saw that she was more modest and less greedy—she gathered two out of three sheaves, and gathered in a more modest fashion" (B. Shab. 113b). Either way, the reader may conclude that Ruth has made herself conspicuous and welcomes attention, since her declared intent is to find favor in someone's eyes (see comment at 2:2). Such a goal would be appropriate in the cultural milieu of ancient Israel and the ancient Near East, where patronage often governed social relationships and provided economic and other advantages.[66]

girl Hebrew *na'arah*. On the nuance of the term, either as young person or subordinate, see under "servant" earlier in this verse.

6. She is a Moabite girl The attending servant or supervisor situates Ruth in a social matrix in terms of her ethnic origin and her relation to Naomi. Again, Ruth continues to be designated as a Moabite (see comment at 1:22; 2:2).

came back with Naomi Ruth's identity is based on her relation to Naomi, not to Mahlon (her late husband) or to her father-in-law. The verb "came back," *shavah,* comports with the narrator's description of her as one returning in 1:22. In keeping with the traditional understanding of Ruth as the archetypical proselyte, the Targum uses "came back" to highlight Ruth's status as a convert. Thus it translates doubly: "who returned with Naomi . . . and has become a proselyte" (*detavat ve-'itgayyerat*).

Naomi from the country of Moab. 7 She said, 'Please
let me glean and gather among the sheaves behind the
reapers.' She has been on her feet ever since she came
this morning. She has rested but little in the hut."

מוֹאָב׃ 7 וַתֹּאמֶר אֲלַקֳטָה־נָּא֙ וְאָסַפְתִּי
בָעֳמָרִים אַחֲרֵי הַקּוֹצְרִים וַתָּבוֹא וַֽתַּעֲמוֹד
מֵאָז הַבֹּ֙קֶר֙ וְעַד־עַתָּה זֶה שִׁבְתָּהּ הַבַּיִת
מְעָט׃

7. She said, 'Please let me glean and gather among the sheaves behind the reapers' It is not clear why the servant continues although he gives the reader an opportunity to see that the hard-working Ruth has gained his respect. We now learn that Ruth had requested permission. But given that permission to glean is granted by law, one wonders why she did so. Is she just polite (as *Iggeret Shemuel* suggests), or is she asking for some special privileges, and if so, what kind? The difficulty lies in deciding what "among the sheaves" (*ba-'omarim*) means here. Aside from where it denotes a unit of measure, the word *'omer* (singular of *'omarim*) occurs only six times in the Bible (plus two times in Ruth, where it is plural).[67] The plural here is understood to refer to bundles of sheaves.[68] Biblical laws demand that "When you reap the harvest of your land, you shall not reap all the way to the edges of your field, or gather the gleanings of your harvest. You shall not pick your vineyard bare, or gather the fallen fruit of your vineyard; you shall leave them for the poor and the stranger: I the LORD am your God." (Lev. 19:9–10; see also 23:22; Deut. 24:19). In verse 15, Boaz arranges for Ruth to glean "among the sheaves" (*bein ha-'omarim*). Does gleaning among the sheaves here mean gleaning among the grain that has already been bundled, thus going beyond the law or custom? This is the conclusion of a number of interpreters.[69] Frymer-Kensky suggests that the answer lies in the phrase "behind the reapers." Ruth is asking for a place immediately behind the reapers so that she can get the first pickings, rather than trailing behind other gleaners. For this she needs permission.

She has been on her feet ever since she came this morning The words in Hebrew are clear, but the precise sense of what Ruth has been doing is not. Has Ruth been standing, waiting to find out if she can enter the fields? (If so, v. 3, which tells us that she has been gleaning, is anticipatory.) Malbim has: "Until this very moment she did not rest."

She has rested but little in the hut Hebrew *zeh shivtah ha-bayit me'at.* As the NJPS translators note, the precise nuance of this phrase is uncertain. The syntax is odd. Further, it is unclear whether *shivtah* comes from *sh-v-t,* "rest" (as in this translation), or from *y-sh-v,* "sit," or from *sh-w-v,* "return." If it comes from *y-sh-v,* then the sense is that "she has sat down in the house [that is, some kind of nearby shelter] only a little." If it comes from *sh-w-v,* then the sense would be that "she has returned home only a little." In any case, the larger picture of a diligent Ruth is not affected. Ibn Ezra expounds that Ruth was minding her own needs in order not to arouse suspicion on account of her beauty.

FIRST DIALOGUE BETWEEN BOAZ AND RUTH (2:8–13)

This is the first part of only two scenes that depict a meeting between Boaz and Ruth. This one, in an open field during broad daylight, has Boaz and Ruth surrounded by witnesses; the other, at a threshing floor, takes place at midnight, deliberately avoiding witnesses (3:8–15). Boaz is the one who initiates both dialogues. In the first, he directs Ruth (for the sake of her well-being); in the second, Ruth directs Boaz for her own sake (3:9). Both scenes conclude with Ruth returning home with grain (2:17–18; 3:15). The meeting in the field consists of two parts. The first extends gleaning privileges to Ruth (2:8–13), and the second provides her with a "free lunch" (2:14–17).

8 Boaz said to Ruth, "Listen to me, daughter. Don't go to glean in another field. Don't go elsewhere, but stay here close to my girls. 9 Keep your eyes on the field they are reaping, and follow them.

8 וַיֹּאמֶר בֹּעַז אֶל־רוּת הֲלוֹא שָׁמַעַתְּ בִּתִּי
אַל־תֵּלְכִי לִלְקֹט בְּשָׂדֶה אַחֵר וְגַם לֹא
תַעֲבוּרִי מִזֶּה וְכֹה תִדְבָּקִין עִם־נַעֲרֹתָי׃
9 עֵינַיִךְ בַּשָּׂדֶה אֲשֶׁר־יִקְצֹרוּן וְהָלַכְתְּ

Boaz's instructions reflect a narrowing of spatial focus: first, he tells Ruth not to go to any other field; then, he instructs her to stay in the vicinity of his fields, and while here, to cling to or "stay" with (*d-b-k*) his "girls." Boaz's eagerness to convince Ruth to stay near is evident. He presents himself as a protector who takes an interest in Ruth's welfare. The reader, like Ruth in the next verse, may wonder about his motive: is he moved by her dramatic story and dire circumstances or charmed by her demeanor? As noted earlier, the Rabbinic sources ponder over his attention to Ruth and identify her modesty as the reason for his interest (see comment at 2:5 above).

8. Listen to me Hebrew *halo shama'at,* literally (as the NJPS notes indicate) "Have you not heard?" In conformity with social decorum, Boaz, as social superior, speaks first. His words take the form of interrogative sentences to express positive wishes in this verse and the next. His diction—like Naomi's—is old-fashioned, even archaic, and it resembles poetic verse. In the Book of Ruth, only Boaz and Naomi use these interrogative forms. This linguistic style appears to signal that Naomi and Boaz belong to the same social or generational cohort, which is distinct from that of the other speaking characters.

daughter Hebrew *biti,* "my daughter." Boaz addresses Ruth just as Naomi did (see comment at 2:2). He uses this term again in 3:10 and 11. This language indicates an age difference, as well as his superior status, but also conveys solicitude.

Don't go elsewhere Or "Do not transgress this directive"; literally, "Do not pass beyond this."

stay here close Hebrew *tidbakin,* "stick" or "cling," from the verbal root *d-b-k.*[70] Earlier, Ruth "stuck" with Naomi (see comment at 1:14); now, says Boaz, she should stick with his girls.

my girls Hebrew *na'arotai.* Designating these female workers as subordinates ("girls" as opposed to "women"; see "servant" at v. 5) is one of several indications that—as the narrator had claimed in verse 1—Boaz is a prosperous paterfamilias, possessing much land and many workers (see also next verse). By having Ruth join his "girls," Boaz moves Ruth closer into the Judean circle and his household. Being alongside the women also offers Ruth greater protection from possible harassment (see below). Equally as important, Ruth is now promoted to a more lucrative position, working as one of Boaz's "girls" rather than as a mere gleaner who gets only what is left behind. These gestures may also reflect some formal reassignment of her status within the corporate household, although it is no longer possible to identify this with precision.

9. they are reaping Hebrew *yiktzorun.* The letter *nun* might signal a masculine plural.[71]

follow them A play on words in Hebrew sharpens the contrast between the two alternatives that Boaz presents to Ruth. In the preceding verse, Boaz instructs her, "Don't go . . . in another field," using the verbal root *h-l-kh* and the adjective *'aḥer;* now he pro-

I have ordered the men not to molest you. And when you are thirsty, go to the jars and drink some of [the water] that the men have drawn."

אַחֲרֵיהֶ֑ן הֲל֥וֹא צִוִּ֛יתִי אֶת־הַנְּעָרִ֖ים לְבִלְתִּ֣י נָגְעֵ֑ךְ וְצָמִ֗ת וְהָלַכְתְּ֙ אֶל־הַכֵּלִ֔ים וְשָׁתִ֕ית מֵאֲשֶׁ֥ר יִשְׁאֲב֖וּן הַנְּעָרִֽים׃

poses that Ruth should instead "follow them" (that is, his girls), using the same two Hebrew roots.

I have ordered Boaz has apparently conveyed these instructions "offstage," as it were, since the reader is not privy to any such directive. Or perhaps this statement is to be construed as a promise that is fulfilled later, in verses 15–16, where he does give such directives.

men Hebrew *ne'arim,* the plural form of *na'ar,* which is a designation for subordinates, as well as for those who are young (see "servant" at v. 5).

molest Hebrew *naga'*. Frymer-Kensky argues against the NJPS translation because it implies that gleaning women would expect to be sexually harassed. She contends, instead, that in this context, Boaz has commanded his workers not to drive Ruth away from the working girls in his employ (where a common gleaner doesn't belong), nor even to drive her away from the water that they have drawn for themselves. But the term *naga'* has a range of nuances. Its primary sense, "to touch" (as it is rendered in the ancient Greek translation), usually refers to inappropriate—that is, sexual—touch (as in Gen. 20:6, when God protects Sarah from Abimelech). The term can also have a more neutral sense but still deal with danger, as in Lev. 5:2, which involves touching impure objects. Naomi's later instructions (v. 22; see comment there), coupled with Boaz's encouragement here, combine to suggest some physical danger in the field for an unaccompanied young woman, possibly because she is a stranger and does not "belong" to anyone (i.e., lacks a patron). (See also the violation of Dinah in the field; Genesis 34.) Several modern commentators add that in distancing Ruth from other (young) males, Boaz subtly discloses his own romantic agenda. Linafelt raises this prospect by stating that "it is up to the reader to decide if Boaz thinks he is protecting Ruth from sexual advances that are unwanted from her perspective, or if he is trying to protect her from sexual advances unwarranted from his perspective because he himself has a romantic or sexual interest."[72] Rabbinic sources, however, highlight Boaz's gallantry, which is more likely the intention of the text. The Targum has Boaz ask her not to go to another nation, and the Midrash has Boaz respond to her modesty and lack of greed (Ruth R. 4.6). Zakovitch concludes that Boaz urges her to remain in his field not because he desires her company but because he is concerned over her provision and safety.[73]

when you are thirsty, go to the jars and drink some of [the water] that the men have drawn A number of biblical narratives depict a "meeting at the well," in which a man travels to a foreign place and meets his future wife at the local well. Typically, the woman draws water for the man. The ancestral stories of Genesis and Exodus include versions of this type of scene, leading to the betrothals of Rebekah and Isaac (Genesis 24), Rachel and Jacob (Genesis 29), as well as Moses and Jethro's daughter (Exodus 2).[74] Note the gender reversals in Ruth. Here Ruth functions in the position of the outsider who is given water and a hospitable welcome. We can also discern another reversal in the motif of generosity. Providing Ruth the Moabite with water harks back to an earlier scene in Deuteronomy, when the Moabites refused water to the Israelites—"they did not meet you with food and

10 She prostrated herself with her face to the ground, and said to him, "Why are you so kind as to single me out, when I am a foreigner?"

10 וַתִּפֹּל֙ עַל־פָּנֶ֔יהָ וַתִּשְׁתַּ֖חוּ אָ֑רְצָה
וַתֹּ֣אמֶר אֵלָ֗יו מַדּ֨וּעַ֩ מָצָ֨אתִי חֵ֤ן בְּעֵינֶ֙יךָ֙
לְהַכִּירֵ֔נִי וְאָנֹכִ֖י נׇכְרִיָּֽה׃

water on your journey" (Deut. 23:5); this is the pretext in the Torah for the ancient ongoing enmity between Israel and Moab.

10. She prostrated herself Ruth's gesture of humility and thankfulness in the presence of an important figure is typical of both men and women in the Bible (see, e.g., Abigail in 1 Sam. 25:23 and Joan in 2 Sam. 14:22).

Why A mere "thank you" would have sufficed, but then the meeting might have ended. Instead, Ruth draws Boaz into an extended conversation in which he is compelled to reveal his motives. By asking a question, Ruth elicits more from Boaz and keeps him engaged.

Why are you so kind Hebrew *madua' matzati ḥen be'einekha?* Literally, "Why have I found favor in your eyes?"[75] Ruth's response does more than graciously acknowledge Boaz's kindness. Her words tell the reader that she has found what she has been seeking. In 2:2, she states that she is looking to find favor in someone's eyes ("someone who may show me kindness," literally, "someone that I may find *ḥen* in his eyes"). Here she declares that she has attained her goal: "I found *ḥen* in your eyes." Elsewhere in the Bible, the most common use of *matzah ḥen* is as a polite preface to a request or as thanks for having received something. There are several occurrences of this phrase that are quite similar to this passage in Ruth. For example, in 2 Sam. 16:4, after King David bestows much reward upon a royal servant, the servant Ziba responds, "I bow down" (as Ruth bows down), and then he continues, "for I have found favor [*ḥen*] in your eyes." And in Gen. 33:15 after Esau offers to give Jacob some of his retinue to accompany him, Jacob answers, "Why have I found favor [*ḥen*]?" While these statements follow proper protocols after receiving largesse, the corresponding statement in Ruth also establishes that Boaz has granted her unexpected privileges. For additional nuances, see comment at 2:2.

to single me out when I am a foreigner The Hebrew *lehakkireini . . . nokhriyah,* both from the root *n-k-r.* The author is discussing a serious issue and, at the same time, is engaging in wordplay. The verb *n-k-r* means to show favoritism. Thus a judge "shall show no partiality [*n-k-r*]" toward a litigant (Deut. 16:19), and a paterfamilias "must acknowledge [*n-k-r*] the first-born" by giving him "a double portion" (Deut. 21:17).[76] But the root is also used as the general term for a foreigner (see next note). In addition, it implies recognition, as when Joseph recognizes his brothers when they come to Egypt (Gen. 42:2). The Targum, following its theme that Ruth is a legal proselyte, explains that Ruth is saying, "Why . . . should you befriend me, seeing that I am of a strange people, of the daughters of Moab; of a people which has not the merit to intermarry with the congregation of the Lord?" Ruth's question shows that Ruth accepts her status as an outsider. It also implies that preferential treatment of the foreigner is not to be expected.

foreigner This term refers to an outsider, often in deprecating contrast to the Israelite (Exod. 21:8; Deut. 17:15; Ps. 69:9; Job 19:15; Ezra 10:10; Neh. 13:26). But according to Isa. 56:6–7, God welcomes the foreigner to God's holy abode. The status of the foreigner was a contested subject in the postexilic period. Ruth, Isaiah 56, and Ezra-

11 Boaz said in reply, "I have been told of all that
you did for your mother-in-law after the death of
your husband, how you left your father and mother

11 וַיַּ֤עַן בֹּ֙עַז֙ וַיֹּ֣אמֶר לָ֔הּ הֻגֵּ֨ד הֻגַּ֜ד לִ֗י כֹּ֤ל
אֲשֶׁר־עָשִׂית֙ אֶת־חֲמוֹתֵ֔ךְ אַחֲרֵ֖י מ֣וֹת
אִישֵׁ֑ךְ וַתַּֽעַזְבִ֞י אָבִ֣יךְ וְאִמֵּ֗ךְ וְאֶ֙רֶץ֙ מֽוֹלַדְתֵּ֔ךְ

Nehemiah each represents a different position (see "Intermarriage" and "Conversion" in the introduction). Sasson suggests that "the term may be better understood as someone who is not recognized as a member of a 'family.' Thus, when Ruth speaks of being 'recognized, noticed,' she may be implying more than Boaz would care to accept."[77] However, the feminine forms of the noun in the Bible elsewhere always carry a negative or dangerous sense.[78] In any case, by calling attention to her outsider status, Ruth compels Boaz to address this point when he responds to her question. The focus of her question indicates that Ruth's foreign status is an issue within the book. And it is to her as an outsider that Boaz extends welcome.

11–12. Boaz's response valorizes and structurally mirrors Ruth's pledge to Naomi (1:16), which expanded from a personal commitment to Naomi herself ("wherever you go I will go"), to the people ("your people shall be my people"), and finally to Naomi's God ("your God, my God"). Boaz first praises Ruth's devotion to her mother-in-law, then her willingness to sever herself from her family and land, and then to come to this unknown people. Boaz's response conveys that Ruth's merit derives from her devotion to Naomi specifically (not to the men of her household). He concludes with a blessing that invites Israel's God to shelter her. Yet what Boaz wishes God to provide for Ruth eventually comes from himself, reflecting a theme about human agency that characterizes the Book of Ruth (see comment at 3:9 and "The Theology of the Book of Ruth" in the introduction).

11. I have been told of all that you did The reader is not informed as to when and how Boaz learned the details about Ruth's history. Because the servant's brief message in 2:6 reveals little, we can suppose that the narrator presumes that the story is well known in the small town of Bethlehem. Boaz now connects the "face," as it were, with what he knows of Ruth by reputation. But the Targum, sensitive to this textual omission, has Boaz specify that he has received a prophecy to this effect and further adds, in line with the Targum's preoccupation with Ruth's Moabite status, that he knows that she is a proselyte. The doubling of the Hebrew verb "to tell" in Boaz's response, ***huggeid huggad li,*** "it was told to me," is interpreted in Rabbinic literature as confirmation that Boaz has received two prophetic revelations: First, it has been revealed to him that the sages will in future times revise the interpretation of the prohibition against marrying Moabites (in Deut. 23:4–7) so that it applies only to male Moabites (see PdRK 16.1; see also Ruth R. 4.1 and 7.7). Therefore, Boaz does not need to exclude Ruth from the Israelite community. Second, it has also been revealed to Boaz that kings and prophets will descend from Ruth.

for your mother-in-law Boaz acknowledges Ruth's devotion to Naomi as a praiseworthy act that deserves recompense. On "mother-in-law," see comment at 1:14.

how you left your father and mother and the land of your birth and came to a people you had not known before As Trible observes, "Boaz's language envelops Ruth in the Abrahamic paradigm," which breaks with the past.[79] Boaz's description of Ruth's merit specifically echoes God's call to Abraham: "Go forth from your native land and from your

וַתֵּלְכִי אֶל־עַם אֲשֶׁר לֹא־יָדַעַתְּ תְּמוֹל
שִׁלְשׁוֹם׃ 12 יְשַׁלֵּם יְהוָה פָּעֳלֵךְ וּתְהִי

and the land of your birth and came to a people you
had not known before. 12 May the LORD reward your
deeds. May you have a full recompense from the

father's house to the land that I will show you" (Gen. 12:1). The noun *moledet* in both verses (translated as "native land" in Genesis and as "land of your birth" in Ruth) underscores this connection. Boaz's words thereby valorize Ruth as another Abraham, ready and able to embark on a journey of faith and commitment. But the comparison highlights Ruth's even greater courage and devotion: unlike the wealthy Abraham, who receives divine promise and blessings (Gen. 12:2–3), Ruth leaves home without any promised security and with every prospect of a future life of poverty and alienation. She is motivated solely by her commitment to another person—a poor, vulnerable widow.

land of your birth . . . people These two terms, *moledet* and *ʿam,* designate the basic identity of persons in the ancient world when viewed by outsiders. Thus, when Esther hides her true identity, she keeps secret her *moledet* and *ʿam* (Esther 2:10 and 20). *Moledet* ("land of birth") is not merely a geographical designation but also a cultural context from which, Boaz acknowledges, Ruth disassociated herself.

12. May the LORD Calling upon Israel's God (twice in this sentence) and asking for divine protection for Ruth, Boaz invokes the theological hope that Ruth herself articulated on the road to Bethlehem. Yet, as the story unfolds, he himself undertakes the task he now ascribes to God, namely, protection, when he acts to secure Ruth's welfare. Whereas some modern commentators suggest that Boaz here shifts responsibility to God for rewarding Ruth more fully, rather than to himself,[80] one medieval interpreter paraphrases Boaz's intent as follows: "No human being is capable of giving a sufficient reward, comparable to what you have done."[81] This interpretation elevates Ruth's devotion even higher.

reward your deeds . . . recompense Hebrew *yeshallem poʿoleikh . . . maskoret.* Two different notions of reward are referenced here: first, "reward" (*sh-l-m,* elsewhere meaning "pay") for "deeds" (*poʿal,* related to *peʿulah,* see below), and second, "recompense" (*maskoret*). In English we distinguish between "wages," normally paid in cash, and "reward," paid in less specific quantifiable goods. In biblical Hebrew, they are both indicated by this root, *s-k-r.*[82] In Jeremiah's vision of Rachel crying for her lost children, the reward of being granted children is extended metaphorically to Israel. God tells Rachel to stop crying, "for there is reward [*sakhar*] for your deeds" (your *peʿulah,* as here), in that the children are coming back from the land of the enemy (Jer. 31:16). This pair of words is picked up in Isaiah in reference to God: "Behold, His reward [*sakhar*] is with Him, His recompense [*peʿulah*] before him" (Isa. 40:10 and 62:11). As in Ruth, Deutero-Isaiah's use of *peʿulah* as God's gesture of reward shows how closely *sakhar* and *peʿulah* are connected. These examples illustrate the broad sense of Boaz's words and the range of intertextual allusions that may be at work. Prompted by Boaz's words "you have come," the Targum specifies that the reward Boaz has in mind is "in the world to come." Ruth will be spared from the "rule of hell (*gehinom*)" and will spend eternity with the matriarchs.

your deeds Hebrew *poʿoleikh*, "deed" (singular). Boaz asserts that it is specifically Ruth's loyalty to Naomi (not what she did for her father-in-law or husband) that deserves a reward.

Lord, the God of Israel, under whose wings you have sought refuge!"
[13] She answered, "You are most kind, my lord, to comfort me and to speak gently to your maid-

מַשְׂכֻּרְתֵּ֔ךְ שְׁלֵמָ֗ה מֵעִ֤ם יְהוָה֙ אֱלֹהֵ֣י
יִשְׂרָאֵ֔ל אֲשֶׁר־בָּ֖את לַחֲס֥וֹת תַּֽחַת־כְּנָפָֽיו׃
13 וַ֠תֹּאמֶר אֶמְצָא־חֵ֨ן בְּעֵינֶ֤יךָ אֲדֹנִי֙ כִּ֣י

from the Lord, the God of Israel By invoking and inviting Israel's God to take action, Boaz indirectly welcomes Ruth into the people Israel.

under whose wings you have sought refuge Literally, "that you have come to take refuge under His wings." In 1:16, Ruth announced her commitment to Naomi's God; now Boaz acknowledges her place under God's wings. The image of God's wings (*kenafaim;* sing. *kanaf*) appears often in the Bible. The notion of God's sheltering wings is especially pronounced in the Psalms, as in "you will find refuge under His wings" (Ps. 91:4; see also 36:8; 57:2; 61:5). One also finds references in Psalms to the shelter provided by the shadow of God's wings (Ps. 17:18; 36:8; 57:2; 63:8). Ruth uses this word (*kanaf*) later when she urges Boaz at the threshing floor to take action for her sake (for a full discussion, see comment at 3:9). The Targum here specifies the "wings of the Shekhinah," a well-developed expression in postbiblical Jewish literature for God's presence among the people Israel. Rashi, commenting on Gen. 12:5, writes of Abraham and Sarah that they took persons in "under the wings of the Shekhinah; Abraham converted the men, and Sarah converted the women."

13. You are most kind Hebrew *'emtza ḥen be-'einekha,* "let me/would that I find favor in your eyes" (or "I have/I will have found favor in your eyes"). Ruth has the last word in this exchange. Like her earlier response to Boaz, this one is carefully crafted, and it is likewise laden with double meanings. Once again Ruth refers to a display of kindness as in 2:2 and 2:10. This time, however, she uses an imperfect form or cohortative mode; Campbell translates: "may I continue to find favor."[83] As Sasson observes, her words also elicit acts of kindness from Boaz.[84]

to comfort me Hebrew *ki niḥamtani,* "for you have comforted me." This term for comfort, *n-ḥ-m,* key in this context, appears in the Bible after major crises. In Isa. 40:1–2, the verb in the plural forecasts God's restoration of Israel, calling messengers to comfort the bereaved Jerusalem after the trauma of exile. Pesikta de-Rav Kahana focuses its sermon on Isa. 40:1–2 with this verse in Ruth. Pointing to the example of how Boaz comforted Ruth, God promises even greater comfort for Israel: "Shall a man's comforting outshine his Maker? By these words the Holy One meant: Boaz comforted, and shall I not—shall I not at the very least—comfort as effectively?"[85]

to speak gently to Hebrew *dibarta al lebh,* "you have spoken to the heart of." Forms of this richly nuanced idiom appear only seven other times in the Bible, always connoting comfort, usually after some kind of breach or disaster. In three of these, the reference expresses encouragement in time of loss (2 Sam. 19:8) or threat of war (2 Chron. 30:22; 32:6). In four of these cases, "speaking to the heart" is the language of courtship, with a male wooing a female. In Gen. 34:3, Shechem, who has violated Dinah but now loves her and longs to marry her, "speaks to her heart" ("spoke to the maiden tenderly"). In Judg. 19:3, a husband "speaks to the heart" of the woman who has left him to win her back ("went after her to woo her"). In Hos. 2:16, God will "speak to Israel's heart" to win her affection and loyalty prior to betrothal ("I will speak coaxingly to her") after listing servant—though I am not so much as one of your maidservants."

14 At mealtime, Boaz said to her, "Come over here and partake of the meal, and dip your morsel in the

נִחַמְתָּנִי וְכִי דִבַּרְתָּ עַל־לֵב שִׁפְחָתֶךָ וְאָנֹכִי
לֹא אֶהְיֶה כְּאַחַת שִׁפְחֹתֶיךָ׃
14 וַיֹּאמֶר לָה* בֹעַז לְעֵת הָאֹכֶל גֹּשִׁי הֲלֹם
וְאָכַלְתְּ מִן־הַלֶּחֶם וְטָבַלְתְּ פִּתֵּךְ בַּחֹמֶץ

v. 14. ה׳ רפה

numerous punishments. In Isa. 40:1–2, God dispatches messengers to "speak to the heart" of Jerusalem ("Speak tenderly to Jerusalem"; elsewhere, God is depicted as Jerusalem's husband, 54:5–4). Thus, with these words, Ruth introduces, or recognizes, an emotional dimension that transcends mere humility or gratitude in her encounter with Boaz.

maidservant Hebrew *shifḥah*. Like the term *'amah* ("handmaid"; see comment at 3:9), *shifḥah* literally refers to a female slave or servant. But when women apply it to themselves, it is usually to show deference toward a powerful male, or to ascribe power to a man, even when the woman speaking is herself privileged. For example, when Abigail and David first meet, she is socially and economically his superior. But to persuade him to spare her household from vengeance, she refers to herself as his *'amah* (1 Sam. 25:24,25,28) and as his *shifḥah* (v. 27). In general, *shifḥah* conveys a lower status than *'amah* does.

my lord, though I am not so much as one of your maidservants Ruth here expresses humility, even obsequiousness. This reflects matters of class: Ruth after all, is the poor outsider. And the language conforms to polite language as we find in other encounters.

though I am not so much as one of your maidservants Literally, "and I will not be as one of your maidservants." The precise intent of Ruth's wording is somewhat obscure, and yet it works well to convey a double message hinting at her desired status. She has just designated herself a maidservant, as befits a well-brought-up beneficiary. But as she now concludes her response, she not only acknowledges Boaz's graciousness, but also—at another level—distances herself from permanent subservience: she is not an actual maidservant and will not become one. The Midrash leans in this direction when it has Boaz respond with wordplay: "You are not from the handmaids (*'amahot*) but with the matriarchs (*'imahot*)" (Ruth R. 5.5).

I am Ruth uses the explicit pronoun *'anokhi,* an emphatic form of "I."

LUNCH IN THE FIELD AND THE BEGINNING OF RUTH'S REWARD (2:14–17)

The scene now shifts to mealtime. Boaz has prayed that God reward Ruth, but now he himself begins to reward her, becoming God's agent. Frymer-Kensky observes that "the characters in the Book of Ruth themselves act to fulfill the blessing that they bestow on one another in God's name."[86] Perhaps, one interpreter ponders, "by having to articulate Ruth's admirable actions and needy situation, Boaz is led to ask himself if he has done enough for his female relatives."[87] The scene conjures up a pastoral setting in which master and workers lunch together in conviviality.

14. Come over here and partake of the meal Once again Boaz initiates the contact. By inviting Ruth to eat at his expense, Boaz extends his solicitude even further, bringing her closer to him both physically and symbolically.

vinegar." So she sat down beside the reapers. He handed her roasted grain, and she ate her fill and had some left over.

15 When she got up again to glean, Boaz gave orders to his workers, "You are not only to let her glean among the sheaves, without interference, 16 but you must also pull some [stalks] out of the heaps and leave them for her to glean, and not scold her."

וַתֵּשֶׁב מִצַּד הַקּוֹצְרִים וַיִּצְבָּט־לָהּ קָלִי
וַתֹּאכַל וַתִּשְׂבַּע וַתֹּתַר׃
15 וַתָּקָם לְלַקֵּט וַיְצַו בֹּעַז אֶת־נְעָרָיו לֵאמֹר
גַּם בֵּין הָעֳמָרִים תְּלַקֵּט וְלֹא תַכְלִימוּהָ׃
16 וְגַם שֹׁל־תָּשֹׁלּוּ לָהּ מִן־הַצְּבָתִים
וַעֲזַבְתֶּם וְלִקְּטָה וְלֹא תִגְעֲרוּ־בָהּ׃

He handed her roasted grain She is no longer an outsider at the margin. Instead, she sits at the master's table, as it were, alongside his reapers. Boaz himself hands her food. He is creating or observing a ceremony of sharing.

handed Hebrew *yitzbot.* Even though this verb does not appear elsewhere in the Bible, its cognate is well known from other Semitic languages (such as Ugaritic and Akkadian) where it means "to seize" or "grab."[88]

she ate her fill and had some left over His generosity in seating her with his entourage and feeding her is exceeded by his generosity in handing her so much food that she has some left over. Such abundance and largesse are rarely mentioned in the Bible.

she ate her fill Hebrew *va-tokhal va-tisbaʿ.* Elsewhere in the Bible, being able to eat until satisfied is often the result of God's generosity (e.g., Deut. 6:11; 8:10; 11:15; 31:20). Thus, Boaz is already cast in the role of an agent bringing to fruition some of the blessings he wished for Ruth in 2:12.

15. After the meal, Boaz continues to act with generosity. He grants Ruth gleaning privileges (as per her request in 2:7), tells the reapers to drop some grain on purpose, and instructs them not to harass her. As a result, Ruth gleans a very large amount.

let her glean among the sheaves Hebrew *gam bein ha-ʿomarim telakket.* According to Boaz's supervisor, Ruth asked permission to "gather among the sheaves [*ba-ʿomarim*]" (v. 7), possibly seeking a better position in the field, with greater access to fruitful gleaning. Here Boaz grants additional privileges (the word *gam* means "also") of gleaning *bein ha-ʿomarim.* While the precise positions in the field are no longer clear for modern readers (see comment at 2:7), the overall message is obvious: Boaz expands the circle of protection and opportunity for Ruth.

interference Hebrew *takhlimuha,* from the verbal root *k-l-m,* which means "humiliate" or "embarrass" in Isa. 54:4, when God promises Zion that she will never again be humiliated now that God is her protector. The idea is also embedded in the Friday night song welcoming the Shabbat bride, "Lekha Dodi": "You will not be shamed and will not be humiliated/embarrassed," *Loʾ teivoshi ve-loʾ tikalmi* (in the sixth stanza).

16. you must also . . . leave them for her This instruction to the reapers makes Ruth's gleaning a much easier task, in that she has more grain to gather with less effort, with the happy result that she will go home with plenty of food.

pull some [stalks] Hebrew *shol tashollu.* The use of the infinitive absolute in its emphatic form emphasizes the seriousness of the command. However, the meaning here is not altogether clear. On the basis of context and the similarity of this verb to the root

[17] She gleaned in the field until evening. Then she
beat out what she had gleaned—it was about an *ephah*
of barley—[18] and carried it back with her to the town.
When her mother-in-law saw what she had gleaned,
and when she also took out and gave her what she
had left over after eating her fill, [19] her mother-in-law

17 וַתְּלַקֵּט בַּשָּׂדֶה עַד־הָעָרֶב וַתַּחְבֹּט אֵת
אֲשֶׁר־לִקֵּטָה וַיְהִי כְּאֵיפָה שְׂעֹרִים׃
18 וַתִּשָּׂא וַתָּבוֹא הָעִיר וַתֵּרֶא חֲמוֹתָהּ אֵת
אֲשֶׁר־לִקֵּטָה וַתּוֹצֵא וַתִּתֶּן־לָהּ אֵת אֲשֶׁר־
הוֹתִרָה מִשָּׂבְעָהּ׃ 19 וַתֹּאמֶר לָהּ חֲמוֹתָהּ

n-sh-l, it can be construed to mean "to fall" (or from *sh-l-l*—so Ibn Ezra), referring to pulling stalks out of the heaps.

not scold her Boaz's protective measures do not merely make Ruth's gleaning more productive but also protect her dignity. The need to ensure that she will not be scolded suggests that people in her position would typically be subject to harassment or admonishment—either because they were poor, women, or foreigners. (For an example of routine harassment of young women, see the story of Jethro's daughters at the well in Exod. 2:17–18.) Perhaps this protection measure is necessary because Ruth's new privileges place her beyond the places allotted to poor gleaners.

17. she beat out This is one method of threshing, which breaks loose the husked grain from its stalks. Compare, for example, Gideon threshing grain in Judg. 6:11.

about an ephah of barley Exod. 16:36 states that an *'omer* is one tenth of an *ephah,* and Exod. 16:16 indicates that the *'omer* of manna is a portion sufficient for one person per day. The *Oxford Annotated Bible* calculates that an *ephah* was about 21 U.S. quarts.[89] Thanks to Boaz's generosity, Ruth is able to glean five times more than she and Naomi need for that day.[90]

HOME AGAIN (2:18–23)

Naomi, who had interpreted her misfortune as God's doing (1:13, 20–21), now shifts to gratitude when she sees the abundant food Ruth brings and hears her report. Only now does Naomi disclose to Ruth that Boaz is a relative and informs her about potential danger in the field—two pieces of information that would have been valuable to Ruth before she went out to glean. The chapter ends as it began, with a focus on the two women at home, but no longer without food. In this closing section, Ruth's success enables Naomi, who had been bitter, to reclaim a capacity to bless and to hope. At the conclusion we learn that Ruth continues to glean throughout the harvest season.

18. her mother-in-law The narrator (here and in 2:19) repeatedly uses the terms "mother-in-law" and "daughter-in-law" even when the person is identified by name, thus emphasizing the relationship between the two women.

what she had left over That is, what remained from the lunch with Boaz (see comment at 2:14). This is food that has already been processed for consumption and requires no further effort—in contrast to the husked, raw grain that Ruth herself has gathered.

after eating her fill Ruth does not neglect herself; she shares leftovers, as it were, but she has eaten sufficiently to have filled herself first (see 2:14). This detail adds a telling dimension to the representation of Ruth as one who is wholly committed but not self-sacrificing.[91]

asked her, "Where did you glean today? Where did you work? Blessed be he who took such generous notice of you!" So she told her mother-in-law whom she had worked with, saying, "The name of the man with whom I worked today is Boaz."

20 Naomi said to her daughter-in-law, "Blessed be he of the LORD, who has not failed in His kindness to

אֵיפֹה לִקַּטְתְּ הַיּוֹם וְאָנָה עָשִׂית יְהִי
מַכִּירֵךְ בָּרוּךְ וַתַּגֵּד לַחֲמוֹתָהּ אֵת אֲשֶׁר־
עָשְׂתָה עִמּוֹ וַתֹּאמֶר שֵׁם הָאִישׁ אֲשֶׁר
עָשִׂיתִי עִמּוֹ הַיּוֹם בֹּעַז׃
20 וַתֹּאמֶר נָעֳמִי לְכַלָּתָהּ בָּרוּךְ הוּא לַיהוָה

19–20. Blessed be he Naomi responds in characteristic fashion to the largesse that she sees by blessing the one who has enabled Ruth to be so successful.

he who took such . . . generous notice of you Hebrew *makireikh,* from the root *n-k-r,* which echoes Ruth's earlier statement to Boaz (see comment at v. 10, "single me out"). Bringing home so much grain indicates that some benefactor must have "noticed" Ruth and given her special privileges. In 2:2, Ruth had announced her intention to find a benefactor.

man Hebrew *'ish*; see comment at 1:1.

20. Blessed be he Repetition of this sentiment discloses Naomi's excitement.

of the LORD For Naomi, God has changed back from an adversary to a source of blessing. After the actions of Ruth and Boaz restore hope, she relinquishes her bitterness, so poignantly expressed in 1:21.

who has not failed in His kindness Literally, "who has not abandoned [*'azabh*] his *ḥesed.*" The sentence structure is such that the pronoun's antecedent is ambiguous. Some commentators have understood this clause as referring to Boaz, who has been kind to both the living (Naomi and Ruth) and the dead (her late husband Elimelech and his sons). They argue that God is never said to show *ḥesed* to the dead in the Bible; rather, this is always an act performed by people—as by Ruth and Orpah to their dead husbands (1:8).[92] However, such a reading presumes that Naomi believes that Boaz had performed acts of *ḥesed* toward her husband while he was still alive. We are given no other evidence that he did so or that Naomi holds to such a belief, which casts some doubt upon the proffered interpretation. Significantly, this phrase "abandoned his *ḥesed*" occurs in the Bible only one other time, where it clearly refers to God. In the other story that has so many parallels to the Ruth story, Abraham's servant is looking for a wife for his master's son. He prays that God "make it happen" and show *ḥesed* to Abraham by bringing the appropriate girl to the well. When Rebekah suddenly appears and meets—even exceeds—his hoped-for qualifications, the servant exclaims, "Blessed be the LORD . . . who has not withheld [*'azabh*] His steadfast faithfulness [*ḥesed*] from my master (Gen. 24:27)."

In our story, Naomi and Ruth don't pray for such a happening, but nevertheless "her happening happened" when Ruth comes to her kinsman's field (v. 3). Furthermore, Naomi has all along perceived the hand of God in the events of her life (see 1:21 above). One would thus expect her to do so in this instance. Taken together, these arguments suggest that the pronoun in Naomi's statement is referring not to Boaz but to God—which is how NJPS renders it. That said, the author may nonetheless intend an ambiguity. Perhaps we are being led to see that, for Naomi, the role of God and the role of a powerful man like Boaz are interchangeable. Such a view would not be exceptional in an ancient, hierarchical the living or to the dead! For," Naomi explained to her, "the man is related to us; he is one of our

אֲשֶׁר לֹא־עָזַב חַסְדּוֹ אֶת־הַחַיִּים וְאֶת־
הַמֵּתִים וַתֹּאמֶר לָהּ נָעֳמִי קָרוֹב לָנוּ

society. Note, for example, the words of the wise woman of Tekoa who says to King David: "My lord the king is like an angel of God" (2 Sam. 14:17).

failed Hebrew *'azabh,* "abandoned." As Frymer-Kensky observes, our narrator likes to play with words and to craft sentences with more than one meaning. Here we see subtle wordplay on Boaz's name: Naomi's fortune has reversed; instead of God's abandoning (*'-z-bh*) his *ḥesed,* there is now Boaz (*b-'-z*). The Hebrew words suggest each other. Boaz, moreover, is acting as God's agent. Frymer-Kensky notes that both Boaz and God are showing *ḥesed,* and so both deserve to be blessed. In 1:16, Ruth uses this verb when she refuses to abandon Naomi. On the covenantal associations of the verb, see also "leave" at 1:16.

the man is related to us; he is one of our redeeming kinsmen Only now does Naomi mention that she has local relatives and that one of them is affluent. In using "us" and "ours," she embraces Ruth as a member of her family and shows that she considers her fate and Ruth's to be linked.

related Hebrew *karov,* "near," a term suggesting kinship. In contrast, Boaz has not used kinship language to explain his generosity to Ruth. Instead, he has singled out Ruth's own merit (v. 11). It is her merit that pries open the gate and paves the way for Ruth's absorption into the community—for her journey from outside Israelite society, to its margins, and then into its center.

redeeming kinsmen Hebrew *go'el,* "redeemer." The term refers both to a person responsible for a relative, and to God in relation to Israel. God as a redeemer acts to rescue Israel (as in the Exodus narrative; see "I will redeem you with an outstretched arm," Exod. 6:6, a passage recited during the Passover Seder). Biblical laws focus on three responsibilities of a redeemer. One pertains to blood vengeance (Numbers 35 and Deut. 19:5–13). The other two designate the redeemer as the person charged with helping destitute relatives, a role pertinent to Naomi's and Ruth's circumstances. The latter roles are most fully developed in Leviticus 25. Leviticus 25:25–34 depicts a number of specific ways that an Israelite is to redeem a kin from financial ruin; verses 35–43 focus on redemption from slavery. The basic role is introduced as follows: "If one of your kin is in straits and has to sell part of a holding, the nearest redeemer shall come and redeem what that relative has sold" (Lev. 25:25, CJPS). This verse uses two of the words that we find in Naomi's response—*go'el* "redeemer" and *karov* "near." Leviticus also specifies other situations in which a redeemer must bail out a destitute relative: "anyone of his family who is of the same flesh [*she'er*] shall redeem him" (25:49). Baruch Levine points out in his commentary on Num. 5:8 that this category of "flesh" relatives is characterized through a list in Lev. 21:2 and that it includes (but is not limited to) one's mother and daughter. Apparently Boaz is within the same broad category, "of the same flesh" as Naomi's deceased husband Elimelech.[93] Naomi also discloses that Boaz is not the only redeeming kinsman.

The role and scope of the redeemer's obligations, as they apply to Ruth and Naomi, have become a subject of scholarly debate (see comment at 3:9 and 4:5–10, as well as "Levirate Marriage" and "Inheritance" and "Redemption" in the introduction). Ibn Ezra specifies here that "redemption is not a levirate marriage but another way." The importance of this observation becomes evident in 3:9, when Ruth invites Boaz to undertake this role. See comment at 3:9. Ruth 4:15 establishes that providing for a needy relative is a crucial aspect of the "redeeming" kinsman in this book. See also Ruth 4:1–7.

הָאִישׁ מִגֹּאֲלֵנוּ הוּא׃ 21 *וַתֹּאמֶר רוּת
הַמּוֹאֲבִיָּה גַּם ׀ כִּי־אָמַר אֵלַי עִם־הַנְּעָרִים
אֲשֶׁר־לִי תִּדְבָּקִין עַד אִם־כִּלּוּ אֵת כָּל־
הַקָּצִיר אֲשֶׁר־לִי׃ 22 וַתֹּאמֶר נָעֳמִי אֶל־רוּת

redeeming kinsmen." 21 Ruth the Moabite said, "He
even told me, 'Stay close by my workers until all my
harvest is finished.'" 22 And Naomi answered her

21. Ruth the Moabite said Why at this moment—when Ruth has been drawn into Boaz's circle, when the redeemer of Naomi and Ruth has been revealed, and when Naomi has fully accepted Ruth as someone tied to her—does the narrator call her "the Moabite"? All three times that the narrator refers to Ruth as a Moabite appear in connection with Naomi (1:22; 2:2, 22). (The other three references to "Ruth the Moabite" are spoken by characters in the story. Boaz refers to Ruth this way twice, in 4:5 and 4:10; and his servant once, in 2:6.) This may signal the extent to which Ruth's "Moabiteness" colors Naomi's relation to her.[94]

He even told me, "Stay close by my workers" Ruth explains that Boaz's graciousness extended beyond the food that she has brought. It also promises a similar harvest throughout the season.

Stay close Hebrew *tidbakin,* from *d-b-k,* the theme word "to stick"; see "clung" at 1:14 and "stay here close" at 2:8.

workers Hebrew *ne'arim,* plural of *na'ar,* meaning young persons or subordinates (see "servant" at 2:5 and 2:15). Ruth employs the same noun as did Boaz in verse 9 and the narrator in verse 15, when Boaz gave orders to his workers. The term used here does not specify the workers' gender. Yet the masculine plural form invites reflection and suggests some specific nuances. For in verse 8, Boaz tells Ruth to stay specifically with his *female* workers (*na'arot*). (Later Naomi will echo Boaz in specifying females; v. 22.) In a story with so many gender displacements, Ruth's "misquoting" of Boaz—not referring specifically to female workers—should not be dismissed too quickly as accidental. Arguably she is simplifying for the sake of brevity—conflating two things that Boaz has said (vv. 8–9). But does this use of the term indicate that Ruth, as family breadwinner, aligns herself with Boaz's men (rather than his "girls") because that is where the better gleaning will be? However one interprets her words, Ruth's language breaks the mold into which Boaz, Naomi, and ancient Israelite culture place her. This trait is consistent with the portrait of Ruth elsewhere in the Book of Ruth. As Trible observes, Ruth must be seen not only "in culture" but also "against culture," as well as "transforming culture".[95] Rabbi Ḥanin bar Levi attributes Ruth's "misquotation" (her using the masculine plural form instead of the feminine plural) to her Moabite origin (Ruth R. 5.1), that is, Ruth is a foreigner who does not know that men and women are meant to inhabit separate social spheres. Given the Bible's claim that the Moabite people are born out of incest—according to the Genesis narrative (see Gen. 19:30–38)—this particular rabbi may be suggesting that Moabites do not observe sexual mores with rigor.

22. Naomi redirects Ruth, making two distinct points: First, that Ruth should attach herself to the "girls" (as opposed to the male workers); second, that doing otherwise by going to another field poses dangers to Ruth. Like Boaz, then, Naomi confines Ruth to the company of women in the field. Both Naomi and Boaz articulate the dominant cultural message to women: if a young woman goes off alone or with men, something unpleasant will happen to her—or be told about her.

daughter-in-law Ruth, "It is best, daughter, that you go out with his girls, and not be annoyed in some other field." 23 So she stayed close to the maidservants

כַּלָּתָהּ טוֹב בִּתִּי כִּי תֵצְאִי עִם־נַעֲרוֹתָיו
וְלֹא יִפְגְּעוּ־בָךְ בְּשָׂדֶה אַחֵר׃ 23 וַתִּדְבַּק

daughter-in-law Ruth As in verse 20, the mention of "daughter-in-law"—which in the Hebrew follows Ruth's name—seems superfluous. This superfluity of names and relationship is present also in verse 19. It serves to highlight the kinship relation.

girls Although Ruth referred to "workers" in general (*neʿarim*), Naomi uses the grammatically feminine form (*neʿarot*), which specifies female workers or young women. This is also what Boaz had instructed Ruth to do (see comment at 2:8).

annoyed Hebrew *yiphgeʿu,* from *p-g-ʿ*. The Hebrew is more forceful, implying "to harass," even to injure. The term indicates, as did Boaz's words in 2:9, that the field was not a safe place for a woman in Ruth's position. (The same verb and preposition are rendered as "molest" in verse 9; see the note there.) The wide range of possible meanings makes it difficult to know the precise nature of Naomi's concern for Ruth. The common interpretation is that Naomi is making explicit the warning embedded in her admonition to "go out with his girls" in the first half of this verse: if you do not stay with the girls, you could be attacked! Frymer-Kensky objects to such a reading for two reasons. First, she argues that it is hard to understand why Naomi would warn Ruth only now, and not when Ruth first went out to glean.

Second, Frymer-Kensky presents philological reasons for not translating the word this way. All occurrences of the phrase *pagaʿ be-* with meaning of "attacked" are found in the historical books (Joshua–2 Kings), which often have their own specialized vocabulary.[96] Frymer-Kensky, therefore, suggests that it should not be applied here. She prefers to translate the words as "lest they disturb you." Frymer-Kensky claims that the author intends that Naomi speak ambiguously, enjoining Ruth on the one hand to stay in Boaz's field (rather than risk encountering people elsewhere who might not be nice to her), while on the other hand encouraging her to develop the linkage with Boaz's household.

However, Naomi's earlier silences suggest a less benign meaning here. Naomi was also silent about Boaz's kinship until now. Just because she didn't warn Ruth earlier about possible molestation in the fields doesn't mean that she cannot be alert to such dangers now.

Frymer-Kensky's second objection to translating the Hebrew verb more forcefully—that the phrase *pagaʿ be-* connotes violence only in the historical books—actually strengthens the case that a violent sense is intended here as well. The Book of Ruth situates itself with the historical books, specifically in the same time period as the Book of Judges, both thematically and linguistically. It begins at that time (see comment at 1:1); and its concluding genealogy (4:18–22) leads to the Davidic dynasty in the Book of Samuel.

With the historical books as the backdrop to Ruth, it seems likely that the phrase *pagaʿ be-* in Naomi's mouth (like Boaz's comment in v. 9) recognizes the presence of danger in the field, from which Boaz provides protection. As an allusion to the world depicted in Judges (see comment at 1:1), the verb reminds the reader of the harsh reality within which the story takes place and serves to magnify the protagonists' acts of kindness.

23. The pace quickens at the conclusion of the chapter. One verse now covers several months, during which Ruth gleans daily for herself and Naomi.

So she stayed close Hebrew *va-tidbak,* from *d-b-k.* For the range of meanings, see comments at 1:14, 2:8, and 2:21. Both Boaz and Naomi have instructed Ruth to do so, and she obeys.

of Boaz, and gleaned until the barley harvest and the wheat harvest were finished. Then she stayed at home with her mother-in-law.

בְּנַעֲרוֹת בֹּעַז לְלַקֵּט עַד־כְּלוֹת קְצִיר־הַשְּׂעֹרִים וּקְצִיר הַחִטִּים וַתֵּשֶׁב אֶת־חֲמוֹתָהּ׃

until the barley harvest and the wheat harvest were finished Ruth's easy access to grain extends through two harvests. According to Oded Borowski, "Barley harvesting (spring equinox to late April)... signaled the beginning of ingathering. Following was the harvesting of wheat (late April to late May), which ended with the celebration of... Pentecost."[97] According to Ruth R. 5.11, the two harvests end after three months, roughly in mid-August.[98] But the end of the harvest season means the end of Ruth's access to food. Beyond the supply of staple grains that the two widows have presumably stored up, no provisions for the future have been made—which is why Naomi takes the next step. This verse thus marks the conclusion of Ruth's work as a gleaner but also functions as the backdrop, and probably impetus, for the plan that Naomi proposes in the following scene.

Then she stayed at home with her mother-in-law This last clause is both the conclusion to what preceded and the introduction or setting of the dialogue that follows in the next chapter. The statement reveals two facts about Ruth at this point in the narrative. First, no matter how well acquainted Ruth has become with the members of Boaz's household, she has not abandoned her primary tie with Naomi. At the same time, Ruth has not been integrated into Boaz's household. The text provides no hint that Boaz has taken further interest in Ruth after the first day. At season's end, she is left without further resources: no future provisions have been made for her. This situation prompts Naomi to hatch a daring plot.

stayed at home Hebrew *va-teishev* (from the root *y-sh-v*, "dwelled" or "sat"). Verbally and thematically, the end of this chapter—which recounts the end of the harvest—echoes the end of chapter one, which mentions the beginning of the barley harvest, the time when Naomi returns (*va-tashov*, from the root *sh-w-v*) to Bethlehem with Ruth. The similar summarizing conclusions of Chapters 1 and 2 serve as framing devices that mark movement in time. The ending also parallels the conclusion of the next chapter, which ends with Ruth and Naomi at home (3:16–18).

with her mother-in-law In contrast to 1:22, this time the narrator emphasizes Ruth's identity not as a Moabite but solely as a relative of Naomi. See also comment at 2:11. But her Moabite status is invoked again, next time by Boaz (4:5 and 10).

CHAPTER 3

The Transformative Midnight Encounter between Ruth and Boaz

A nighttime meeting between Boaz and Ruth occupies center stage in this chapter. Ruth, in compliance with Naomi's directives, secretly approaches Boaz, who is asleep on the threshing floor. When Boaz suddenly awakens, Ruth requests that he act on her behalf, and he enthusiastically consents. Yet the reader is left in the dark as to what exactly transpires; the precise nature of her actions and request are concealed by innuendos.

This chapter begins and concludes, like Chapter 2, with Naomi and Ruth at home. At its beginning, Naomi orchestrates the nighttime meeting between Boaz and Ruth (3:1–5). At its end at dawn, Ruth returns home with grain and hope-filled news (3:16–18, as in 2:18–22). In this second meeting Ruth enlists Boaz's support as redeemer, ready to champion her cause at the city's gate.

OUTLINE OF CHAPTER 3

I. Naomi's daring plan for desperate times (1–5)
II. Ruth and Boaz on the threshing floor (6–15)
III. Homecoming with good news and grain (16–18)

NAOMI'S DARING PLAN FOR DESPERATE TIMES (3:1–5)

We begin with Naomi and Ruth at home and alone. Much has happened since Ruth first went out to glean (2:2), and yet the women's fundamental circumstances remain the same: the two depend for their survival on Ruth's daily gleaning during the harvest seasons, enhanced by Boaz's generosity, which ensures that she brings home sufficient grain. However, with the grain harvest at an end (2:23), the prospects for future provisions are slim. The women who had surrounded the two widows when they first arrived (1:19) have long since disappeared. Apparently nothing has been done for Ruth and Naomi in Bethlehem—"the house of bread"—to secure their economic position.

Yet Naomi, revitalized by Ruth's success as a breadwinner (2:20–22), and perhaps feeling desperate as she looks ahead to their future, now proposes that Ruth solicit Boaz, although she stops short of any explicit reference to sexual seduction. She instructs Ruth to groom herself and to approach Boaz under the cover of night. Naomi's instructions conclude with "and he will tell you what to do" (3:4). It is difficult to miss the sexual overtones in her instructions: Ruth is to undertake a risqué and risky mission. Boaz's later eagerness to keep Ruth's visit a secret (3:14) confirms the reader's impression that this meeting is at least unconventional and perhaps scandalous. Sasson and Campbell conclude, after reviewing the interpretations of this chapter by numerous commentators, that "the storyteller meant to be ambiguous and hence provocative."[99] Rabbinic sources tend to downplay the sensual overtones; nevertheless, they too acknowledge the innuendos when they explain that Ruth modifies Naomi's instructions lest she be mistaken for a prostitute (see Rashi on 3:6, also Ruth R. 5.13–14, and below at vv. 3, 6).

In this section Naomi explains that she wishes to provide Ruth with *manoaḥ,* translated here (v. 1) as "home." In Naomi's frame of reference, as we have seen, this means marriage (see comment at 1:9). But respectable marital arrangements are usually not contracted in such a stealthy fashion as the one Naomi proposes here. Perhaps the reader is

3 Naomi, her mother-in-law, said to her, "Daughter, I must seek a home for you, where you may be happy.

ג וַתֹּאמֶר לָהּ נָעֳמִי חֲמוֹתָהּ בִּתִּי הֲלֹא

meant to infer that Ruth's Moabite status makes her an unlikely candidate for a legal union—or even for good standing in the Israelite community (Deut. 23:4 specifically excludes Moabites from ever entering the community; see "Intermarriage" and "Conversion" and "The Status of the Moabites" in the introduction). Perhaps Naomi aims to skirt this issue by contriving a less formal and more personal arrangement for Ruth as Boaz's protégée. Some commentators suppose that Naomi is arranging a levirate marriage.[100] Yet neither she nor Ruth or Boaz mentions the subject. Furthermore, Boaz does not qualify as a levir. Rather, both Naomi (2:20) and Ruth (3:9) refer to Boaz as a "redeemer"—a kinship role that does not, in the Bible, pertain to marriage (see comment at 3:9 and "Levirate Marriage" in the introduction). Finally, if Boaz were a levir, then why such unusual means to make the point? The narrator leaves the reader pondering what Naomi expects. Alsheikh fills in the gaps by elaborating on Naomi's instructions. He has Naomi mention levirate marriage and also speak about the value of coupling with Boaz on other grounds. Commenting on 3:2, Alsheikh has Naomi explain to Ruth that to be actualized, holiness must be mixed with something that seems forbidden. As examples, she discusses the marriage of Jacob to two sisters (forbidden in Leviticus) and the union of Judah and Tamar which, in this retelling, was sanctioned by an angel who told Judah to unite with Tamar so that the consummation would not be entirely as it should (*she-lo ke-hogen*). "The entire house of Israel depends on your coupling," says Naomi. The very holiness of something great (the birth of the Messiah) requires it to contain sin.

3:1. Daughter Hebrew *biti,* "my daughter," the term with which Naomi regularly addresses Ruth, expressing both solicitude and connection (see comment at 2:2). Boaz likewise has used this term with Ruth (e.g., 2:8) and uses it again (3:10 and 11).

I must seek Hebrew *halo 'abhakesh,* "Must I not seek?" A distinctive interrogative style characterizes both Naomi's and Boaz's speech (see also Naomi in 3:2 and Boaz in 2:8). The author may intend this shared pattern to signal that Boaz and Naomi are cohorts, belonging to the same (older) generation.

seek Hebrew *'abhakesh*. When the verbal root *b-k-sh* is used with a person of relatively low social status, it suggests an entreaty posed to a more powerful figure, as when the Psalmist pleads to God (e.g., Ps. 27:4), or when King Ahasuerus asks Esther, "What is your request [*bakashateikh*]?" (Esther 5:3).

a home Hebrew *manoaḥ,* "rest" or "repose." The use of this word harks back to the related word *menuḥah,* "security," which Naomi wishes for her daughters-in-law in Moab (1:9). Elsewhere in the Bible, *manoaḥ* carries a wide range of expectations and references concerning the nature of "rest." In Gen. 7:9, the dove that Noah sends out cannot find *manoaḥ,* a place to rest, until the waters subside. In Deut. 28:65, Israel is warned that it will not find *manoaḥ,* a place to rest its feet, unless it obeys God. Naomi associates home or "rest" with the protection of a man. As she says to her widowed daughters-in-law: "find security [*menuḥah*] in the house of a husband" (1:9). Ibn Ezra echoes this view, explaining in his commentary to this passage that *manoaḥ* means a husband, for "a woman has no rest [*menuḥah*] until she is married." Although such a conventional view is to be expected in a society where men are typically the providers, the Book of Ruth gently, yet

[2] Now there is our kinsman Boaz, whose girls you
were close to. He will be winnowing barley on the
threshing floor tonight. [3] So bathe, anoint yourself,

אֲבַקֶּשׁ־לָךְ מָנוֹחַ אֲשֶׁר יִיטַב־לָךְ׃ 2 וְעַתָּה
הֲלֹא בֹעַז מֹדַעְתָּנוּ אֲשֶׁר הָיִית אֶת־
נַעֲרוֹתָיו הִנֵּה־הוּא זֹרֶה אֶת־גֹּרֶן הַשְּׂעֹרִים
הַלָּיְלָה׃ 3 וְרָחַצְתְּ ׀ וָסַכְתְּ וְשַׂמְתְּ שמלתך

firmly, illustrates that Naomi's security depends first and foremost on another woman, Ruth, who is eventually acknowledged as better for Naomi "than seven sons" (4:15).

for you Those who consider Naomi altruistic find support here. As in 1:8–13, Naomi expresses her concern solely for Ruth's welfare. But those who view Naomi's reaction as more self-serving consider this statement disingenuous.[101] Yet there is no need to choose between these two extremes: Naomi can seek to improve Ruth's lot, and anticipate that such improvement also will benefit her, given Ruth's utter commitment to her mother-in-law. After all, if Boaz takes kindly to Ruth and helps her, then Ruth is better able to support Naomi. This point is indeed confirmed in 3:17 when Ruth interprets her meeting with Boaz as ensuring that she not return "empty handed" to Naomi.

2. ***kinsman*** Hebrew *moda'at.* Like the narrator's term *moda'* ("kinsman") in 2:1, this is an unusual form of the verbal root *y-d-'*, "to know."[102] Naomi also employs other forms of this verb in verses 3 and 4. Naomi conspicuously does not refer to Boaz as a *go'el* ("redeemer") as she did earlier (2:20), or evoke levirate relation (which she had used previously in reference to Orpah in 1:15). Given her unusual designation for Boaz here, it is reasonable to conclude that she has something other than redemption or levirate marriage in mind for this rendezvous.

winnowing barley on the threshing floor tonight Literally, "scattering (with) [*zoreh*] the threshing floor of barley tonight." The verb *z-r-h* often applies to people, as when God scatters Israel among the nations (Ezek. 12:15), but the present verse illustrates the agricultural basis of the term, which frequently is used metaphorically. In ancient Israel, harvested and bound sheaves of grain were carried by hand or cart to a large, flat area (see next comment), where the grain was pounded on the ground ("threshing") to loosen the kernels from their hard husks and other chaff. Then, as the prevailing winds of late afternoon came up, the threshers winnowed the threshed grain by throwing it upward. They collected the heavier grain kernels, which fell to the ground; the chaff, being lighter, was carried downwind.

threshing floor A large, flat, outdoor space where many farmers and farmhands would gather together at the end of the harvest to perform the seasonal task of processing harvested sheaves into usable grain berries. A large communal facility, a threshing floor tended to be located outside of town.[103] According to the Book of Kings, the northern Israelite capital of Samaria had a threshing floor near its gate; it was so big that two kings of Israel and Judah could sit there and survey four hundred prophets arrayed before them (1 Kings 22:10). Jeremiah likewise associates threshing with town gates (Jer. 15:7). The Mishnah requires a town's threshing floor to be set fifty cubits from its gate (BB 2.8)—close enough for easy access and protection, yet far enough away to keep the chaff from blowing into town or onto the roadway. To an ancient audience, mention of a threshing floor would evoke associations of fecundity (see, e.g., Joel 2:24: "And threshing floors shall be piled with grain, / And vats shall overflow with new wine and oil"). And given its considerable size, it was the natural site for certain communal and ritual gatherings and feasting. (Not surprisingly, the site of the Jerusalem Temple was originally a threshing floor, according to dress up, and go down to the threshing floor. But do not disclose yourself to the man until he has finished

שִׂמְלֹתַיִךְ עָלַיִךְ וירדתי וְיָרַדְתְּ הַגֹּרֶן אַל־
תִּוָּדְעִי לָאִישׁ עַד כַּלֹּתוֹ לֶאֱכֹל וְלִשְׁתּוֹת׃

2 Samuel 24.[104]) Being set apart from daily activity, the threshing floor, was also a liminal, or transitional, space. Thus, the threshing floor could also be the site of transgression, since it was also associated with freedom from ordinary constraints (see Hos. 9:1).

*3. **So bathe, anoint yourself, dress up*** Although this triplet of verbs designates a sequence of common actions, it is also an ancient Near Eastern literary trope that foreshadows a major change in an individual's life. This sequence is known already from Old Babylonian marriage ceremonies (twentieth century B.C.E.).[105] In Ezekiel, God's metaphoric betrothal of Jerusalem echoes this pattern: "I bathed you in water . . . and anointed you with oil . . . I clothed you with embroidered garments" (Ezek. 16:9–10). And the same series of verbs is also used when David ends a period of mourning, arising unexpectedly after his infant son's death: "he washed and anointed himself and changed his clothes" (2 Sam. 12:20). The sequence shows that Naomi is telling Ruth to groom herself to look her best. The Targum makes Naomi's instructions more concrete: "wash yourself with water, anoint yourself with perfumes, and put on your jewelry." However, the Midrash—in keeping with its characteristic pattern of portraying Ruth as the righteous convert—explains that washing refers to purification from idolatry, while anointing means adornment with "*mitzvot* and righteous deeds" (Ruth R. 5.12).

anoint yourself Several translations render this as "perfume yourself" to make the point explicit:[106] Ruth is to make herself attractive to Boaz.[107] In the ancient Near East, people rubbed olive oil into their hair and skin to protect them from damage in the hot, dry, sunny climate. Men would also anoint their beards. (The wealthy mixed their oil with fragrance, which was costly.)[108] Given that olive oil was a precious commodity, ordinary Israelites most likely reserved this practice for special occasions. In the public life of the nation, priests and kings were anointed with olive oil when they took office (for which the Bible uses another verb, *m-sh-ḥ*). But as S. Greengus observes with regard to ancient Babylonian marriage rites, one must separate a person's toilette from ritual anointing; "in the former a woman anoints herself, while in the latter situation the anointing is done to her by another."[109] In Eccles. 9:7–8, Kohelet counsels anointing for a man's toilette as well: "Let your head never be without oil," meaning that every day should be celebrated festively as a special occasion. In his comment on Ruth 3:3, Rashi, following the Rabbinic sages, also understands anointing as a way of adorning oneself (see at v. 6).

dress up Hebrew *ve-samt simlotayikh 'alayikh,* literally "put your garments on." The grooming that Naomi proposes has been interpreted as an invitation to Ruth to shed her widow's garments (compare the case of Tamar in Gen. 38:12–14, who wears such clothes for years), whereas others assume bridal preparations.[110] Yet if we take our cues from the connotations implicit in the previous two verbs, it is reasonable to translate this next phrase as "dress up" festively. Rashi, echoing the Midrash (Ruth R. 5.12), elaborates: "as for Shabbat." Ibn Ezra explains that this phrase refers simply to donning clothes other than the everyday clothes worn while gleaning. (In Ibn Ezra's day, as in the ancient Near East, few people owned more than one change of clothing.)

go down to the threshing floor Most interpreters consider this instruction to be astonishing. We learn later that Boaz likewise considers Ruth's visit to be suspect, thinking to himself, "Let it not be known that the woman came to the threshing floor" (v. 14). However, one recent interpreter regards Naomi's intentions as practical and discreet.

eating and drinking. [4]When he lies down, note the place where he lies down, and go over and uncover his feet and lie down. He will tell you what you are

4 וִיהִ֣י בְשָׁכְב֗וֹ וְיָדַ֙עַתְּ֙ אֶת־הַמָּקוֹם֙ אֲשֶׁ֣ר
יִשְׁכַּב־שָׁ֔ם וּבָ֛את וְגִלִּ֥ית מַרְגְּלֹתָ֖יו ושכבתי
וְשָׁכָ֑בְתְּ וְהוּא֙ יַגִּ֣יד לָ֔ךְ אֵ֖ת אֲשֶׁ֥ר תַּעֲשִֽׂין׃

Because a threshing floor is outdoors and because Boaz would presumably be sleeping at some distance from workers of lower status, this offers Ruth her one opportunity to approach Boaz privately without going to his house (an even riskier step). That is, a threshing floor was less compromising than other settings because it was essentially public yet offered a measure of privacy at night.[111] The Rabbinic sages tone down the eyebrow-raising implications of Naomi's instructions by different means (see below).

go down The Masoretic text includes two versions of this word, as it does for the verbs "lie down" in verse 4 and "acquire" in 4:5. At first glance, it seems as if the *ketiv* ("written") version is in first person, with Naomi as the subject—namely, "I will go down" (*yaradeti*). But some scholars consider this to be an archaic second-person feminine form, meaning "you will go down," in the singular.[112] Such usage would be consistent with the other archaic verb forms that characterize the speech register of Naomi and of Boaz, (see comment at 2:8), both of whom are from an older generation. In any case, the *kerey* (read aloud) version indicates a second-person singular. The ancient Greek translation, the Septuagint, consistently uses second person for these verbs, but in this case has "go up" instead of "go down." This makes better sense, given that threshing floors are likely to be at an elevated spot to catch the wind.[113] Rashi in this instance authorizes the first-person form of the written text (but not others in this section) by further elaborating on Naomi's words: "my merit will go with you." Such a rendition not only provides Ruth with a symbolic chaperone but also hints at her need for protection, signaling the riskiness of the venture ahead.

threshing floor See comment at verse 2 and below at verse 6.

Do not disclose yourself Hebrew *ʾal tivvadeʿi,* "do not make yourself known," using another form of the multilayered verb "to know" (*y-d-ʿ*); see comment at "kinsman" in verse 2. The *niphʿal* form of the verb used here does not ever refer to carnal knowledge as does the *kal* form, but the repetition of the verb throughout this section is nonetheless suggestive. In addition, secrecy now begins to shroud the anticipated scene, foreshadowing an encounter that breaks with convention and so cannot withstand public scrutiny in broad daylight. It is not clear to the reader whether Ruth is to hide from view all evening, or to mill about anonymously among the threshers. If the latter, then we can assume that it was socially acceptable for a woman to be present at the threshing floor—at least until nightfall.

the man Naomi does not mention Boaz by name at this juncture. The term signals not only gender but also his status as someone who can provide security (as her use of this word in 1:9 also indicates).

until he has finished eating and drinking Naomi wishes Boaz to be in a good mood when he notices Ruth. Such timing increases the chances that he will respond out of a sense of fullness rather than deficiency—in a spirit of generosity rather than indifference. When biblical narrators draw attention to eating and drinking, they usually do not refer to ordinary meals but rather to formal acts of commensality. Given the setting at the threshing floor during the harvest, "eating and drinking" implies festivities, with "drinking" as reference to some intoxicating beverage (as in the Golden Calf episode, Exod. 32:6).[114]

4. ***note the place where he lies down*** As a prosperous landowner, Boaz would place himself at night apart from the common workers. With advancing darkness, Ruth would soon be unable to find him unless she were to take note during daylight where he chooses to make his bed.

note the place Hebrew *ve-yadaʿat ʾet ha-makom,* "know the place," using the verb "know" that resonates throughout this section. In later Rabbinic parlance, the designation "*ha-makom*" would evoke God or God's presence (see also Gen. 28:16–19, when Jacob encounters God). The word becomes one of several ways to refer to God, as in condolences: "May *ha-makom* comfort you [plural] among the mourners of Zion and Jerusalem."

lies down This verb, *sh-k-b,* appears with striking frequency, a total of eight times, in this chapter (v. 4, three times; v. 7, twice; vv. 8,13,14). The narrative passage that most intensively displays such usage elsewhere in the Bible (seven times in four verses) is Gen. 19:32–35, where the verb refers to the illicit sexual union between Lot and his daughters, which results in the births of Moab (Ruth's ancestor) and Ammon (Gen. 19:30–38). Through this verbal allusion, the narrator may intend for the reader to link together these two "Moabite" episodes. Other comparable passages are 2 Samuel 11–12, the story of David and Bathsheba, with eight instances of *sh-k-b,* and 2 Samuel 13, Amnon's rape of Tamar, with six. Although this verb can be used without sexual connotation (as in Gen. 28:11, when Jacob lays down alone to sleep),[115] it almost always carries sexual overtones when a woman is involved. (The exception is when it refers to a woman in a state of impurity, as in Lev. 15:20.) Typically, the sexual meaning is made explicit through the use of a preposition (usually *ʾet* or *ʿim*). The absence of such a preposition in this passage somewhat distances the verb from its sexual subtext, but the verb nonetheless combines with other terms (threshing floor, know, uncover) to evoke a charged situation.

uncover his feet and lie down Naomi's provocative instructions now climax with this directive, which is loaded with possible double entendre. (See the following three comments.) Ultimately, however, it is not clear precisely what Ruth is supposed to do when she meets with Boaz.

uncover Hebrew *gilit,* a common transitive verb. In its *piʿel* stem (as here) and (rarely) in the *kal,* it means "uncover," "reveal," and in the *niphʿal,* "be revealed." Its best-known object is *ʿervah,* literally, "nakedness," in the expression *gilah* (or *galah*) *ʿervah,* "uncovered nakedness." The term can mean to expose private body parts to sight (Ezek. 16:37, 23:10,19) or, when used euphemistically, to engage in illicit sex (Lev. 18:6–19, 20:11, 17, 19–21; Ezek. 22:10). Similarly, in Deut. 23:1 and 27:20, to uncover a father's "garment" means to have sex with his (presumably former) wife. To be sure, *gilah* does not always have a sexual connotation. One can "uncover" an eye, allowing someone to see (e.g., Num. 22:31; Ps. 119:18), or an ear, letting someone hear (Ruth 4:4; 1 Sam. 9:15). Other metaphorical acts using this verb include "revealing" righteousness (Ps. 98:2). But in the ancient world, to speak of a woman uncovering any part of a man's body at night (when that man is not her husband) was highly suggestive.

feet Hebrew *margelot,* here translated "feet," occurs only in Ruth (3:4,7,8, and 14) and in Dan. 10:6, where (in the latter) it is paired with "arms." It refers either to legs or to the space on the ground around them. Given the Bible's use of the related root word *regel,* "foot," elsewhere as a euphemism for genitalia (as in Isa. 6:2 and 7:20), *margelot* could carry this connotation here. On the other hand, the author or editor may have deliberately placed this term for legs in Naomi's mouth, instead of the more familiar word *regel,* precisely to exclude a sexual connotation, calling the reader's attention to the ground around Boaz's feet. Although it is unlikely that Naomi would explicitly instruct Ruth to expose Boaz's genitalia,[116] this freighted and ambiguous language further intensifies the sexually charged atmosphere.[117] Midrash Ruth Zuta acknowledges the scandalous, perhaps even preposter-

5 וַתֹּאמֶר אֵלֶיהָ כֹּל אֲשֶׁר־תֹּאמְרִי [אֵלַי*]
אֶעֱשֶׂה׃

to do." 5 She replied, "I will do everything you tell
me."

v. 5. קריא ולא כתיב

ous, nature of Naomi's directions when it has Ruth exclaim: "If I uncover his *margelot,* they will kill me!" To which Naomi replies that her own righteousness will "go down" with Ruth (hence the first-person written form of that verb; see the previous verse).

lie down For Ruth to lie down next to Boaz at night is clearly a breach of conventional norms. In an ancient society, such an act would be viewed as reprehensible, with dire consequences for the woman. (For the range of connotations for this verb, see comment on "lies down" earlier in this verse.) On the apparent first-person form of the Masoretic *ketiv* (written version of this verb), see at "go down" in v. 3. Ruth's Moabite status exposes her to even greater danger, given the poor reputation of Moabites in the Bible (see "The Status of the Moabites" in the introduction).[118]

He will tell you what you are to do The narrator does not spell out what Naomi expects Boaz to say once he is approached by a woman in such compromising circumstances; and Naomi does not spell out what Ruth is to say or ask. Even if one questions whether Naomi has set the scene for a sexual assignation (within the limits posed by the physical setting of the threshing floor), it is nonetheless clear that Naomi is advising Ruth to become passive after she initiates the encounter, waiting for Boaz to take the lead. The Targum, clearly aiming to defuse the erotic charge, makes Naomi's instructions less open-ended and more businesslike: "Then ask advice of him, and in his wisdom he will tell you what to do."

5. I will do everything you tell me Hebrew *kol 'asher to'mri ['elai] 'e'eseh,* "all that you say [to me] I will do." Ruth's response, followed by the ensuing compliance sequence in verse 6, shows once again her utter commitment to Naomi (see 1:16–17) and her readiness to obey completely. Boaz gives the same response to Ruth's request (see 3:11).

me Hebrew would normally include the indirect object *'elai* "to me," but the Masoretic text as written (*ketiv*) does not include it. The actual word appears only in the version for reading aloud (*kerey*). Grammatically speaking, its presence would normally be expected, although its absence does not actually affect the plain sense. (See also Exod. 18:24; Deut. 5:24; 1 Kings 5:20; Jer. 42:20; Esther 2:13.) Noting the missing written word, Midrash Ruth Zuta (3.2) suggests that Ruth has determined to do whatever Naomi has asked of her, even if it is not sanctioned by the tradition (see also Alsheikh in the introduction to 3:1–5 above).

RUTH AND BOAZ ON THE THRESHING FLOOR (3:6–15)

Boaz and Ruth meet once again, although this time it is not by "chance." This second recorded encounter both evokes and invokes the earlier one (2:3–16). Both meetings are framed by conversations between Ruth and Naomi at home. In the two meetings, Ruth acts first and Boaz initiates the dialogue in response; she speaks briefly, whereas he speaks at length. In both, there is mention of sheltering wings (see below). Such similarities throw into sharper relief the contrasts between the two scenes: in this second meeting, midnight replaces broad daylight; a secret location replaces the open, populated field; the private replaces the public. Unlike the first encounter, this new one is literally shrouded in darkness and suffused with mystery.

6 She went down to the threshing floor and did
just as her mother-in-law had instructed her. 7 Boaz

6 וַתֵּ֖רֶד הַגֹּ֑רֶן וַתַּ֕עַשׂ כְּכֹ֥ל אֲשֶׁר־צִוַּ֖תָּה
חֲמוֹתָֽהּ׃ 7 וַיֹּ֨אכַל בֹּ֤עַז וַיֵּשְׁתְּ֙ וַיִּיטַ֣ב לִבּ֔וֹ

Naomi's plan sends Ruth to Boaz at night. Yet although Ruth has promised to do as Naomi has commanded her, at the crucial moment she departs from her mother-in-law's instructions: instead of waiting for Boaz's guidance, Ruth takes the initiative and tells him what *he* should do, reminding him that he is a redeemer. However, her words also contain an ambiguity, or rather, a double entendre, by including a word that could refer to protective wings or allude to marriage. How readers interpret Ruth's request here influences also how they understand the broader messages of the book (see below at v. 9). Boaz resolutely agrees to her request and undertakes responsibility for Ruth's welfare; his subsequent actions on her behalf, including marriage, demonstrate how profoundly the encounter has affected him.

To put the matter succinctly, Ruth *solicits* Boaz. In American parlance, "to solicit" often means an attempt to sell something, including sex. In England, however, "to solicit" also means to advocate; hence, a lawyer is called a solicitor. A third, archaic sense of the verb is also germane: "to draw out with gentle force" (*Oxford English Dictionary*). This array of possible meanings seems to fit Ruth's proposal: advocacy is at its heart, yet it is hard to miss other connotations as she elicits Boaz's commitment.

What might the narrator be communicating with allusions laden with sexual connotations? The narrator may be highlighting the proper behavior of Boaz and Ruth despite the charged circumstances. As commentators repeatedly note, Boaz and Ruth contrast with their ancestors, Lot and his daughters or Judah and Tamar. The proper behavior of both Boaz and Ruth under compromising circumstances stands out more clearly because of the potential for transgression depicted in those related narratives. Boaz's restraint and readiness to undertake responsibility contrasts with Judah's shirking his duty and with his sexual encounter with Tamar. Ruth's dignified exchange with Boaz at night contrasts with Lot's daughters' seductions of drunken Lot. At a symbolic level, the encounter on the threshing floor also reverses and acts as a corrective to those other stories of ancestors and thereby "repairs" them (see "Ruth's Relationship to Other Biblical Books," in the introduction).[119]

OUTLINE

I. The setting at the threshing floor (3:6–7)
II. Second dialogue between Boaz and Ruth (3:8–13)
III. Conclusion (3:14–15)

THE SETTING AT THE THRESHING FLOOR (3:6–7)

Later in this chapter, Boaz expresses his concern about the impropriety of his meeting Ruth on the threshing floor: "Let it not be known that the woman came to the threshing floor" (v. 14). From this we can conclude that ancient readers would have known (as a matter of cultural norms) that after nightfall, a threshing floor was not a suitable place for a respectable woman. (For a fuller explanation of the setting at the threshing floor and its connotations, see comment at verses 2 and 3.)

6. The narrator emphasizes Ruth's compliance in a typical rhetorical fashion. But a slight change in the reported sequence suggests to early commentators a significant difference. Thus Rashi notes that the narrator first states that "she went down" before adding that "she did just as her mother-in-law had instructed her." (An expected sequence, ate and drank, and in a cheerful mood went to lie down beside the grainpile. Then she went over stealthily and

וַיָּבֹא לִשְׁכַּב בִּקְצֵה הָעֲרֵמָה וַתָּבֹא בַלָּט

Rashi's remarks imply, would have been to be told first that she did as she was instructed—bathed and so forth—and only then that she went to the threshing floor.) Rashi explains the perceived difference as follows: Ruth reasoned that "If I adorn myself so [before I go down], anyone who meets me will take me for a prostitute [*zonah*]." Therefore, Rashi continues, Ruth adorns herself only *after* she reaches the threshing floor. Rashi here construes that Naomi's instructions in verse 3 involve putting on jewelry or cosmetics. Thus, even though Rashi earlier "tames" Naomi's instructions—by taking "anointing" there as a reference to mitzvot—here he amplifies their erotic implications.

just as Hebrew *ke-khol 'asher,* literally, "like all that." It could suggest "approximately," a qualification, implying that Ruth does almost everything Naomi asks of her (otherwise we would expect *kol 'asher,* "all that," as in 3:5). However, this idiom elsewhere in the Bible is commonly used to mean "doing everything."[120]

instructed Hebrew *tzivvattah,* "commanded," from *tz-w-h.* This is the verbal root from which *mitzvah,* "commandment," comes. Its use here reflects the authority that Naomi's words carry for Ruth. The use of the verb corresponds to how Naomi has been addressing Ruth all along and is the expected verb form, given these characters' relationship in their household hierarchy.[121]

7. ***went to lie down beside the grainpile*** The narrator may signal here that Boaz's location allowed for privacy.[122] On "lie down," see comment at 3:4.

beside Hebrew *bi-ktzeih,* "at the edge."

Boaz ate and drank, and in a cheerful mood These details establish that Boaz is in a receptive frame of mind, possibly even tipsy. As noted above, these terms suggest feasting, not merely an ordinary meal (see also comment on v. 3).

in a cheerful mood Hebrew *va-yiytav libo,* "his heart became good," a condition associated with joy and pleasure, as in Eccl. 7:3 and 11:9. When combined with drinking, the phrase might imply being too drunk to make a good decision (Esther 1:10) or to defend oneself (2 Sam. 13:28). However, the phrase can also indicate joy unrelated to the consumption of wine (Judg. 18:20; 1 Kings 8:66; Prov. 15:15; Eccles. 9:7). One contemporary interpreter describes Boaz here as "relaxed," a suggestive paraphrase even if not exact.[123] By contrast, Rabbinic traditions, followed by Rashi, contend that Boaz's heart was made "good" by his study of Torah (Ruth R. 5.15).

she went over stealthily As Naomi has instructed, Ruth secretly comes to Boaz.

stealthily Hebrew *balat,* a word whose precise meaning is difficult to determine but most likely refers to something done to someone without that person's knowledge.[125] Obviously, Ruth exercises caution as she moves toward Boaz. The clause "she went over stealthily" (*va-tavo' balat*) alludes to another biblical scene, Judg. 4:16–23. When Jael approaches the sleeping general Sisera before killing him, "she approached him stealthily" (4:21, *va-tavo'... bala't,* with a variant spelling). In both accounts, a foreign woman approaches a sleeping man after he has had something to drink; and she takes the initiative in a way that ultimately benefits Israel. Jael comes to kill; Ruth, to offer life. In addition, *balat* alludes to a story about Ruth's most famous descendant, David, during the period

וַתְּגַל מַרְגְּלֹתָיו וַתִּשְׁכָּב׃ 8 וַיְהִי֙ בַּחֲצִ֣י
הַלַּ֔יְלָה וַיֶּחֱרַ֥ד הָאִ֖ישׁ וַיִּלָּפֵ֑ת וְהִנֵּ֣ה אִשָּׁ֔ה
שֹׁכֶ֖בֶת מַרְגְּלֹתָֽיו׃

uncovered his feet and lay down. 8 In the middle of
the night, the man gave a start and pulled back—there
was a woman lying at his feet!

that he is an outlaw. In 1 Sam. 24:5, David cuts off the wing (*kanaf*) of King Saul's garment while the latter is "covering his legs"—that is, relieving himself—in a presumably dark cave. (Note that Ruth uncovers Boaz's legs when she comes upon him in the dark and is about to ask him to cover her with his *kanaf*.) David's action is modified by the adverb *balat*. In both accounts, an underdog acts with evident good will before initiating a negotiation with a powerful person, who then invokes God's blessing upon the first party.[126]

uncovered One presumes that Boaz is asleep by the time Ruth uncovers a portion of his body. Some commentators suggest that Ruth uncovers much more of Boaz than his feet, or that Ruth undresses herself.[124] Although such speculations go beyond the plain sense of the text, they reflect the scene's suggestive undertones. It is difficult to ignore the audacity of such an act and its intimate nature.

feet See at verse 4 for the range of meanings and implications of this unusual term. See also at verse 14.

SECOND DIALOGUE BETWEEN BOAZ AND RUTH (3:8–13)

Eventually, Boaz stirs. Perhaps the reader is meant to conclude that his uncovered legs feel cold; or perhaps it is the midnight hour itself—an hour of mystery, a time of peril or possibilities—that explains his awakening.

The dialogue that ensues is rich in reversals and meanings. Ruth does not wait for Boaz to tell her what to do but instead gives him instructions. Yet, it is difficult to know precisely what she asks him to do. The words she uses, especially *kenaphekha*, can refer to protective wing(s) or to a technical sense of the word "robe," which might imply marriage. As a result, interpreters disagree as to whether Ruth boldly proposes marriage to Boaz, subtly alludes to marriage, invokes levirate marriage, or simply asks for protection. Possibly the author wants the reader to consider that Ruth is speaking explicitly only about redemption but suggestively using language that also evokes marriage. Boaz, like the reader, is given room to interpret her words.

8. In the middle of the night Hebrew *va-yehi be-ḥatzi ha-laylah*. This phrase also occurs in Exod. 12:29, which records the killing of the firstborn of Egypt with the tenth plague. In the Bible, ordinary men are afraid of what lurks in the night (Ps. 91:5). Here, Boaz trembles, startled, in the face of the unknown. In the Passover haggadah, this expression—often translated as "and it came to pass at midnight"—is the refrain of a popular *piyut* (liturgical poem) that recounts momentous events that supposedly have taken place at this hour. Ruth Rabbah 6.1 lists numerous righteous deeds that were supposed to have transpired at midnight.

the man gave a start and pulled back Hebrew *va-yeḥerad* and *va-yillafet*. The first verb (lit. "trembled") is common and well understood. The second verb, however, appears only three times in the Bible and its precise force is not clear.[127] The author's choice of such an obscure verb adds to the mystery of the midnight hour (so Frymer-Kensky notes). What frightens Boaz? The darkness? The sudden jolt of awakening from a deep sleep after having eaten and drunk? A palpable presence of another? His uncovered limbs? The presence

9 "Who are you?" he asked. And she replied, "I am
your handmaid Ruth. Spread your robe over your
handmaid, for you are a redeeming kinsman."

9 וַיֹּאמֶר מִי־אָתְּ וַתֹּאמֶר אָנֹכִי רוּת אֲמָתֶךָ
וּפָרַשְׂתָּ כְנָפֶךָ עַל־אֲמָתְךָ כִּי גֹאֵל אָתָּה׃

specifically of a woman? Does Boaz wonder what he has done when asleep or drunk? Any and all of these could account for his alarm.[128] Rashi explains that Boaz fears the presence of a *sheid,* an evil spirit. Rashi draws out a double sense from the obscure verb *va-yillafet*: One sense means "to hold" as in Judg. 16:29, which Rashi cites as an explanation; the second sense comes from the third-person *niph'al,* implying that something is done to Boaz. Then, through similarity in sound, Rashi construes *yillafet* as if it were *yitalef,* "was enwrapped." He explains that Ruth calmed Boaz by holding him in her arms.

there was Hebrew *hineih,* often translated as "Behold!" or "Look!" and is best captured by the French *Voila!* (See there!). Linguists and literary critics describe the function of *hineih* as a "focalizer," acting like a camera's zoom lens to give readers the perspective of the protagonist(s). The interjection shifts our perspective, focusing on what Boaz now suddenly perceives, namely a woman.

a woman lying at his feet! We are not informed as to how Boaz realizes that the nearby presence is female. Is it her scent, the oil with which she has anointed herself? Or her clothes or body pressed against him? Or her general shape? Ibn Ezra speculates that Ruth may have said something or that Boaz could see in the moonlight that the person had no beard or that the figure was dressed in women's clothing. These explanations keep the encounter chaste. The Targum makes such chasteness explicit. It adds at this point that Boaz's "flesh" became "like a turnip" but that he restrained himself, as did Joseph (when tempted by Potiphar's wife)[129] and Palti (the latter, according to Rabbinic tradition, places a sword between himself and his wife Michal to make sure he does not touch her, respecting her prior marriage to David).[130]

9. ***Who are you?*** Hebrew *miy 'att,* a request for clarification whose nuance depends upon the context (see comment at v. 16). The pronoun's grammatical form presumes a female addressee. Perhaps we are to suppose that Boaz does not recognize Ruth because it is dark and he is startled. Or perhaps because she is so transformed in her new garb that he cannot tell she is the woman he has previously met in the field. The Midrash suggests that Boaz may not realize that this night visitor is human. Ruth Rabbah and later Rashi explain that Boaz fears it is a female demon. Such figures appear in ancient Near Eastern sources (and also in Isa. 34:14); one of these is Lilith, whose very name is evoked by the night (*layla*). Ruth Zuta 3.4 imagines him saying, "If you are a spirit, go away! And if you are human, let me know." Ruth Rabbah 6.1 takes *va-yillafet* ("pulled back") to mean that Ruth clings to him, so that he feels her hair and reminds himself that spirits have no hair. He then asks her, "Who are you, a spirit or a woman?" When she answers, "A woman," he says, "A free woman or married?" and she answers, "Free." Finally, he asks: "Ritually pure or impure?" "Pure."[131] Only then does she tell him who she is (Ruth R. 6:1).

your handmaid Hebrew *'amatekha,* "your *'amah.*"[132] The term is one of two that designate a subordinate woman, usually a servant; the other term being *shifḥah* (as in Ruth 2:13). In a number of non-legal contexts, *'amah* is interchangeable with *shifḥah,* "maidservant," but possibly in Ruth, *'amah* occupies the higher rung.[133] To Hubbard, *'amah* here implies that she was no longer a lower class "servant," but, instead, "identified herself among those eligible for marriage or concubinage."[134] To call oneself *'amatekha* was a woman's normal way of expressing proper deference to a social superior, used in the Bible especially in relation to a man to whom she wishes to ingratiate herself. (Men used a corresponding masculine term *'eved,* often translated as "servant.") It is part of the biblical rhetoric of persuasion. Hannah calls herself *'amatekha* (your *'amah*) in her addresses to God (1 Sam. 1:11) and to the priest Eli (1:16). Both queens (1 Kings 1:13,17) and prostitutes (1 Kings 3:20) call themselves *'amatekha* when speaking to kings. But women who petition men use this deferential title even when the man is not necessarily a superior: thus Abigail defers to David when she is a wealthy landowner's wife, and he is still an outlaw leader (1 Sam. 25:24–5, 28,31,41). Archaeologists have found a clay seal from about the fifth century B.C.E. that belonged to a noblewoman, possibly the wife of the Jewish governor. It refers to her as his *'amah,* another sign of the use for women in high position.[135] Ruth's emphasis on her status as *'amah* (using it twice in the same brief statement) suggests that she is using it in its more formal sense, in deference to Boaz's social position.

Spread your robe over your handmaid, for you are a redeeming kinsman Hebrew *ufarasta kenafekha 'al 'amatekcha ki go'el attah.* At this point Ruth no longer follows Naomi's directives; she has been instructed to have Boaz tell her what to do. Instead, she takes charge and tells him what *he* should do. The nature of Ruth's request is the puzzle at the heart of the book and also a key to the interpretation of the book.

Many interpreters (ancient[136] and modern[137]) read Ruth's request as implying a marital liaison. They understand the word *kenafekha* as "your robe," referring to an act of espousal as per Ezek. 16:8 (so the NJPS translators' note; see below). But the noun *kanaf* typically refers to wing(s). Ruth is asking for protection or patronage, without spelling out how Boaz is to provide this support. Earlier Boaz prayed that God, under whose wings (*kanaf* in the plural) she was seeking shelter, would reward Ruth (2:12). Here, she is asking him to spread *his* wings (*kanaf*) over her, thus inviting him to become God's agent. Even if Naomi has designed a sexual strategy for this encounter (3:1–4), Ruth de-sexualizes her plan by calling Boaz to responsibility, not romance. The Targum reflects the more typical Rabbinic interpretation. It omits the phrase "Spread your robe over your handmaid" and replaces it with "Let your name be called over your maidservant, by taking me to wife, inasmuch as you are a redeemer."

According to Rashi, Ruth asks Boaz to acquire the family's field, then asks that Boaz should also acquire her in marriage to perpetuate her dead husband's name. She explains (according to Rashi) that the deceased's name would be recalled when people would see Ruth in the field and say: "Here is Mahlon's wife." Rashi's elaboration anticipates and obviates the contradictions created in 4:5 and 10 when Boaz links acquiring Ruth with perpetuating the name of the deceased. Through this explanation, Rashi eliminates levirate marriage as the goal of a marriage with Ruth by accounting differently for how the deceased's name is to be perpetuated (see further comment at 4:5 and "Why and How Boaz Marries Ruth" in the introduction).

As for modern commentators, Bush, for example, argues that Ruth must be suggesting marriage: "Naomi has marriage in mind for Ruth in the beginning of the chapter, and Boaz immediately thinks of marriage upon hearing Ruth's words; hence marriage must be implied in some way."[138] But it would be a mistake to conflate Ruth's goals with either those of Naomi or Boaz. Neither Ruth nor the author uses the common terms for betrothal, nor does Boaz in his response to Ruth in Chapter 3.[139]

Spread Hebrew *ufarasta.* The Hebrew does not use the imperative at this point but rather the more indirect sense. Ibn Ezra notes here an allusion to matrimony.[140]

your robe Hebrew *kenafekha,* meaning either "your robe" or "your wings" (or "wing"), is problematic and subject to debate. In the Bible the noun *kanaf* in the plural most frequently refers to God's wings (as in Ps. 57:2). When one translates the noun as "wings" (or "wing"), then Ruth is expressly echoing Boaz's earlier blessing of Ruth in 2:12: "May you have full recompense from the LORD, the God of Israel, under whose wings [*kenafaim*] you have sought refuge." Ruth thus urges Boaz to undertake the protective role that he has ascribed to God. This pattern of persons carrying out the blessings they had earlier bestowed is also familiar from Naomi's actions. In 1:9 Naomi wishes that God provide *menuḥah* ("security" or "rest") for her daughter(s)-in- law; in 3:1 she herself acts so as to make *manoaḥ* ("home" or "rest") possible for Ruth (see further comment on "security" at 3:1 and "The Theology of the Book of Ruth" in the introduction).

On the other hand, *kanaf* as a singular form of the noun, can mean "robe" or "garment." Although not as frequent as the reference to wing(s), the noun *kanaf* can mean an ordinary garment or its corner (as in 1 Sam. 15:27). But in a few cases it pertains to sexual relations (as in Deut. 23:1; 27:20). The mention of *kanaf* in Ezek. 16:8 strongly influences the prevailing understanding of its meaning here. Thus the NJPS note at 3:9: "A formal act of espousal; cf. Ezek. 16:8." Rashi interprets *kanaf* as a *talit* (prayer shawl), referring to the practice of covering a woman with a *talit* as an act of espousal (*nis'uin*).

for you are a redeeming kinsman The second part of Ruth's request is unambiguous: act like the redeemer that you are. Boaz is one of this family's redeemers—according to Naomi (2:20)—and as such has certain responsibilities. Ruth makes no mention of what Boaz is to do as a redeemer, beyond conveying a general sense of protection. Perhaps the writer deliberately keeps Ruth's request vague, or perhaps a redeemer's obligations were so obvious to ancient readers that no explanation was necessary. Even though some biblical obligations of the redeemer are specific (see next comment), both ancient and modern interpreters often expand the role when analyzing Ruth's proposal, usually combining it with levirate marriage, which was an entirely different practice (as Ibn Ezra rightly notes in his comment to 2:20, "redemption is not a levirate marriage but another way").

redeeming kinsman Hebrew *go'el,* "a redeemer," a term that occurs nine times in Ruth as a noun and another twelve times as a verb (constituting proportionately the highest concentration of the term in the Bible).[141] Redemption, then, has strong resonance for this book and is one of its key themes. In the Bible, a redeemer/*go'el* is charged with protecting vulnerable relatives. As S. Bahar notes, the protection a *go'el* provides can take many forms, depending on circumstances. It can have physical, economic, or spiritual dimensions.[142] Biblical laws describe three specific responsibilities of a human redeemer: (a) settling blood vengeance (see esp. Numbers 35), (b) redeeming a relative from servitude (see esp. Lev. 25:35–43), and (c) buying back a poor relative's land that was sold (see esp. Lev. 25:25–34).[143] It seems that any relative who can afford to is obliged to offer help in these cases.[144] In the Prophets and the Psalms, *go'el* most often refers to God metaphorically as the redeemer of Israel and, sometimes, of the just or of the poor in particular (see further comment at 2:20, 4:4, and 4:5 and "Redemption" in the introduction). Several of these meanings are at play in Ruth's request: she calls Boaz to his responsibility to protect a poor relative, and she also alludes to the opportunity for him to act as a redeemer in God's stead. But is she asking for something more specific? Although many ancient and modern interpreters think that she is proposing marriage, that conclusion is not warranted by what the Bible discloses about redeemers and by the details in the Book of Ruth; at most, marriage might be hinted at by the double meaning of spreading the *kanaf/kenafaim* in the same verse (see "robe" above).

10 He exclaimed, "Be blessed of the LORD, daughter! Your latest deed of loyalty is greater than

10 וַיֹּאמֶר בְּרוּכָה אַתְּ לַיהוָה בִּתִּי הֵיטַבְתְּ
חַסְדֵּךְ הָאַחֲרוֹן מִן־הָרִאשׁוֹן לְבִלְתִּי־לֶכֶת

10–13. For Boaz's response, a brief "I will" would have sufficed. But instead we hear a veritable outpouring of praise, assurances, explanations, and promises—all sealed with an oath and ending with instructions. This is Boaz's longest speech in the book, by far, and the most effusive. (It is longer than anyone else's utterances as well.) Its key point is at the center: he will do whatever Ruth requests ("All that you say I will do for you." See comment at 3:11).

*10. **He exclaimed*** Literally, "He said." The translation rightly conveys the exclamatory force of his response. Boaz seems grateful and flattered by Ruth's request. The open-ended nature of her request, with its room for interpretation, may be integral to his gratitude.

Be blessed of the LORD Literally, "Blessed are you to YHWH." This blessing formula parallels Naomi's blessing of Boaz in 2:20 ("blessed is he to YHWH"). In both cases, one detects surprise, relief, gratitude, and delight; and both proceed to mention *ḥesed.* Boaz's words make Ruth one of only seven individual women in the Bible who are directly blessed. Rebekah is blessed by her family when she leaves home to marry Isaac (Gen. 24:60), Laban blesses his daughters Leah and Rachel when parting (Gen. 32:1), Deborah blesses Jael for killing Israel's enemy (Judg. 5:24), the priest Eli blesses Hannah (1 Sam. 2:20), and David blesses Abigail when she prevents him from needless bloodshed (1 Sam. 25:32–33). Yet Ruth is the only individual woman who is blessed by invoking God's name in this manner, which directly connects her to God.

daughter Hebrew *biti,* "my daughter," a term he will use again in 3:11. Boaz resumes his role as benevolent patriarch. See comment at 2:8.

deed of loyalty Hebrew *ḥesed,* a theme word in this book. *Ḥesed* in Ruth refers to benevolent action beyond cultural expectations or contractual obligations (see comment at 1:8, 2:20, and *"Ḥesed"* in the introduction).

latest . . . the first What exactly constitutes "the first" instance of *ḥesed,* and what constitutes the second ("latest")? The NJPS translation includes a note about the second *ḥesed*: "i.e., she sought out a kinsman of her dead husband; see note at 2:20 above. Her first loyalty had been to return with Naomi." This is also Rashi's view regarding the first *ḥesed*. Frymer-Kensky likewise considers "the first" act of *ḥesed* as directed toward Naomi: Ruth's refusing Naomi's offer of release, re-obligating herself to Naomi by oath, and accompanying her to Bethlehem. This is what Boaz had previously acknowledged in 2:12 when he wished that God reward Ruth. But what Boaz means by the second *ḥesed* is not as obvious. Although it may also involve generosity toward Naomi, Boaz's mention of "younger men" (see next comment) suggests that he regards the second, "latest" *ḥesed* as directed toward himself. The Targum removes the ambiguity. Aligning Boaz's blessing with the Targum's overriding concern about Ruth's conversion, it adds to Boaz's remarks: "The first being that you became a proselyte," and the second, her seeking a levir. A number of other ancient and modern interpreters consider the second *ḥesed* to pertain either to Naomi or to the deceased husband.[145] Ibn Ezra, however, also considers the first *ḥesed* as the unspecified kindness that Ruth directed toward her late husband (pointing back to Naomi's words in 1:8).

the first, in that you have not turned to younger men, whether poor or rich. [11] And now, daughter, have no fear. I will do in your behalf whatever you ask, for

אַחֲרֵי הַבַּחוּרִים אִם־דַּל וְאִם־עָשִׁיר׃
11 וְעַתָּה בִּתִּי אַל־תִּירְאִי כֹּל אֲשֶׁר־תֹּאמְרִי
אֶעֱשֶׂה־לָּךְ כִּי יוֹדֵעַ כָּל־שַׁעַר עַמִּי כִּי

in that you have not turned to younger men Literally, "to not go after the young men." Boaz's blessing makes it abundantly clear that Ruth could have gone after other men, that she is not legally obliged to bind herself to a relative. The idiom "to go after" (*lalekhet aḥarei*) often implies allegiance and commitment. Thus Jeremiah describes faithless Jerusalem as saying, "I love foreigners and will go after them" (Jer. 2:5). It is to such passionate pursuit (on the human plane) that Boaz is presumably referring. Malbim notes that Ruth's choice of an older man is "a tremendous act of kindness to him" (on 3:10).

younger men Hebrew *ha-baḥurim.* This word generally refers to young men (see Eccles. 11:9). The Bible repeatedly and widely pairs the term *baḥur* (young man) with *betulah* (maiden). (See Deut. 32:25; Isa. 23:4, 62:5; Jer. 51:22; Ezek. 9:6; Amos 8:13; Zech. 9:17; Ps. 78:63, 148:12; Lam. 1:18, 2:21; 2 Chron. 36:17.) The biblical narrator does not actually tell us Boaz's age—nor whether he is married or widowed, or whether he has children. All we know is that he is a man of property, who owns fields and directs laborers (2:19,20), that is, he is a man of substance (*gibor ḥayil,* 2:1). Ruth Rabbah specifies that he was eighty years old and a widower (Ruth R. 6.2). The mention of young men indicates that age is an issue.

whether poor or rich According to Frymer-Kensky, Boaz understands that Ruth has come to him not because he is the only one who could marry her, but because as Naomi's kinsman, he is the one who can help Naomi by aligning himself with Ruth. Her coming to him represents an act of *ḥesed* for Naomi, and he blesses her for this (Frymer-Kensky; notes). However, here in the privacy of the threshing floor, Boaz seems not concerned with Naomi's welfare but only with Ruth. Ibn Ezra adds that everyone (i.e., "whether poor or rich") loved Ruth because of her beauty, a detail about Ruth that significantly goes unmentioned in the biblical text. It is noteworthy, therefore, that in the Book of Ruth a woman's success—even one who is a poor widow—does not depend upon her physical appearance (true also of the *'eshet ḥayil* in Proverbs 31).

11. And now The sense here is "on to practical matters." This type of rhetoric usually expresses steps to be followed in light of the preceding events (see, e.g., Gen. 12:19).

daughter Hebrew *biti,* "my daughter." Boaz continues to display solicitude in his stance toward Ruth (2:8; 3:10).

have no fear God and Israel's prophets most often offer these words of encouragement and assurance of benevolence (e.g., Gen. 26:24; Deut. 1:21; Isa. 54:4). Despite their alluring nighttime encounter, Boaz, like Ruth, is not saying anything that suggests romance. Ruth Zuta 3.10 adds that Boaz hastens to reassure Ruth because she feared that he would kill her.

I will do in your behalf whatever you ask Hebrew *kol 'asher to'meri 'e'eseh lakh,* "All that you say I will do for you." Boaz's statement is identical to Ruth's earlier assent to Naomi's instructions (v. 5), but with a crucial addition: not only will he do everything she asks, but also he will do it *for her.* Ruth is the subject of his commitment—not Naomi, Elimelech, or Mahlon. This statement, however, stands in tension with his later public announcement that he is marrying Ruth "so as to perpetuate the name of the deceased upon his estate" (4:10).

all the elders of my town know what a fine woman
you are. 12 But while it is true I am a redeeming
kinsman, there is another redeemer closer than I.
13 Stay for the night. Then in the morning, if he will

אֵשֶׁת חַיִל אָתְּ׃ 12 וְעַתָּה֙ כִּי אָמְנָם כִּי
אם* גֹאֵל אָנֹכִי וְגַם יֵשׁ גֹּאֵל קָרוֹב מִמֶּנִּי׃
13 לִינִי ׀ הַלַּיְלָה וְהָיָה בַבֹּקֶר֙ אִם־יִגְאָלֵךְ

v. 12. כתיב ולא קריא

all the elders of my town know Literally, "the whole gate of my people knows," that is, those who sit at the gate. The reference is not primarily to a geographical space but to "the legally responsible body of this town," which gathers there[146] (see "gate" in 4:1). The town's gate is the site of his negotiations on Ruth's behalf. The Septuagint reads "tribe" instead of "gate." The Targum, adapting the verse to its own period, iterates the legal sense of "gate" and translates the phrase as "the great Sanhedrin" of my people. Boaz's words convey more than first meets the eye. They signal that Ruth's virtuous behavior and her good reputation will help him to carry out his plans.

fine woman Hebrew *'eshet ḥayil,* often translated as "a woman of valor" in older translations of Ruth and in Prov. 30:10. This phrase is the feminine form of the equivalent term *'ish ḥayil.* As such, it echoes the narrator's introduction of Boaz as an *'ish gibor ḥayil* (2:1, translated there as "a man of substance"). Boaz's language thus casts Ruth's worthiness as comparable to his own. The midrashic work Lekach Tov[147] makes the point explicit: "you are an *'eshet ḥayil* and deserve an *'ish gibor.*" Furthermore, Boaz's reference to Ruth as *'eshet ḥayil,* together with his mention of the "gate" (see previous comment), also alludes to Prov. 31:10–31. That final section of Proverbs extols the *'eshet ḥayil,* "a capable wife."[148] The Proverbs passage begins by prizing an *'eshet ḥayil* above rubies and concludes by stating that "her works praise her in the gates." Ruth's good reputation "in the gates" is germane here, given the potential taint of her Moabite origin (see "The Status of the Moabites" in the introduction).

12. ***But while it is true that I am a redeeming kinsman*** The Hebrew is less tidy. The *ketiv* (written tradition) is *ki 'omnam ki 'im go'el 'anokhi,* whereas the *kerey* (recited tradition) omits the particle *'im,* yielding *ki 'omnam ki go'el 'anokhi.* The *ketiv* can be read literally as "truly, if I am a *go'el,*" meaning "even if." The *kerey* would mean "truly, indeed, though I am a *go'el.*"[149] Either way, Boaz concurs that he is a redeemer. (On that role and its duties, see comment at verse 9 and 2:20, "redeeming kinsman.")

there is another redeemer closer than I Boaz has already committed himself to honor Ruth's wish that he be a redeemer; he now explains that the situation is not that straightforward. Yet he neglects to clarify what is meant by "closer" (*karov,* from "near," the same noun Naomi used for Boaz in 2:20). The biblical text never spells out the precise kinship relations; the narrator and Naomi designate Boaz's relationship to Naomi only in vague terms (see comment at 2:1,20; 3:2). The Rabbis, however, are keen on figuring out the genealogical connection among Boaz, the unnamed redeemer, and Elimelech. Rashi, following several midrashic traditions (see, e.g., Ruth R. 6.3), explains here that the unnamed redeemer is a brother (presumably of Elimelech), whereas Boaz is the son of a brother, that is, Elimelech's nephew.

13. ***Stay for the night*** Boaz now turns to practical matters. However, his reasoning here is unclear. We can surmise from the next verse that he wants to prevent others from knowing about Ruth's visit. Why then does he ask her to stay for the night? Perhaps

טוֹב יִגְאָל וְאִם־לֹא יַחְפֹּץ לְגָאֳלֵךְ וּגְאַלְתִּיךְ
אָנֹכִי חַי־יְהוָה שִׁכְבִי עַד־הַבֹּקֶר׃

act as a redeemer, good! let him redeem. But if he does not want to act as redeemer for you, I will do so myself, as the LORD lives! Lie down until morning."

it is too dangerous for a woman to travel alone at night. Perhaps she could be attacked or shamed, as is the young woman in Song of Songs when wandering around town at night (Songs 5:7). Or she may be simply maligned (Hubbard considers the type of gossip that would harm Ruth should her visit be made public; see comment at 3:14). In any case, Boaz's suggestion is a gesture of hospitality and protection—proving to Ruth (or to the reader) that he is indeed taking her under his wing.[150]

Stay Hebrew *lini,* from the verbal root that Ruth herself uses in 1:16 when she declares to Naomi: "Wherever you lodge. . . . " Some manuscripts enlarge either the letter *lamed* or the *nun*. This Masoretic tradition draws attention to the verb but doesn't explain why it is specifically singled out.

act as a redeemer Literally, "will redeem you." Boaz refers three times in one sentence to redeeming Ruth (not Naomi or the land). She is clearly his main concern. It is significant that he is meeting her on her own terms, talking about redemption rather than attraction.

good Hebrew *tov.* Based on the phrasing, some Rabbinic sages conclude that "Tov" is the name of the other redeemer (see Ruth R. 6.3). Hebrew syntax allows the clause to be construed as: "If Tov will act as a redeemer, let him redeem!"

let him redeem As noted earlier, redemption elsewhere in the Bible pertains primarily to supporting a needy relative in crisis but does not appear to pertain to marriage (see comment at 2:20). Yet both ancient and modern interpreters often claim that Boaz is talking about marriage here. In Bush's opinion, for example, "to redeem" in Boaz's speech means "to act as a *go'el* by marrying the widow of the deceased relative."[151] But this argument is unconvincing. Moreover, if Boaz construes Ruth's request as a marriage proposal (as Bush supposes), and if redemption refers to marriage, Boaz would seem remarkably sanguine about the prospect of Ruth's marrying another man.

But if he does not want to Hebrew *ve-'im lo' yaḥpotz.* This terminology is found in only one other biblical passage: the clause of release from levirate marriage (Deut. 25:7). This singular connection, coupled with Boaz's announcements at the gate (4:5 and 4:10), persuades interpreters to link the union of Boaz and Ruth to levirate marriage. But this conclusion is unwarranted; see "Levirate Marriage" in the introduction.

I will do so myself . . . ! Literally, "I will redeem you, I!" The second "I" is the emphatic *'anokhi,* which underscores Boaz's own commitment to Ruth. This is the third time in this one verse that Boaz mentions redeeming Ruth—and her alone. (Contrast this with the motives he presents in public in the next act in Chapter 4.)

as the LORD lives! This oath further underscores Boaz's emphatic promise to do what Ruth has requested. In the Rabbinic view, the invocation of God's name is an extreme act, which prompts Rabbinic interpreters to offer various explanations for Boaz's utterance. The Midrash offers a "back story" in which Boaz is fighting his *yetzer* (inclination toward sensory gratification): The *yetzer* challenges him: "You are free and seeking a woman; and she is free and seeking a man." But Boaz resists temptation and swears that

14 So she lay at his feet until dawn. She rose before one person could distinguish another, for he thought, "Let it not be known that the woman came to the threshing floor." 15 And he said, "Hold out the shawl you are wearing." She held it while he measured out six measures of barley, and he put it on her back.

14 וַתִּשְׁכַּ֤ב מרגלתו מַרְגְּלוֹתָיו֙ עַד־הַבֹּ֔קֶר
וַתָּ֕קָם בטרום בְּטֶ֛רֶם יַכִּ֥יר אִ֖ישׁ אֶת־רֵעֵ֑הוּ
וַיֹּ֙אמֶר֙ אַל־יִוָּדַ֔ע כִּי־בָ֥אָה הָאִשָּׁ֖ה הַגֹּֽרֶן׃
15 וַיֹּ֗אמֶר הָ֠בִי הַמִּטְפַּ֨חַת אֲשֶׁר־עָלַ֧יִךְ
וְאֶֽחֳזִי־בָ֖הּ וַתֹּ֣אחֶז בָּ֑הּ וַיָּ֤מָד שֵׁשׁ־שְׂעֹרִים֙
וַיָּ֣שֶׁת עָלֶ֔יהָ

he is not going to touch her (Ruth R. 6.4). Thus, Boaz's oath, in the midrashic interpretation, refers to his chaste invitation that Ruth spend the night. According to Rashi, however, Ruth has just challenged Boaz, objecting that he is dismissing her with empty promises. By his oath, Boaz aims to assure her that these are not mere words.

Lie down The verb *sh-k-v* appears with unusual frequency in this chapter (see comment at 3:4 for connotations and intertextual allusions). In a scene already erotically charged with sexual possibilities, the choice of this Hebrew word is inescapably suggestive. Yet the context favors the prevailing plain-sense interpretation—that is, that Boaz is simply inviting Ruth to lie on the ground. For up until now, Ruth and Boaz have pointedly confined their conversation to matters of redemption. And Boaz's enthusiastic response has assured the reader, as much as Ruth, that he will act honorably on her behalf.[152]

CONCLUSION (3:14–15)

14. she lay at his feet For the third time we learn that Ruth is lying at Boaz's feet (see vv. 4 and 8 above), this time with what we might call "mutual consent." On the complex range of connotations for "feet," see comment at 3:4.

before one person could distinguish another This detail could help explain why Boaz did not recognize Ruth earlier in verses 8–9: personal identification was impossible under cover of night. The verb "distinguish" (*yakir,* from *n-k-r* "recognize") recalls the wordplay at 2:10 where it was also used (translated there as "single").

he thought, "Let it not be known that the woman came to the threshing floor" This statement indicates that Ruth's visit was compromising and needed to be kept private. Boaz is motivated by the wish to protect Ruth's respectability as an *'eshet ḥayil,* and perhaps his own as well. Whereas Boaz's thinking reflects his solicitude for Ruth, the comment also serves to highlight the risky nature of this nocturnal visit for Ruth's position within society. Hubbard writes, "one can easily imagine what impression their meeting would create among the Bethlehemites—an old man victimized by a seductive Moabitess, a clandestine lovers' tryst, a conspiracy to get around the law.... The repercussions could be catastrophic"[153] (see "The Status of the Moabites" in the introduction).

15. shawl Hebrew *mitpaḥat.* The word's meaning is uncertain because this is a hapax legomenon, a word used only once in the Bible. The translation follows postbiblical use, which suits the context.

She held it while he measured out Boaz pours grain onto the fabric that Ruth spreads before him. Coming as it does at the end of a scene so laden with erotic innuendo, this gesture is inevitably suggestive.[154] But it is also an act of restraint, symbolizing the

When she got back to the town, [16] she came to her
mother-in-law, who asked, "How is it with you,

וַיָּבֹא* הָעִיר׃ 16 וַתָּבוֹא אֶל־חֲמוֹתָהּ
וַתֹּאמֶר מִי־אַתְּ בִּתִּי וַתַּגֶּד־לָהּ אֵת כָּל־

v. 15. בנוסח אחר "ותבא"

redirection that has taken place, pointing to the prospect of future plenitude. Until this moment, there has been no easy access to bread in "the House of Bread" (Bethlehem) for the widow, the poor, and the stranger. But now this state of affairs is beginning to change. Boaz is here making an immediate and personal demonstration of this change and of his commitment to Ruth. In addition, if the quantity of grain is to be regarded as large, then the bundle of grain may provide Ruth with cover as she returns home: a woman walking at dawn carrying grain might not seem suspect.

six measures of barley Hebrew *shesh se'orim,* "six barleys." Surely, six grains of barley do not require anything besides Ruth's hand to hold them (which may account for the mention of the shawl, i.e., to signal that there was no direct physical contact between them). Most interpreters, therefore, presume that the phrase refers to a larger unit of grain. Although we do not know precisely what these six "measures" amount to, the context suggests that it is generous and serves to express Boaz's *ḥesed.* The Targum makes the sense of plenitude explicit, saying that Boaz poured out six *se'ahs* of barley, a very large amount.[155] It adds that God gave Ruth strength to carry such a heavy load. The Targum and Ruth R. 7.2 interpret the six measures of barley as symbolizing the six great men who would descend from Ruth: David, Daniel and his three companions (Hananiah, Mishael, and Azariah), and the future King-Messiah. Rashi, however suggests instead that the six hint at the six blessings for the future king, Ruth's offspring. Ruth herself will provide yet another interpretation of this gesture (see 3:17).

When she got back Hebrew *va-yavo',* "and he came." The implied subject is Boaz, not Ruth. The extant Tiberian Masoretic manuscripts thus depict him as eagerly going to work on her behalf. The Targum likewise reflects such a reading and even inserts Boaz's name. The translation here follows certain later manuscripts, reading the verb form as grammatically feminine, *va-tavo',* which is also consistent with the ancient Syriac and Vulgate (Latin) translations and fits the context better.

HOMECOMING WITH GOOD NEWS AND GRAIN (3:16–18)

At the conclusion we find ourselves again with Ruth and Naomi at home, as we did at the beginning of this chapter (3:1–5). But so much has changed! Ruth tells Naomi what has happened on the threshing floor. Reassured, Naomi advises a "wait and see" course of action, counting on Boaz to do whatever is necessary to help their circumstances. A number of scholars note parallels between this concluding section and the conclusion of Chapter 2, as well as with Naomi's earlier instructions in this chapter,[156] highlighting the symmetrical nature of the book's structure. As at the conclusion of Chapter 2 (2:18–23), Naomi is filled with hope.

16. How is it with you Hebrew *mi 'att,* "Who are you?" This is a request for clarification whose nuance depends upon the context. Boaz asked the same question in 3:8, before Ruth identified herself. But the question is sometimes posed even to persons whom

daughter?" She told her all that the man had done for
her; 17 and she added, "He gave me these six measures
of barley, saying to me, 'Do not go back to your

אֲשֶׁר עָשָׂה־לָהּ הָאִישׁ׃ 17 וַתֹּאמֶר שֵׁשׁ־
הַשְּׂעֹרִים הָאֵלֶּה נָתַן לִי כִּי אָמַר [אֵלַי*]

v. 17. קריא ולא כתיב

a speaker already recognizes.[157] Naomi obviously knows that she is speaking to Ruth (see next comment), thus the translators' idiomatic rendering. What Naomi does not know is who Ruth has become as a result of her daring nighttime meeting with Boaz. Naomi's question expresses an anticipated transformation. The Midrash bluntly specifies what kind of clarification Naomi is here seeking: "She meant: 'Are you still a virgin, or a married woman?' to which Ruth replied: 'A virgin'" (Ruth R. 7.4). For LaCocque, the three questions about who Ruth is (here, and at 2:5 and 3:8) illustrate that Ruth's slippery identity is a theme in the book.[158]

daughter Hebrew *biti,* "my daughter." Naomi consistently addresses Ruth this way (2:2, 3:1, and 3:18) and so does Boaz (2:8; 3:10,11). Restricting this form of address to Naomi and Boaz aligns the two as a cohort. At this juncture, calling Ruth "my daughter" shows that Naomi knows whom she is addressing.

She told her all that the man had done for her The focus is on what Boaz has done, not on Ruth's directive to Boaz. But the reader knows that contrary to Naomi's instructions, Ruth did not wait passively for Boaz to act; instead she told him what to do. And the reader also knows that it was Ruth's words, her chutzpah, in fact, that elicited Boaz's commitment and promises. Perhaps Ruth's silence about her own role in the encounter with Boaz is to illustrate in yet another way her *ḥesed*: her generosity in giving all the credit to another.

17. ***and she added*** Literally, "and she said." As the translation indicates, the subsequent words are implicitly an addition to the dialogue that was recorded in 3:8–15.[159]

He gave me these six measures of barley, saying to me, 'Do not go back to your mother-in-law empty-handed' These are Ruth's last words in the book. Significantly, neither Ruth nor Boaz had mentioned Naomi in their threshing floor exchange (3:9–15). Therefore, Ruth's explanation of the grain has been subject to differing interpretations. Some scholars conclude that Ruth fabricates this statement to reassure a self-centered Naomi.[160] Others find another example of Ruth's generosity. Alsheikh suggests that Ruth adds these words to assure Naomi here that marriage with Boaz will not distance Ruth from Naomi, for Boaz cares about Naomi's welfare, hence the grain. Some approach the statement as reflecting a matter of narrative technique.[161] Thus, Coxon concludes that the writer is highlighting the key thematic issue of a journey from emptiness to fullness.[162] Bush argues that Boaz had in fact said these words, but the narrator uses direct speech at this point "to communicate to us (and to Naomi!) the seriousness of Boaz's intentions."[163]

Linafelt considers Ruth's statement a betrayal of her own integrity "once she has secured the coveted 'seed.'"[164] With these as Ruth's concluding words, Linafelt argues, the story mirrors "the course of many women's lives in the ancient world—and even, one supposes, today—in which procreation is thought to be the only worthwhile goal."[165] This conclusion, Linafelt adds, is both poignant and disturbing in a book "that constructs such a strong and shrewd female character."[166] Linafelt's conclusion, however, overlooks an important point: the word "seed" is not used in these passages, only the word "barley." The text's focus remains on bread—on household economy, not procreation. Indeed, ac-

mother-in-law empty-handed.'" 18 And Naomi said,
"Stay here, daughter, till you learn how the matter
turns out. For the man will not rest, but will settle the
matter today."

אַל־תָּבוֹאִי רֵיקָם אֶל־חֲמוֹתֵךְ׃ 18 וַתֹּאמֶר
שְׁבִי בִתִּי עַד אֲשֶׁר תֵּדְעִין אֵיךְ יִפֹּל דָּבָר
כִּי לֹא יִשְׁקֹט הָאִישׁ כִּי־אִם־כִּלָּה הַדָּבָר
הַיּוֹם׃

cording to the women in Ruth 4:15, the ultimate purpose of Ruth's child (once she bears a son) is also economic and female-centered: to provide for Naomi's old age.

In this fashion, the Book of Ruth challenges the view of women primarily as the bearers of sons (a view represented by Naomi) and replaces it with the image of woman as breadwinner.[167] It makes sense to regard Ruth's elaboration in this verse as her own interpretation of Boaz's silent gesture: Ruth's last words offer a clue to her overarching motive, which the book otherwise conspicuously fails to articulate explicitly. (Although Ruth eloquently vows to join Naomi permanently [1:16–17], she never explains her reasons why.)

your mother-in-law Hebrew *ḥamoteikh*. In the Hebrew text, this is Ruth's last word (following *reykam* "empty"), a fitting conclusion to her project, which has focused so heavily on helping her mother-in-law. Ruth assures Naomi that she will not be abandoned (see 1:16), even after Ruth's own future is secure.

empty-handed Hebrew *reykam,* "empty." Naomi described herself as empty when first returning to Bethlehem: "I went away full, and the Lord has brought me back empty [*reykam*]" (1:21). The verbal link implies that Ruth and the author are here commenting on Naomi's earlier self-description. But now, thanks to Boaz, Ruth comes, not empty but bearing grain for Naomi. Ruth's statement is a harbinger of fulfillment, cast in Naomi's own frame of reference. Ruth signals that the time of fullness has finally begun.

18. daughter Hebrew *biti,* "my daughter," as in 3:1 and 16 (see there).

the man As in 2:19–20 and 3:3, Naomi does not refer to Boaz by name but in terms of his social role and therefore his importance for her plans.

will not rest, but will settle the matter today Ruth's apparently detailed report about the encounter on the threshing floor assures Naomi that Boaz will act swiftly.

will not rest Hebrew *lo yishkot*. The verb *sh-k-t* (be calm) refers to settling down after turmoil, as when the land rests from the turmoil of war (Judg. 5:31).

matter turns out Hebrew *yippol ha-davar*, "the matter will fall." This expression elsewhere refers to precise execution of a plan, as when the king instructed Haman to make sure everything was done accordingly to plan (Esther 6:10).

will settle the matter Hebrew *killah ha-davar,* "bring the matter to a close; finish it." Possibly also a concluding pun on the name Chilion (1:2,5). These, Naomi's final words in the book, rightly sum up the present situation—and Naomi's own perception of how the world works: women need a man to bring matters to a happy conclusion. However, this is not the book's last word on this subject.

CHAPTER 4

Redemption and Restoration

The last chapter of Ruth moves from the world of women to the world of men (although women will have the last word; see comment at 4:17). The private maneuverings by Naomi and Ruth give way to public negotiations in which the two women remain silent. Their personal plight now becomes a communal concern that broadens into a welcoming *ḥesed.* Some contemporary readers consider this shift a resumption of patriarchal slant, familiar from the rest of the Bible but contrary to the earlier portions of the Book of Ruth.[168] Such a response overlooks an important feature of this book: what seems like a public world dominated by certain men is also a façade for the work of women behind the scenes. Thus, Boaz appears as a free agent, executing justice on behalf of dead relatives, but in fact he functions as a willing agent of Naomi and Ruth, marshalling the entire community in their support.

And if the reader misses this point, the witnesses at the gate do not—as we shall see from their blessing, which calls attention to the irregular nature of the union between Boaz and Ruth, even though celebrating it (see comment at v. 12). In this manner, while acknowledging that gender strongly determines social roles and responsibilities, the Book of Ruth also unmasks its limits with gentle irony. More to the point, this chapter integrates the worlds of men and of women into a harmonious whole, rather than presenting polarized realms in tension with each other. The expressed intent of each group finds here satisfactory resolution. The men rejoice at the perpetuation of the male line, and the women celebrate Naomi's prospects of sustenance.

As each of the previous chapters, this one can be divided into three parts. But whereas Chapters 2 and 3 are symmetrical or circular, beginning and ending with Naomi and Ruth at home, this one moves forward linearly into the future. In this way the epilogue connects to the prologue in Chapter 1, and births replace the deaths with which the book began (1:1–5); the force of life prevails, to everyone's benefit.

OUTLINE OF CHAPTER 4

I. Negotiations at the gate: redeeming Ruth (1–12)
II. Betrothal, birth, and more blessings (13–17)
III. Epilogue: reweaving the web of life—the concluding genealogy (18–22)

NEGOTIATIONS AT THE GATE: REDEEMING RUTH (4:1–12)

The scene shifts to the city gate—a public arena where legal transactions are negotiated and where Ruth's nighttime visit to Boaz finds its resolution. In a brief colloquy before ten town elders, Boaz, Ruth's chosen patron, convinces Elimelech's nearer kinsman to relinquish his responsibility to act as redeemer, then grandly announces that he will marry Ruth "in order to preserve the name of the dead" (4:10). At the end of the negotiations, the entire community witnesses and affirms Boaz's decision to marry Ruth (vv. 11–12), clearing the way for Ruth to enter the community. This gesture of inclusion contrasts sharply with other biblical texts that object to a union with Moabites (Ezra 9–10 and Neh. 13:1–3; see also Deut. 23:4, which excludes Moabites from the community).

At the same time, this scene has parallels to Isa. 56:1–7, which welcomes the foreigner. Here, the marriage of Ruth and Boaz—an act that would constitute a scandal in Ezra 9–10

4 Meanwhile, Boaz had gone to the gate and sat down there. And now the redeemer whom Boaz had mentioned passed by. He called, “Come over and sit

ד וּבֹעַז עָלָה הַשַּׁעַר וַיֵּשֶׁב שָׁם וְהִנֵּה
הַגֹּאֵל עֹבֵר אֲשֶׁר דִּבֶּר־בֹּעַז וַיֹּאמֶר סוּרָה

(where such unions are deemed destructive to the communal fabric and to God’s law)—portrays Boaz as a paragon of virtue. Although this section seems preoccupied with legal matters, the narrator’s aim is not to inform the reader about ancient laws, but rather to show how Boaz cleverly brings about his desired end: to see to Ruth’s welfare, to which he had committed himself in 3:10–13. The opening section (vv. 1–12) is divided into five parts.

OUTLINE

I. Setting the stage (4:1–2)
II. Dialogue to discourage the would-be redeemer (4:3–6)
III. Legalizing the agreement about redemption (4:7–8)
IV. Legalizing Boaz’s marriage to Ruth (4:9–10)
V. Communal ratification and blessing of the marriage of Boaz and Ruth (4:11–12)

Boaz confronts the unnamed kin with a proposition: redeem, that is, buy, the family land. When the man agrees, Boaz presents a complication: he declares that redeeming the land that belongs to Elimelech’s and Naomi’s household entails also acquiring Ruth. Yet, it is not self-evident in the biblical text and context whether Boaz is claiming that he plans to acquire Ruth, or whether the nearer kin is obligated to do so; nor is it obvious why Boaz combines redemption of land (the initial subject of the negotiations in Ruth 4) with the acquisition of the woman and perpetuating the name of the deceased (Ruth 4:5 and 10). However, the unnamed redeemer withdraws his offer to redeem, thereby clearing the path for Boaz to act as redeemer and announce his marriage to Ruth.

SETTING THE STAGE (4:1–2)

On what appears to be the next day, Boaz summons Ruth’s would-be redeemer together with an assembly of Bethlehemites to sort out the matter of Ruth’s redemption.

4:1. Meanwhile, Boaz Literally, “and Boaz.” The conjunction, *vav,* effects narrative and thematic continuity, while being temporally ambiguous—like “thereupon” or “meanwhile.” Compare Gen. 31:19,34; 34:7; 37:6.

the gate The town’s gateway, equivalent to the later town square, was the locale in the ancient world where people (typically men) congregated for commerce and other exchanges such as news. In addition, it was where authorized leaders met to conduct legal proceedings and decide on official matters. Thus, Deuteronomy situates a lawsuit before the elders “at the gate” (22:15). Likewise, when the prophet Isaiah denounces corruption, he accuses evildoers of “laying a snare for the arbiter at the gate” (Isa. 29:21). Archaeological excavations show that these gateways typically consisted of a large uncovered space like a plaza. The ancient city gates of Gezer and Dan also show stone benches along the walls facing the plaza. Symbolically and practically, the gate also constitutes an interface between individual households and the larger clan and between that clan and the outside world. The Targum, although anachronistic vis-à-vis the Book of Ruth, nonetheless accurately characterizes the formal and legal significance of the gate when it “translates” it as “the Beth Din

down here, So-and-so!" And he came over and sat
down. 2 Then [Boaz] took ten elders of the town and
said, "Be seated here"; and they sat down.

שְׁבָה־פֹּה פְּלֹנִי אַלְמֹנִי וַיָּסַר וַיֵּשֵׁב׃ 2 וַיִּקַּח
עֲשָׂרָה אֲנָשִׁים מִזִּקְנֵי הָעִיר וַיֹּאמֶר שְׁבוּ־
פֹה וַיֵּשֵׁבוּ׃

[court of law] of the Sanhedrin [central governing council]." In the previous chapter, Boaz refers to Ruth's good reputation among "all the elders"—literally, in the Hebrew, "the whole gate" (3:11). Alsheikh adds that Boaz went to the gate to inquire whether he is permitted to marry Ruth.

And now Hebrew *ve-hinneih.* Often rendered in older translations as "Behold!" It focuses attention in this case on what Boaz sees. See "there was" at 3:8.

the redeemer...passed by One can suppose that Boaz expected this redeemer to come by. Yet, perhaps, like Ruth's "happening" upon Boaz's field (2:3), this is a possible allusion to providence. Ruth R. 7.7 makes divine intervention explicit, stating that since Ruth, Naomi, and Boaz had done their part, God determined to do God's part, which is how the unnamed kin suddenly appeared.

Come over and sit down Boaz here employs cohortative verb forms of invitation, which could also be rendered as "Would you come over and sit down?" The redeemer consents without a word. Boaz's abrupt summons reaffirms the reader's understanding that Boaz is a man to be reckoned with (2:1). Everything that follows confirms that he possesses clout and that other men follow his lead.

Come over From Hebrew *s-w-r,* a verb that means "to swerve." It suggests diverting one's course from an expected path, as when Lot invites the divine messengers to digress from their path and enter his home (Gen. 19:2–3) and when Moses turns aside upon seeing the burning bush (Exod. 3:4).

So-and-so! Hebrew *ploni 'almoni,* an expression used when a name (of a person or place) is immaterial to the narrative (see 1 Sam. 21:3). Here, however, the term is intentionally and conspicuously used to avoid naming the character. The purpose for the anonymity of the man remains a mystery. As scholars note, it is not likely that Boaz does not know the man's name. If the name were insignificant to the author, the designation could simply have been eliminated. Some Rabbinic sages, as well as modern scholars (e.g., Hubbard), suggest that not naming implies measure-for-measure justice: the one who refuses to "preserve the name" of a kin (see below) deserves to have his own name vanish. Others argue that the narrator may wish to protect him from the embarrassment resulting from his inability or unwillingness to undertake responsibility for Ruth and Naomi (see comment at 4:6 when he relinquishes his redemption rights). Campbell, who reviews the various proposed explanations, rightly concludes that none is satisfactory.[169] Some Rabbinic sources suppose that the man's name was Tov (as per 3:13). The Targum, howevr, has: "you, whose ways are secret."[170] The same notion is reflected in some Septuagint manuscripts,[171] as well as suggested by Rashi. Rashi also explores the etymology from *'alman* (a play on *'almoni*) which means "widower" and "a mute," a reference to the man's lack of awareness that exclusion in Deut. 23:4 applies solely to males.

2. ***[Boaz] took ten elders of the town*** Literally, "he took ten men *('anashim)* from the elders of the town." Boaz's authority is underscored by his capacity to "take," that is, summon, control, and command the elders. In this context, *'anashim* (which NJPS does not render literally) designates persons authorized to speak and act on behalf of the whole body—in this case, the body of elders.[172]

ten elders In the pre-monarchic period when the Book of Ruth is set, namely, the time of "the chieftains" (1:1), the elders constituted a town's formal authoritative body.[173] The precise qualifications for the position of elder in ancient Israel remain a matter of conjecture. Nili Fox notes that the term applies to sub-tribal units (extended families), as well as tribal and clan leaders; the term indicates either longevity or high status within the group. An adult man, she writes, "could qualify as an elder if he belonged to a family recognized by the group as prominent."[174] Certain biblical texts suggest that assemblies of elders were usually summoned *ad hoc,* as the need arose to adjudicate cases. Thus, in Judges 11, it is the elders who negotiate with Jephthah and, as it were, hire him to protect the community. See also Ezra 10:14, where the elders determine the status of marriages in the case of suspected intermarriage. In summoning elders to function as witnesses, Boaz here sets the stage for a legal transaction where their presence legitimizes the proceedings. In an ironic twist, perhaps not accidental, elders here legitimate precisely the kind of marriage that Ezra 10 delegitimizes (see "Intermarriage," "Conversion," and "The Status of the Moabites" in the introduction). The number ten implies that this is an official legal assembly of elders. Rabbinic texts conclude from the present case that a quorum is required for reciting marriage benedictions (Ruth R. 7.8). In later Jewish tradition, the number ten constitutes the minimum number required to make up a community. Rabbinic Judaism establishes ten adults as a minimum, a ***minyan,*** required for certain acts of public worship such as Mourners' Kaddish and reading the Torah publicly (see B. Meg. 23b).

and said, "Be seated here"; and they sat down Boaz's commanding presence is even more clearly evident as he selects and seats the ten elders, who readily comply with his demand. Boaz uses the imperative form of the verb, which conveys both formality and authority, indicating that the arrangement is not merely social but an official convocation. The assembling of elders has a ripple effect on the townspeople. Soon, the reader discovers that "all the people" (4:11) are present along with the elders, presumably in anticipation of what is about to happen.

DIALOGUE TO DISCOURAGE THE WOULD-BE REDEEMER (4:3–6)

Boaz announces that Naomi is selling land and invites the unnamed kin to act as redeemer and buy the land. But when the man consents, Boaz adds a condition: acquisition of the land is combined with acquisition of Ruth. The key statement (4:5) is problematic. One problem results from the difficulty in deciding between the written form (*ketiv*) of the main verb *kaniti*, meaning "I acquire(d"), and the reading instructions (*kerey*), *kanita,* "you acquire(d)" (see the commentary at 4:5); consequently, it is difficult to know whether the unnamed kin must take Ruth or whether Boaz himself plans to take her. Another problem results from the difficulty in determining what assumptions and practices account for Boaz's claim about acquiring Ruth.

A number of interpreters suggest that lack of familiarity with the operative traditions in ancient Israel, and with changes in Israelite legal customs, account for the confusion that modern readers face in this section.[175] Others suggest that the narrator deliberately uses ambiguity as a literary strategy.[176] As we shall see, an element of confusion results not so much from ignorance of ancient custom (although this plays a role) but from introjecting the notion of levirate marriage into the scene—which most definitely is not applicable. (See further at vv. 5 and 10 as well as "Levirate Marriage," "The Marriage of Boaz and Ruth," and "Why and How Boaz Marries Ruth" in the introduction.)

3 He said to the redeemer, "Naomi, now returned
from the country of Moab, must sell the piece of land

3 וַיֹּאמֶר֙ לַגֹּאֵ֔ל חֶלְקַת֙ הַשָּׂדֶ֔ה אֲשֶׁ֥ר
לְאָחִ֖ינוּ לֶאֱלִימֶ֑לֶךְ מָכְרָ֣ה נָעֳמִ֔י הַשָּׁ֖בָה

3. Naomi... must sell the piece of land which belonged to our kinsman Elimelech The sudden mention of Naomi selling a field belonging to Elimelech is surprising. The reader has been led to believe that Naomi has no resources whatsoever; she is so poor that Ruth must go gleaning daily. Yet, given biblical laws restricting the dispersal of inherited land, it is reasonable that Elimelech would have property, to which his heir would have some right (see the laws in Leviticus 25 which safeguard the inalienability of family land) and to which Naomi would have returned. Nevertheless, we have not been informed about the legal status of Elimelech's land after his death or about Naomi's entitlement to it. The most common view is that Elimelech had sold either the land or its usufruct (i.e., the yield of the land to those who work the land) prior to leaving for Moab, and that the land is now under an "outsider's" control, that is, someone who is not a member of this family. Bush, for example, concludes that "Naomi as the wife of the deceased has the right to the usufruct of the field of Elimelech and, hence, the right to redeem it, i.e., buy it back from whoever now is in possession of it."[177] However, since Naomi does not have the means to do so, Boaz invites the near redeemer to undertake this task.[178] Malbim offers a different explanation: "it should be understood that it [the land] was being offered for sale by Naomi and that it had already been publicly declared for sale." Both explanations, as well as others, still leave many questions unanswered, especially: Why was the land not mentioned sooner by the narrator or protagonists? Or why is the land the subject now, when earlier (3:10–13) Boaz spoke only about redeeming Ruth? The text offers no answer. Significantly, the question of the land and its disposition is largely eclipsed once the issue of Ruth's status surfaces in the negotiation.[179]

The narrator does not spell out the legal status of the land nor Naomi's entitlement to it. Some modern scholars conclude that ancient readers of Ruth would not have needed more explanation on this point because they would have been familiar with Israelite laws pertaining to inheriting land.[180]

must sell Hebrew *makherah,* meaning "[has] sold" (perfect tense, third person feminine); with a slight change of vowels, it can be read as *mokhrah,* "is selling" (participle, third person feminine). Either way, "must" should be omitted. If we read the imperfect ("sold"), we still do not know when and how Naomi sold the land. The present participle "is selling" makes the most sense in this context, given that the gleaning season is now over and food sources are drying up.[181] Regaining control of the land would safeguard Naomi's economic survival. The suggestion that Naomi is entitled to land rights baffles some modern commentators, who question the plausibility that a widow would inherit her husband's land in ancient Israel. Although several biblical texts indicate that women could own land (2 Kings 8:1–6), and inherit it (Numbers 27 and 36), no biblical text refers specifically to a situation comparable to that of Naomi and Ruth.[182] However, extra-biblical Jewish sources from the fifth century B.C.E. document that women owned and were able to transfer property.[183] See "Inheritance" in the introduction. (It is noteworthy that neither the unnamed redeemer nor Boaz is understood to be automatically entitled to the land, a detail that supports the assumption that the land does not revert to a male relative when there is a widow.)

land In this first round of the negotiation, Boaz mentions only the redemption of land.

which belonged to our kinsman Elimelech. 4 I thought
I should disclose the matter to you and say: Acquire
it in the presence of those seated here and in the
presence of the elders of my people. If you are willing
to redeem it, redeem! But if you will not redeem, tell

מִשְּׂדֵה מוֹאָב׃ 4 וַאֲנִי אָמַרְתִּי אֶגְלֶה אָזְנְךָ
לֵאמֹר קְנֵה נֶגֶד הַיֹּשְׁבִים וְנֶגֶד זִקְנֵי עַמִּי
אִם־תִּגְאַל גְּאָל וְאִם־לֹא יִגְאַל* הַגִּידָה

v. 4. בנוסח אחר "תגאל"

our kinsman Hebrew *'aḥinu,* often rendered elsewhere as "our brother." In the Bible, the singular noun *'aḥ,* when referring to specific individuals, applies to males who share the same father or mother. The semantic range of the noun can therefore encompass fellow Israelites in general, given that all are regarded as offspring of the same patriarch(s). Thus Abram refers to his nephew Lot by this term (Gen. 13:10). This usage is frequent in Deuteronomy, as part of the rhetoric that urges all Israelites to care for each other like "brothers." More to the point here, *'aḥ* is the term used in the laws of redemption to refer to members of one's clan (Lev. 25:25,47). Boaz uses the term here in that wider sense, and again in verse 10. In terms of social hierarchy, this noun is used to refer to social equals, even if unrelated (e.g., Gen. 29:4). Rabbinic sages, who interpret the negotiations in Ruth through the lens of levirate union, suppose that Elimelech and the unnamed redeemer are both brothers of Salmon, the father of Boaz; Boaz, then, is a nephew of Elimelech (B. BB 91a). But the text in its plain sense does not imply such a conclusion (see "Levirate Marriage" in the introduction).

4. In this verse, Boaz employs forms of the verb *ga'al* ("redeem") five times. The language of redemption dominates also verse 7 and constitutes the heart of the negotiations in this scene. Redemption is what Ruth has requested and what Boaz promised (3:9–13). The question remains, however, as to what or who is to be redeemed: on the threshing floor, Boaz spoke solely about Ruth. Here redemption pertains to the land. As the story unfolds, it becomes evident that negotiations about the land are a means to redeeming Ruth, that is, of securing her social and economic position and rescuing her and Naomi from poverty.

disclose Hebrew *'egleh,* which is composed of the same consonants as the verb *ga'al,* "redeem" (see above). Such sound repetition further reinforces the theme of redemption in this section.

Acquire Hebrew *keneih,* from the verbal root *k-n-h.* This is the verb that describes Abraham's acquisition of the burial cave (Gen. 25:10) and Joseph's acquisition of land in Egypt (Gen. 47:19–20). The term can be used not only for commercial purchases but also for taking charge or assuming responsibility in a more general sense. For details, see "acquire" at 4:5 and 4:10, where it is applied also to Ruth.

in the presence of those seated here and in the presence of the elders of my people Boaz underscores the legal nature of the proceedings by emphasizing twice that the redeemer's response is to be made *neged,* "in front of" (translated as "in the presence of"), the elders. The negotiations are public and, as Boaz makes clear, carry legal consequences. There is no need to suppose a reference to two different groups. As Campbell rightly concludes, those sitting represent the larger group of elders of the people.[184] Reference to the elders also intensifies the pressure upon the unsuspecting redeemer who may prefer to reflect on the matter.

redeem See comment at 2:20 and 3:9.

me, that I may know. For there is no one to redeem
but you, and I come after you." "I am willing to
redeem it," he replied. 5 Boaz continued, "When you
acquire the property from Naomi and from Ruth the

לִ֣י ואדע וְאֵֽדְעָה֒ כִּ֣י אֵ֤ין זוּלָֽתְךָ֙ לִגְא֔וֹל
וְאָנֹכִ֖י אַחֲרֶ֑יךָ וַיֹּ֖אמֶר אָנֹכִ֥י אֶגְאָֽל׃
5 וַיֹּ֣אמֶר בֹּ֔עַז בְּיוֹם־קְנוֹתְךָ֥ הַשָּׂדֶ֖ה מִיַּ֣ד
נָעֳמִ֑י וּמֵאֵ֨ת ר֤וּת הַמּוֹאֲבִיָּה֙ אֵֽשֶׁת־הַמֵּת֙

But if you will not redeem Hebrew *ve-'im lo' yig'al* literally "But if he will not redeem." The NJPS translators choose to use the second-person pronoun, following many late-medieval manuscripts, the Septuagint, and the Targum, which reflect the second-person inflection—a difference of one Hebrew letter. Some contemporary scholars justify the Masoretic third-person form by construing it as a stage whisper, aimed at the distinguished witnesses.[185]

tell me, that I may know. For there is no one to redeem but you, and I come after you Boaz's willingness, even eagerness, to undertake the redemption of the land creates an opening for the other person to save face if he relinquishes the opportunity to redeem the land. The very need to inform the other party that there are no nearer kin implies that he, like Boaz, is not an actual brother of Elimelech but a more distant relation.

I am willing to redeem it Hebrew *'anokhi eg'al,* "I will redeem." The speed and brevity of the response betrays no hesitation, characterizing the redeemer as a householder willing to undertake family responsibility even at short notice. In the group-oriented societies of the ancient Near East and Mediterranean, honor would accrue to a person as a result of such actions, increasing his social standing and influence. In this case, if there are no other heirs, it would also increase the size of a person's estate. The acquisition would be rewarding on many levels. For now everyone knows that the parcel will still remain within (or be restored to) the purview of the larger clan, which is a highly valued outcome.[186] Note, however, that the price of the land is never mentioned, another sign that the narrator's focus is on the human drama, not the land.

5. ***Boaz continued*** Literally, "and Boaz said."

When you acquire the property from Naomi and from Ruth the Moabite Boaz introduces a complication, the purpose of which is clear to the reader: to dissuade the other man from becoming the *go'el.* Boaz has expanded the ownership of the field (here translated as "property") to include Ruth, the real subject of his actions. Like Naomi's entitlement to the land, so too Ruth's rights to the land are obscure in the text (for some interpretations, see above, "Naomi . . . must sell" at 4:3, and "Redemption" and "Inheritance" in the introduction). The present situation is all the more ambiguous given Ruth's Moabite status.[187] Presumably, as the widow of Mahlon, she too shares in the inheritance now under Naomi's jurisdiction. At least, this is how Boaz presents the case.

Ruth the Moabite This is the first time that Boaz mentions Ruth's problematic Moabite status. On the exclusion of Moabites from the Israelite community, see Deut. 23:4–7 and "The Status of the Moabites" in the introduction. Some midrashic sources suggest that this Moabite status prompts the other redeemer to reconsider (see, e.g., Ruth R. 7.7). But in Boaz's strategic, carefully worded pronouncement, this reference serves to affirm Ruth's pivotal place in the process despite, or in full cognizance of, her Moabite status. This is one of several places where it is evident that despite her commitment to Israel and its God, Ruth remains a Moabite in the eyes of the community.

Moabite, you must also acquire the wife of the deceased, so as to perpetuate the name of the deceased

קניתי קָנִ֫יתָה לְהָקִ֥ים שֵׁם־הַמֵּ֖ת עַל־

you must also acquire the wife of the deceased Boaz introduces a complication, which Nielsen considers to be a "masterstroke of dramatic irony."[188] As in 3:9, the reader encounters apparent ambiguities in the text precisely at a decisive moment.[189] The first problem is textual, determining who is to "acquire" Ruth—Boaz or the other redeemer? The second problem concerns the basis for the "acquisition."

you . . . acquire The written form of the verb (*ketiv*) as printed is *kaniti,* grammatically a first-person form of the verb *k-n-h,* elsewhere translated as "I acquire(d)" (as is the case in 4:10). But the recited tradition (*kerey*) has *kanita,* "you acquire(d)" (second person), as per the translation here. As a rule, the Masoretes and Rabbinic halakhah consider the *kerey* the preferred reading of the text.[190] However, it is granted that in a few instances, the *ketiv* form is more logically suited to the context.[191] According to the *kerey*, Boaz here informs the unnamed redeemer that the latter will now have responsibility for Ruth as part of his household. This raises the second major interpretive problem: what is the basis for Boaz's claim about this obligation? Frymer-Kensky points out that "Boaz's statement does not sound quite right. Why should a kinsman have to marry Ruth in order to buy the land for the family? A redeemer is not a levir."[192] Biblical laws about redemption of land or slaves say nothing about marrying the widow. And levirate marriage does not apply here. Moreover, the term for levirate marriage (*yibbum*) does not appear in this section (see "Levirate Marriage" in the introduction).

Four general explanations have been proposed to resolve this problem:

A. Boaz is referring to contemporary customs of levirate unions (supposing that practice and laws changed over time or are not fully represented elsewhere in the Bible).[193]

B. Boaz is alluding to levirate marriage (even though it does not quite apply) as a way of extending moral responsibilities.[194]

C. Boaz is alluding to levirate marriage even though it does not quite apply, in order to justify his marriage with Ruth.

D. Boaz is not referring to marriage but to taking economic responsibility as a *go'el*/redeemer.[195]

All of these interpretations have their advocates, and each could work to deter the unnamed kin from acquiring the land. The third view is adopted here. The community's response shows both an awareness of this irregularity and a support for it (see comment at 4:12).

Many Rabbinic sources suppose a levirate obligation (with the unnamed kin as a brother of Elimelech).[196] The Targum makes this point explicit by adding here: ". . . you are required to perform the duty of a levir with her," using the technical term for levirate union, *y-b-m.*[197] Rashi does not suppose a levirate obligation. Instead, he has Boaz add that Ruth will not relinquish the land unless the redeemer marries her. This addition justifies the "acquisition" of Ruth by a different rationale. Salmon ben Yeroḥam likewise rejects levirate obligation here.

A different explanation emerges if one reads the *ketiv* as referring to Boaz. In this case, Boaz is informing the other man that he, Boaz, is taking Ruth. The implied scenario includes an expectation that the land would later revert to an offspring of Boaz and Ruth (as per the laws of Lev. 25:28), rendering the redeemer's investment a loss.[198] Ibn Ezra is among the few traditional commentators who prefer the written form to the recited, as do a number of modern scholars.

must The translator's addition. Better omitted.

acquire the wife The Hebrew verb *k-n-h* typically refers to the acquisition of property, as in 4:4. However, its semantic range is broad, which clouds Boaz's intent regarding Ruth's future legal status. This word first appears when Eve names her son Cain, explaining that "I have gained [*kaniti*] a male child" (Gen. 4:1). The word also refers to God's possession of heaven and earth in Abram's oath ("I swear to the LORD, God Most High, Creator [*koneh,* i.e., participle of *k-n-h*] of heaven and earth" (Gen. 14:22), as well as to God's "acquisition" of the people Israel (Exod. 15:16). The commercial use of the term is common in postexilic texts but is also used, as in Proverbs, for virtues ("Acquire [*keneih*] wisdom, acquire discernment"; Prov. 4:5). In subsequent Rabbinic literature, this verb regularly appears in transactions related to marriage, although it is not the main or only such term, and does not itself mean "marriage."[199] (See also "acquiring Ruth the Moabite" at 4:10.) One modern scholar observes that this term differs from terms that clearly refer to full transfer of possession, arguing that neither *k-n-h* ("acquire") nor *g-'-l* ("redeem") refers to complete control or disposal of property.[200] The term is especially important in two texts that pertain to land redemption: in Leviticus 25, it details the laws of land redemption (where the term is used eight times), as well as acquiring persons of low status, namely slaves (25:44–45); and in Jeremiah 32, the story of Jeremiah's redeeming of family land (eight times). Only in Ruth 4:10 is this term linked with marriage.

wife of the deceased Boaz highlights Ruth's status as Mahlon's wife, a reminder that she, too, has claim to the patrimony. By referring to her this way, Boaz situates Ruth explicitly with the family of Elimelech. Furthermore, as Rashi's addition to 3:9 indicates, Ruth's status as Mahlon's wife also serves as the vehicle for perpetuating the name of the deceased. See comment below and at 3:9.

so as to perpetuate the name of the deceased upon his estate This part of Boaz's statement raises another legal issue. The language is nearly identical to that in Deut. 25:5–6, which delineates levirate marriage as the responsibility of a brother to produce a child with his deceased brother's widow. This similarity prompts interpreters to conclude that Boaz refers to levirate marriage. However, the term "redemption" elsewhere in the Bible entails neither marriage nor a commitment "to perpetuate the name of the deceased" through marriage. Boaz's statement, if understood in the context of levirate marriage, is thus inconsistent with known biblical traditions and laws. Significantly, the deceased's name is not perpetuated in the genealogy that ends the book (see comment at 4:21). Rashi understands the perpetuation of the name to come from Ruth's role as Mahlon's wife, not through levirate marriage.

perpetuate Hebrew *lehakim;* or "to establish." This verb appears in a variety of biblical contexts concerned with making something endure: God's covenant with Noah and his descendants (Gen. 9:9), the Davidic throne (2 Sam. 3:10), the Davidic dynasty or seed (2 Sam. 7:12), or the renewed covenant with Israel (Ezek. 16:60). In the two cases where it specifically refers to levirate marriage (Gen. 38:8 and Deut. 25:5–10), this verb indicates that the resulting offspring continue the lineage of a deceased man, becoming his heirs. See also comment at verse 10.

upon his estate." 6 The redeemer replied, "Then
I cannot redeem it for myself, lest I impair my own
estate. You take over my right of redemption, for I am
unable to exercise it."
7 Now this was formerly done in Israel in cases of
redemption or exchange: to validate any transaction,

נַחֲלָתוֹ׃ 6 וַיֹּאמֶר הַגֹּאֵל לֹא אוּכַל֙ לגאול
לִגְאָל־לִ֔י פֶּן־אַשְׁחִית אֶת־נַחֲלָתִ֑י גְּאַל־לְךָ֤
אַתָּה֙ אֶת־גְּאֻלָּתִ֔י כִּ֥י לֹא־אוּכַ֖ל לִגְאֹֽל׃
7 וְזֹאת֩ לְפָנִ֨ים בְּיִשְׂרָאֵ֜ל עַל־הַגְּאוּלָּ֣ה וְעַל־
הַתְּמוּרָה֙ לְקַיֵּ֣ם כָּל־דָּבָ֔ר שָׁלַ֥ף אִ֛ישׁ נַעֲל֖וֹ

6. ***I cannot . . . lest I impair my own estate*** The unnamed redeemer relinquishes his role in response to unexpected, new information that places his interests at risk. What is this information? If we accept the ***kerey*** reading that Boaz says, "you acquire," then the redeemer reneges because he has just been informed that he must care for additional persons in his household. If we accept the text according to the ***ketiv,*** construing the verb as "I acquire," then the unnamed redeemer is surprised by Boaz's intention to acquire (or marry) Ruth. In this reading, the narrative at this point demonstrates coherence and consistency. For the other man now realizes that buying the land would be a foolhardy investment: sooner or later, the land will revert back to Elimelech's proper heir through Ruth, whom Boaz is now taking as his wife (according to Leviticus 25, land reverts to the original owner in the jubilee's year; see further "Inheritance" and "Redemption" in the introduction). The narrator portrays the unnamed redeemer as an ordinary, decent person, not as a villain. Like Orpah, he seeks to do the right thing but eventually gives up, thereby serving as a foil for the greater magnanimity of the story's heroes. One Rabbinic midrash advances this sympathetic view. Capitalizing on the ambiguity of the verb "acquire," and responding to both senses (as "I acquire" and "you acquire"), this midrash explains that the other man, as a gentleman, withdraws his bid to act as redeemer in order to help Boaz (Ruth R. 7.10). According to another midrashic opinion, however, the unnamed redeemer reneges because of Ruth's Moabite status; Rabbi Shemuel castigates him for being ignorant in matters of Torah, for he should have known that the halakhah interprets the passage in Deuteronomy as excluding only Moabite men (*mo'avi*), not Moabite women (*mo'avit*) (Ruth R. 7.10).

You take over my right of redemption Hebrew *ge'al . . . 'et ge'ulati,* "redeem . . . my redemption." The verbal root *g-'-l* appears five times in this verse (as it does in v. 4 above). By relinquishing his role as a redeemer and transferring the right or obligation to Boaz, the unnamed redeemer helps fulfill Ruth's wish that Boaz be her redeemer (3:9). Brichto rightly observes, and this translation indicates, that what is transferred is the right (or duty) to redeem, not the specific items that are to be redeemed.[201] This distinction influences how one understands 4:10, when Boaz "acquires" Ruth.

LEGALIZING THE AGREEMENT ABOUT REDEMPTION (4:7–8)

7. ***Now this was formerly done*** The narrator intrudes into the story to inform the reader that these events are taking place at a time well before the narration itself. In other words, so much time has passed that customs have changed and have even been forgotten, thus requiring explanation. Ruth 1:1 locates the time of the story as the period of the chieftains (or judges). The genealogy that ends the book makes clear that the present narration is set at a time after David (4:17 and 22). The story itself spans nearly one hundred years from beginning to end (from Elimelech's departure for Moab to the birth of

one man would take off his sandal and hand it to the other. Such was the practice in Israel. [8] So when the redeemer said to Boaz, "Acquire for yourself," he

וְנָתַ֣ן לְרֵעֵ֑הוּ וְזֹ֥את הַתְּעוּדָ֖ה בְּיִשְׂרָאֵֽל׃
8 וַיֹּ֧אמֶר הַגֹּאֵ֛ל לְבֹ֖עַז קְנֵה־לָ֑ךְ וַיִּשְׁלֹ֖ף

David, a period of five generations). Modern scholars estimate that the book in its current form was written about five hundred years after the time of David (see "Authorship and Date" in the introduction), that is, sometime in the fifth century B.C.E.

in cases of redemption or exchange: to validate any transaction, one man would take off his sandal and hand it to the other The narrator elaborates on the details of the agreement to establish that proper procedure was followed. The only other passage in the Bible that mentions a sandal ritual is Deut. 25:5–10. There, a sandal is removed in the release ritual performed when a man refuses to carry out his prescribed duties as a levir (Rabbinic sources call the release ritual in Deuteronomy *ḥalitzah*). The parallels between the redemption ritual in Ruth 4 with that in Deuteronomy prompt many scholars to infer that the unnamed redeemer in Ruth is relinquishing specifically his levirate obligation. In fact, however, this verse makes just the *opposite* point: it specifies that the sandal ritual is used for *kol* (any or every) kind of transaction or transfer. If such was the case in ancient Israel, then Deut. 25:5–10 represents an instance of this general rule, adapted to the levirate situation. The transaction ratified here represents a different sort of case.[202] (On the function of the sandal, see below. For more on the ritual in Deut. 25:5–10, see "Levirate Marriage" in the introduction.)

one man would take off his sandal and hand it to the other Oral cultures rely on witnesses and symbolic gestures to ratify legal agreements. Although such rituals are not always described in preserved writings (since writing displaced them), we can assume that these practices continued, especially in agrarian communities, long after writing was adopted for formal legal matters. A sandal in particular lends itself easily to be used as such a symbol. Ibn Ezra observes more than a millennium later that a sandal is a common personal item that can be removed without leaving a person naked.[203] Nonetheless, there exists no reliable extra-biblical evidence for sandals being used in legal transactions in the ancient world.[204]

the practice Hebrew *te'udah,* a noun related to the word *'ed,* "witness" (see also Isa. 8:16 and 20). In modern Hebrew, *te'udah* designates official written proof, such as a graduation certificate. Both the ancient ritual gesture and the modern legal document serve the same function: to record or validate an agreement.

8. The narrator depicts a consensual, gentlemanly agreement here, in which no one is portrayed as guilty of dereliction. This is in sharp contrast to the sandal ritual of release described in Deut. 25:5–10, in which the widow spits on the levir who refuses to marry her and thus publicly shames him. This striking difference reinforces the conclusion that Ruth 4 is not depicting a levirate situation.

he drew off his sandal The pronoun is ambiguous, that is, it is not clear which man removes his sandal. Rabbinic sources record a debate on this matter (B. BM 47a). Some argue that Boaz removes his own sandal as an exchange for what he is receiving. Others argue that the unnamed redeemer removes his own sandal to symbolize what he is transferring. Rashi takes no side, whereas Ibn Ezra concludes that Boaz removes his sandal to symbolize an exchange.

drew off his sandal. 9 And Boaz said to the elders and
to the rest of the people, “You are witnesses today
that I am acquiring from Naomi all that belonged to
Elimelech and all that belonged to Chilion and
Mahlon. 10 I am also acquiring Ruth the Moabite,

נַעֲלֽוֹ׃ 9 וַיֹּאמֶר בֹּעַז לַזְּקֵנִים וְכָל־הָעָם
עֵדִים אַתֶּם הַיּוֹם כִּי קָנִיתִי אֶת־כָּל־אֲשֶׁר
לֶאֱלִימֶלֶךְ וְאֵת כָּל־אֲשֶׁר לְכִלְיוֹן וּמַחְלוֹן
מִיַּד נָעֳמִֽי׃ 10 וְגַם אֶת־רוּת הַמֹּאֲבִיָּה

LEGALIZING BOAZ’S MARRIAGE TO RUTH (4:9–10)

9. And Boaz said to the elders Boaz has convened ten representative elders to constitute a legal assembly at the city’s gate (see “gate” at 4:1 and “elders” at 4:2) to underscore the legality of the transaction. The pronouncement he now utters is thus addressed to a court, as it were, calling for formal ratification of his action. In the later halakhah, a “court” panel serves to witness whatever agreement parties work out themselves. Its members also assist the parties to come to an enduring agreement, within the bounds of precedent and communal norms. A similar mediating role may be supposed for the earlier Israelite tradition.

and to the rest of the people Presumably, a crowd has gathered at the gate after Boaz has summoned the elders. Boaz now addresses the entire community, to ensure broad communal support for the daring step he is taking.

You are witnesses *‘eidim ’attem.* Boaz’s speech begins and ends with this call to witness (see also 4:10 below). Obtaining the elders’ approval legalizes the arrangement. In the oral culture depicted in Ruth, such verbal affirmation confirms that a binding agreement has been reached and duly established. In literate cultures, witnesses memorialize their participation by signing their names on legal documents. In the fifth-century-B.C.E. Jewish community of Elephantine, Egypt, contracts, including marriage contracts, are always accompanied by several witnesses who sign their names.

that I am acquiring from Naomi all that belonged to Elimelech Boaz now casts his proposal in the broadest possible terms: redemption covers Elimelech’s entire patrimony and that of his sons.

and all that belonged to Chilion and Mahlon The mention of the two deceased brothers is relevant because Boaz will present Mahlon’s widow Ruth as a legitimate link in the chain of acquisitions and family lineage, a claim that helps him justify his next, rather radical step. Moreover, their father’s patrimony may count as the sons’ since he predeceased them.

10. I am also acquiring Ruth the Moabite, the wife of Mahlon, as my wife One contemporary reader has opined that Boaz’s marriage announcement must be one of the least attractive in Western literature.[205] But in its own literary context, Boaz’s declaration heralds a happy ending where everyone walks away content, satisfied that the right thing has been done and in the right fashion. Yet despite this happy ending, it is impossible to overlook the fact that Boaz’s announcement stands in tension with Deut. 23:4, which unequivocally states that “No Ammonite or Moabite shall be admitted into the congregation of the LORD; none of their descendants, even in the tenth generation, shall ever be admitted into the congregation of the LORD.” (See further at “The Status of the Moabites” in the introduction.) It is noteworthy that Boaz divides his transaction into two separate legal formulations: the acquisition of the land and his announcement of marriage. The two are distinct and subject to different presumptions.

the wife of Mahlon, as my wife, so as to perpetuate the name of the deceased upon his estate, that the

אֵ֫שֶׁת מַחְל֗וֹן קָנִ֨יתִי לִ֣י לְאִשָּׁ֔ה לְהָקִ֤ים
שֵׁם־הַמֵּת֙ עַל־נַ֣חֲלָת֔וֹ וְלֹֽא־יִכָּרֵ֥ת שֵׁם־

also Hebrew *ve-gam.* Campbell's translation as "And more important"[206] is overly emphatic but rightly draws attention to the force of this particle.

acquiring...as my wife Hebrew *kaniti li le-'ishah,* "acquired for myself as wife/woman." Significantly, the word "acquire" appears in Ruth only in this chapter (seven times). Elsewhere "acquire" can refer to acquiring property (Lev. 25:15) or slaves (Jer. 32:7–44), but also to wisdom (Prov. 4:5); for a fuller discussion of the semantic range, see "acquire the wife" comment at 4:5). Biblical texts usually refer to marriage with the verbs *lakaḥ*), as in Gen. 24:7, or *nasa'* as in Ruth 1:4, followed with the noun *'ishah* (woman or wife; see below). Although the verb *k-n-h* does not refer to marriage elsewhere in the Bible, the syntax and formulation Boaz employs are used elsewhere for marriage in the Bible and extra-biblical sources. D. H. Weiss points out that *k-n-h* is typically used in cases of multiple transactions, one of which involves the acquisition of land or slaves. Weiss and Brichto understand the verb to mean "acquiring the rights to/for" (see, e.g., comment at 4:6).[207] That is, Boaz is here declaring only that he has the right to marry Ruth and that no legal obstacles stand in the way. Although such an interpretation may be more palatable for modern readers than the idea of an outright acquisition of a wife, it remains speculative because the combination of "acquire" and "wife" in the Bible is unique to Ruth 4.[208] For further discussion, see "The Marriage of Boaz and Ruth" in the introduction.

Ruth the Moabite Boldly identifying Ruth as a Moabite at this point is essential for Boaz's plan. For him to obtain the community's approval of this unusual marriage with a Moabite, he must make full disclosure of all relevant factors in full view. It is clear from this declaration (as well as from 2:2,6,21; 4:5) that Ruth is not publicly regarded as an Israelite, even though she earlier committed herself to Naomi, to Naomi's people, and to Naomi's God (1:16). This challenges the view that Ruth has converted earlier in the story (see also "Intermarriage" and "Conversion" in the introduction). However, she is not identified as a Moabite from this point on. See "Ruth" at 4:13.

wife of Mahlon This relationship is critical for Boaz's plan to succeed. See comment at 4:10.

as my wife Hebrew *le-'ishah,* "as wife." This is formulaic language for marriage. The word *'ishah* can be translated as "woman" or "wife."[209] Context and preposition determine whether "wife" or "woman" is meant. For the first time (and one might be tempted to add, at last!), Boaz makes explicit the nature of his intended relationship with Ruth. Why is Boaz marrying Ruth? Zornberg judiciously concludes that Boaz does not marry Ruth out of obligation but rather out of *ḥesed.*[210] The entire negotiation has paved the way for this moment.

so as to perpetuate the name of the deceased upon his estate This public justification for his marriage to Ruth stands in tension with Boaz's private promise to her at the threshing floor (3:10–13), when he identified her as his sole concern. But by acknowledging his allegiance to community traditions, Boaz integrates his personal goal with larger, communal values, and thus defuses potential objections to this marriage. Boaz's statement evokes levirate marriage in Deut. 25:7: "to establish a name in Israel for his brother" (*lehakim le-'aḥiv shem be-yisra'el*) and also Gen. 38:8. By claiming this as his goal, Boaz links his marriage to Ruth with the well-known values of preserving a man's line, name, and

הַמֵּ֛ת מֵעִ֥ם אֶחָ֖יו וּמִשַּׁ֣עַר מְקוֹמ֑וֹ עֵדִ֥ים
אַתֶּ֖ם הַיּֽוֹם׃
11 וַיֹּ֨אמְר֜וּ כָּל־הָעָ֧ם אֲשֶׁר־בַּשַּׁ֛עַר וְהַזְּקֵנִ֖ים
עֵדִ֑ים יִתֵּן֩ יְהוָ֨ה אֶת־הָאִשָּׁ֜ה הַבָּאָ֣ה אֶל־

name of the deceased may not disappear from among his kinsmen and from the gate of his home town. You are witnesses today."

11 All the people at the gate and the elders answered, "We are. May the LORD make the woman

property beyond his death. (For details, see "perpetuate" at 4:5). Yet how is the marriage perpetuating the deceased's name? That name, after all, does not appear in the book's concluding genealogy (4:18–22). Appealing to the venerable goal of perpetuating the name of the deceased nonetheless enables Boaz to overcome a possible prohibition concerning marriage to Moabites (Deut. 23:4–7) or simply to render such a ban irrelevant.

that the name of the deceased may not disappear What looks like a restatement of the prior phrase may in fact refer to a different part of this transaction: first the acquisition of property and then the "acquisition" of Ruth. The two slightly different rationales for Boaz's actions would ensure that all legal conditions are covered.

may not disappear Hebrew *lo yikkaret,* "not be cut off." The same phrase appears in Isa. 56:5, where God promises certain eunuchs, who are unable to procreate, that God will give them an everlasting name [*yad va-shem*] that shall not perish (*lo yikkaret*). Numerous biblical texts depict the destruction or loss of name as a dreadful fate and a sign of utter annihilation (e.g., 2 Sam. 14:8; 2 Kings 14:27). In appealing to Moses to recognize their right to inherit, the five daughters of Zelophehad similarly point to the potential loss of their father's name as justification for receiving his inheritance/patrimony (Num. 27:4).[211] Jacob Milgrom, who explores the *karet* in the context of Leviticus, defines it as "excision and deprival of afterlife."[212] As extirpation, it can mean that the line of a person is terminated (so Ibn Ezra and also Tosefta on B. Shab. 25a); the deprivation can refer to not being able to join ancestors in death (whereas ordinarily one is gathered after death into one's family).[213]

from among his kinsmen and from the gate of his home town Boaz augments the intended results of his action to include the larger community as the repository of the deceased's name and memory. The language may be integral to the procedures of transferring rights legally.

You are witnesses today This second call to witnessing completes Boaz's announcement and frames it, emphasizing the legality of the proceedings. See comment at 4:9.

COMMUNAL RATIFICATION AND BLESSING OF THE MARRIAGE OF BOAZ AND RUTH (4:11–12)

11. All the people at the gate and the elders answered The unanimous consent by the entire assembly, especially the elders, formally ratifies the legitimacy of the union between Ruth and Boaz. Their support reinterprets or bypasses the law that excludes Moabites from the Israelite community (Deut. 23:4). However, at no point in this scene is that other law specifically mentioned. The main hint suggesting that Deuteronomy's law is a subtext here stems from the unusual steps that Boaz has taken in order to marry Ruth. His round-about negotiations with the would-be redeemer and his grand public declarations about his intentions are best explained if interpreted as attempts to circumvent an obstacle. The opposition to Moabites would constitute such an obstacle.

We are Hebrew *'eidim,* "witnesses." The Hebrew original conveys the emphatic legal support of the elders and the people who explicitly declare themselves "witnesses," as

בֵּיתֶ֔ךָ כְּרָחֵ֤ל ׀ וּכְלֵאָה֙ אֲשֶׁ֨ר בָּנ֤וּ שְׁתֵּיהֶם֙
אֶת־בֵּ֣ית יִשְׂרָאֵ֑ל וַעֲשֵׂה־חַ֣יִל בְּאֶפְרָ֔תָה

who is coming into your house like Rachel and Leah, both of whom built up the House of Israel! Prosper in Ephrathah and perpetuate your name in Beth-

Boaz demands. They repeat the very word, *'eidim,* with which Boaz begins and concludes his announcement (4:9 and 10), thereby formally sanctioning his proposal. With this one Hebrew word, the legal matter is sealed. With the blessings that follow, one can imagine the entire town cheering. The formulaic language in Boaz's announcement of his betrothal and the subsequent affirmation by witnesses may constitute the marriage ceremony itself. Such a simple public ritual would be consistent with marriage rituals from the ancient world (see comment below at 4:13). Unfortunately, the Bible itself is silent regarding marriage customs. The betrothal of Rebekah (Genesis 24) is the only detailed example pertaining to a marriage ritual, but it sheds no light on the present union (see comment below at 4:13 and "The Marriage of Boaz and Ruth" in the introduction). The unusual wording of the blessings that follow suggests that the community fully recognizes that this marriage is irregular but, nonetheless, chooses to validate it (see comment at 4:12).

May the Lord make the woman who is coming into your house like Rachel and Leah, both of whom built up the House of Israel! The communal blessings that follow the formal witnessing exude delight (as eleventh-century Jewish commentary Lekaḥ Tov makes the implicit sense explicit by adding "all rejoiced"). The blessings focus on prospects of birth. They also show that the people warmly welcome Ruth into the community. When Ruth first set out from Moab, she committed herself to Naomi's people ("your people shall be my people;" 1:16). But as Glover observes in his essay on ethnic identity, affiliation cannot be decided unilaterally.[214] The community has to be willing to accept that individual. The blessings offered by the people of Bethlehem signal acceptance and enact Ruth's integration into the community. In the remainder of the narrative, Ruth is no longer identified as a Moabite.

May the Lord make Hebrew *yitten YHWH,* "May YHWH give [the opportunity]" See the same phrase in 4:13, translated there as "The Lord let her."

the woman who is coming into your house Alsheikh makes the transgressive nature of the decision explicit when he adds the words "even though she is a Moabite." The biblical text is more subtle. See below.

the woman Hebrew *'ishah.* Elsewhere Ruth is called *na'arah,* "girl" (first by Boaz in 2:5 and again by the community in 4:12), suggesting an age difference between her and Boaz. The use of *'ishah* here, a term that can mean woman or wife, refers to her new status as a wife.

like Rachel and Leah These two sisters whom Jacob married are (together with their maidservants Bilhah and Zilpah) the progenitors of the twelve tribes of Israel (see Genesis 29–30). References to the matriarchs in the Bible outside of Genesis are quite rare. They appear in only three other places: 1 Sam. 10:2 mentions Rachel's tomb; Isa. 51:1–2 recalls Sarah as a source of hope for the postexilic community; and Jer. 31:15–20 announces that God responds to Rachel's bitter weeping over her children with a promise of hope and restoration. (Although Hosea undeniably refers to Rachel in Hos. 12:13, he does not name her.) Rachel is listed first because Jacob is first betrothed to her (even though the marriage with Leah is consummated first). Her priority is indicated, for example, in Gen. 31:4 ("Jacob had Rachel and Leah called to the field"). She is also Jacob's favorite wife, the one

lehem! 12 And may your house be like the house
of Perez whom Tamar bore to Judah—through the

וּקְרָא־שֵׁם בְּבֵית לָחֶם׃ 12 וִיהִי בֵיתְךָ
כְּבֵית פֶּרֶץ אֲשֶׁר־יָלְדָה תָמָר לִיהוּדָה

he loves (Gen. 29:18–20) and repeatedly recalls (48:7). The reference to Rachel and Leah honors Ruth by aligning her with the ancient matriarchs. Pesikta de-Rav Kahana emphasizes this alignment by having Boaz assure Ruth, who had called herself "foreigner," of her place with the matriarchs.[215] But the blessing goes even further: "These wishes not only make the Moabite woman Ruth, a 'foreign' woman, equal to the female ancestors of Israel: they also provide Ruth with the genealogy based on women."[216]

Malbim adds two additional, different perspectives. First, commenting on this verse, he notes Rachel and Leah's idolatrous origin as daughters of Laban; nevertheless (he says), they built the house of Israel: "So, too, should there be built from Ruth a faithful home." Second, commenting on the concluding genealogy, which he connects with transmigration of souls, Malbim interprets the reference to Rachel and Leah as part of David's defense of his Moabite ancestry: all Israelites (says David to his accusers) are the offspring of a prohibited union between a man and two sisters (see Lev. 18:18). In Ruth (Malbim expounds), the people and the elders "understood that all of this 'deceit' was necessary to bring forth precious souls from the hands of oppressors."[217]

both of whom built up the House of Israel The two sisters in Genesis 29–30 initially compete with each other but channel that competition into producing children (see 29:34; 30:8). This verse celebrates the productive nature of their rivalry and its fertile results. The built-up house of "Israel" refers either to Jacob himself or (more likely) to the people as a whole.

Prosper Hebrew *'aseh ḥayil,* literally "do [something] mighty." The NRSV translates this phrase as "produce children," an interpretation that cannot be justified, given how *ḥayil* is used elsewhere in this book (see comments at 2:1; 3:11). Here it probably implies both economic prosperity and social virtues.

Ephrathah An old name for Bethlehem and also the name of a biblical ancestress, Ephrat, wife of Caleb, whose lineage leads to Boaz. See further "Ephrathites" at 1:2. This linguistic association with a female ancestress may be deliberate.

perpetuate your name The Hebrew *u-kera shem,* "and call a name" (imperative, second person singular, masculine). This phrase could also be interpreted as "be called by name." Although the present translation specifies that the blessing calls for Boaz's name to be perpetuated, the Hebrew is more ambiguous. The NRSV translation has "bestow a name," and the KJV has "be famous." Rashi explains that it means "your name will be great." Brichto favors "continue/perpetuate the family line," similar to "perpetuate the name" (*lehakim shem*) in 4:5 and 4:10.[218]

12. may your house be like the house of Perez Perez is the offspring of an illicit union and a failed levirate arrangement, which is nonetheless affirmed in the biblical text as right (Genesis 38; see below). By choosing this transgressive episode as a model for their blessing, the witnesses here may be acknowledging the irregular nature of the union between Boaz and Ruth, yet nonetheless affirming its rightness (see below).

Perez The name means "a breach" or "a break." Perez is so named because he pushes his way out of the womb ahead of his twin brother. When his head appears, the midwife says, "'What a breach you have made for yourself!' So he was named Perez" (Gen. 38:29). Outside of Genesis and Ruth, Perez appears only in a few genealogies (e.g., 1 Chron.

offspring which the LORD will give you by this young woman."

מִן־הַזֶּ֗רַע אֲשֶׁ֨ר יִתֵּ֤ן יְהוָה֙ לְךָ֔ מִן־הַֽנַּעֲרָ֖ה הַזֹּֽאת׃

2:4–5), a total of twelve times in the entire Hebrew Bible, three of them in Ruth. In Genesis 38, Perez is a sign of both rupture and blessing because the birth of twins usually symbolizes divine blessings or approval. His prominence in Ruth, evident in this blessing and also in the concluding genealogy (4:18), serves a double function. His story helps legitimize the union of Ruth and Boaz, a union that is likewise under the cloak of suspicion yet is here welcomed and affirmed. In addition, it underscores the unusual nature of this union and the ways in which it breaches the wall that has excluded Moabites.

whom Tamar bore to Judah According to Genesis 38, Judah impregnates Tamar without knowing that she is his widowed daughter-in-law (see "Ruth's Relationship to Other Biblical Books" in the introduction). The intricate story in Genesis begins as an attempted but failed levirate marriage (38:7–10). The story reaches its climax when Tamar's pregnancy by Judah becomes obvious, and Judah (still ignorant of his role) condemns her to death for harlotry (38:24). Tamar proves to Judah that he is the father, at which point he proclaims: "She is more in the right than I, inasmuch as I did not give her to my son Shelah" (38:26). The story of Judah and Tamar is a trickster's tale that rights a wrong (done to Tamar, who was not given her due as a childless widow) by non-conventional means. In the end, Tamar is pronounced righteous by Judah. The birth of twins, one of whom is Perez, signals divine favor as well. As a descendant of Perez, Boaz continues the line of that earlier incestuous union. (Ruth herself is a descendant of earlier incest between Lot and his older daughter; see "Moabite women" at 1:4 and "The Status of the Moabites" in the introduction.)

Reference to this particular episode discloses communal awareness that this present union also crosses certain boundaries; at the same time, such reference justifies such crossing. Yet who is the trickster in this tale? Ruth, like Tamar, takes risks; she provokes a patriarch (on the threshing floor) to do the right thing. But Adler suggests that this time the trickster is Boaz, who manipulates the negotiations at the gate through rhetoric and other means (intimidation?) so as to justify his marriage to Ruth in spite of the prohibition concerning Moabites.[219] At a symbolic level, the allusions to, and connections between, these different "tricksters" reverse and undo the earlier "histories." As Ruth's acts of generosity toward Naomi reverse the inhospitable behavior that first led to the exclusion of Moabites (see Deut. 23:4–9), so too the actions of Boaz "reverse" the story of Judah, who acted so precipitously and dishonorably when he unexpectedly encountered a woman.

through the offspring A blessing for progeny concludes the scene at the city gate. The stranger—poor and a widow—has now been welcomed heartily into the community. A hoped-for child will restore a link to the broken genealogy with which the book began. As for "offspring," Hebrew: *zer'*, "offspring" or "seed," the Bible repeatedly attributes *zer'* not only to men but also to women. For both men and women have offspring. Instances include the following:

- God speaks regarding the first woman: "her seed or offspring" (*zar'ah;* Gen. 3:15);
- An angel speaks to Hagar: "your offspring" (*zar'ekh;* Gen. 16:10);
- Rebekah's family blesses her: "your offspring" (*zar'ekh;* Gen. 24:60);
- Regarding a priest's daughter: "and she has no offspring" (*ve-zera' eyn lah;* Lev. 22:13); and
- Zion is personified as a woman: "your offspring" (*zar'ekh;* Isa. 54:3).

13 וַיִּקַּ֨ח בֹּ֤עַז אֶת־רוּת֙ וַתְּהִי־ל֣וֹ לְאִשָּׁ֔ה
וַיָּבֹ֖א אֵלֶ֑יהָ וַיִּתֵּ֨ן יְהוָ֥ה לָ֛הּ הֵרָי֖וֹן וַתֵּ֥לֶד

13 So Boaz married Ruth; she became his wife, and
he cohabited with her. The LORD let her conceive,

which the* LORD *will give you Biblical texts frequently connect pregnancy with God's actions in the world. In doing so, they distance procreation from mere biology. The well-known biblical stories about barren women exemplify this perspective. Thus, for example, Sarah conceives only when God "takes note" of her (Gen. 21:1; see also Rebekah in Gen. 25:21, Rachel in Gen. 30:32, Hannah in 1 Sam. 1:19, and Manoah's wife in Judges 13). On the significance of God's role in Ruth's pregnancy, see "the LORD let her conceive" below at 4:13.

young woman Hebrew *na'arah*. See also 2:6. Ruth's youthfulness is evoked also in Boaz's first address to her as "my daughter" (2:8 and 3:10,11). But note that she is referred to as a "woman" when Boaz finds her at his feet on the threshing floor (3:8), when he contemplates her return to Naomi's home (3:14), and in the people's blessing in 4:11. Calling her young is relevant in the context of childbearing.

BETROTHAL, BIRTH, AND BLESSINGS (4:13–17)

The final scene celebrates marriage and birth, as well as the prospect of redemptive sustenance for Naomi's old age. As in a Jane Austen novel, all ends well: the wise and worthy woman without means is safely lodged in the arms and home of the best possible husband, and the woman for whose sake she risked all is likewise secure. The future looks bright, made even brighter by the disclosure that these events ultimately lead to the birth of Israel's most beloved king.

Throughout the chapter, Ruth and Naomi remain silent. In this section they are surrounded by the town's women who will have the last reported words in the book, as they name Ruth's child and interpret his significance. Earlier, the scene at the gate focused primarily on perpetuating a deceased man's name, with Boaz's marriage to Ruth as the means to this end (4:5 and 4:10). The present scene focuses on providing sustenance for living women, especially Naomi. In the Book of Ruth, male agenda and female agenda differ yet do not conflict; both eventually find their happy resolutions and combine into a harmonious whole.

Verse 13 is Janus-faced, serving as the conclusion to the proclamations at the gate, and introducing the consequences that follow. This verse tersely spans about nine months and major events in the protagonists' life. One can see parallels with the passage 1:1–5 that sums up more than ten years in a rapid-fire manner before similarly slowing down to focus on Naomi. But whereas Naomi in Chapter 1 is the first and central spokesperson, this time the microphone (as it were) has been handed to the neighboring women who have the last words in the book. Like the chorus in classical Athenian drama, these women give voice to the meaning of what has transpired: through the newborn, Naomi's lifeline that had been cut at the beginning of the book (1:1–5) is renewed. The book's conclusion, then, mirrors and symbolically rectifies the events of its beginning, bringing the story full circle: Naomi's hopeless situation and emptiness (see especially 1:11–13 and 1:21) are transformed as she embraces the child who now is reckoned as hers.

13. So Boaz married Ruth; she became his wife Literally, "And Boaz took Ruth, and she became to him a wife/woman." The language is formulaic (see below) and thereby underlines the legality of the union as a marriage. Unfortunately, the Bible does not define legal marriages or describe wedding ceremonies that make them legal. Very likely the scene witnessed in 4:10–12 constitutes the wedding ceremony, with the narrator confirming in 4:13 that it was properly enacted. [220]

Evidence from other ancient cultures is not always clear or applicable. Yet the preserved marriage contracts from a Jewish military colony in Elephantine, Egypt, in the fifth century B.C.E. shed interesting light on the subject. In these documents, dated roughly to the time of the likely composition of Ruth, the man declares that he was given the woman as wife by a member of her family (e.g., a brother).[221] He also declares his intention (in print and before witnesses) to take her as wife. The document lists the items that she brings to the joint household and establishes that she is entitled to take them back if the couple divorces. We learn that either spouse may end the marriage by declaring their intention to do so to the congregation, which will act as witness. Yet although specific witnesses sign the marriage contract, there is no indication whether a wider congregation also witnesses the marriage ceremony and offers verbal ratification.[222] (See also "Marriage" in the introduction.)

married Hebrew *lakaḥ,* "he took," the typical biblical term for marriage, occasionally without the addition of "as wife" (Exod. 2:1, 1 Kings 3:1, Hos. 1:3). To modern readers, "take" conjures up a setting wherein the woman is a passive object to be taken or given at will. In the Bible, however, this language aptly represents the social world in which the woman moves to her husband's household. The more felicitous term from a modern perspective, *nas'a,* literally, "carried" or "lifted up" (see comment on "married" at 1:4), suggests that marriage elevates the woman. The word *nas'a* as a term for marriage appears only in late biblical texts but has become the more common term for marriage in postbiblical Hebrew (*nissu'in*).[223] Interestingly, *nas'a* in the Bible appears only in the context of mixed marriages—in Ruth 1:4; Ezra 9:2,12; and 10:44, all referring to Judahite men marrying non-Judahite women. It may suggest that in marrying a non-Israelite, the man elevates his wife who, as a foreigner, is perhaps regarded as of a lower status.

she became his wife The narrator indicates that the marriage between Ruth and Boaz is not a unilateral act by one spouse but one in which each actively participates. In biblical parlance, the statement "Boaz took Ruth" (with or without the addition of "as wife"; see Exod. 2:1) suffices to signal marriage. Yet the narrator adds that she became his wife, underscoring not only the legality of her new status but also her active role in this transaction. This emphasis may relate to Ruth's being an adult who enters the relationship on her own accord. A similar idiom is used for David's marriages with Abigail in 1 Sam. 25:42 and with Bathsheba in 2 Sam. 11:27. In all three cases, the bride is a widow (in Num. 30:10, a widow is independent enough to be entitled to make vows without male consent). Another place where this expression appears is Num. 36:11, when Zelophehad's daughters, as land-owners, marry relatives, choosing husbands for themselves. This particular formulation, therefore, may be preferred in cases when the woman is her own agent or when there is no male who exercises authority over the woman. See also 1:12–13.[224]

he cohabited with her Literally, "he came to her" or "he entered her," using the verb *b-w-'* (see Gen. 6:18, regarding Noah's entering the ark; or Exod. 12:25, regarding the Israelites' entering the land of Israel). This expression sometimes indicates a sexual union. In later Rabbinic law, such "entering" (*bi'ah*), understood as consummation, is one of the acts that constitute marriage (see M. Kid. 1.1).

The LORD let her conceive Literally, "YHWH gave [*va-yitten*] her pregnancy." In verse 11, the people wished that God will make (*yitten*) Ruth fertile. Now God acts to grant Ruth pregnancy. God's role in conception is frequently highlighted in the Bible in the case of barren women who subsequently give birth to sons, indicating that these births

and she bore a son. 14 And the women said to
Naomi, "Blessed be the LORD, who has not withheld a redeemer from you today! May his name be

בֵּֽן׃ 14 וַתֹּאמַ֤רְנָה הַנָּשִׁים֙ אֶֽל־נָעֳמִ֔י בָּר֣וּךְ
יְהֹוָ֗ה אֲשֶׁר֩ לֹ֣א הִשְׁבִּ֥ית לָ֛ךְ גֹּאֵ֖ל הַיּ֑וֹם

are specifically sanctioned by God (as in the stories of Sarah, Rebekah, Rachel, and Hannah). Yet although Ruth is childless after ten years of marriage (1:4), the narrator never states that she is barren. Such an omission already differentiates this mother's story from those of others who conceive after long delay. In addition, the expression used here is unique in the Bible: God directly bestows pregnancy upon Ruth (not simply opens her womb, as is more common; see Gen. 29:31). God's presence at this juncture unequivocally signals God's blessing of Ruth. Her integration is now complete. Ruth's initial vow (1:16) had expressed her commitment to Naomi, to Naomi's people, and to Naomi's God. Now all three recipients of her loyalty have reciprocated—Naomi, the people (4:11–12), and God. Furthermore, this divine action also highlights the book's distinctive theology: although the various figures in the book—Naomi, Ruth, Boaz, and the people—mention God frequently, it is only here that the narrator credits God with intervention in human affairs. For instance, in 1:6, God is only the subject of hearsay: Naomi has "heard that the LORD had taken note of His people and given them food." Elsewhere God's name is invoked when people bless each other. Here, however, God's action follows the generous actions of those people for whom God is a blessed reality.

A midrash makes a similar point. Commenting on the fortuitous appearance of the would-be redeemer in 4:1, the midrash has God proclaim: "Boaz did his [part], and Ruth did hers, and Naomi did hers; [then] the Holy One said: 'I too will do mine'" (Ruth R. 7.7; see also Lekach Tov on 4:1). This sequence of actions in Ruth, climaxing with God's intercession only after the human protagonists have done their best, is one of many reasons why calling Ruth "a human comedy" (as Trible does)[225] is so apt. This phrase (in a clear allusion to Dante's "Divine Comedy") underscores the book's focus on ordinary human beings whose actions bring God's presence into the world. (See further "The Theology of the Book of Ruth" in the introduction.)

and she bore a son The birth of a son in the Bible typically signifies divine favor. This event could have served as the conclusion to the book. But as befits a tale about *ḥesed,* about exceeding expectations, the narrative does not stop here, but returns to the still vulnerable and bereft Naomi to address her plight.

14. the women said to Naomi Like Ruth, the narrator does not forsake Naomi. As its climax, the book's conclusion lingers on the restoration of Naomi's life and lineage, surrounding Naomi with women who make her the center of their concern. The old, childless widow whose hopes have been dashed by life's severe blows is not to be left behind. She now becomes the recipient of blessings as well as a progenitor.

Blessed be the LORD, who has not withheld a redeemer from you today! The townswomen of Bethlehem have the last speeches in the book (see also comment at 4:17). Earlier blessings were conferred upon Boaz, blessings that included Ruth (4:11–12). Now the women bestow blessings on Naomi as well and cast her as the chief beneficiary of all that has transpired. They witnessed her "emptiness" when she first returned from Moab (1:19–21); now they celebrate her "redeemer." In this sense, the book ultimately becomes Naomi's story, with Ruth serving as a vehicle for Naomi's restoration.

withheld Hebrew *hishbit,* "to bring to a cessation." The verbal root *sh-b-t* refers to bringing to an end or conclusion, as God did on the seventh day of creation (Gen. 2:2), perpetuated in Israel! 15 He will renew your life and sustain your old age; for he is born of your daughter-

וְיִקָּרֵא שְׁמוֹ בְּיִשְׂרָאֵל׃ 15 וְהָיָה לָךְ לְמֵשִׁיב
נֶפֶשׁ וּלְכַלְכֵּל אֶת־שֵׂיבָתֵךְ כִּי כַלָּתֵךְ

from which the term "Shabbat" comes. In the present situation, it means that the promise of a redeemer for Naomi has not come to end, even though it may have looked that way earlier (in Chapter 1).

a redeemer Hebrew *go'el,* the same term translated elsewhere in the book as a "redeeming kinsman" (e.g., 3:9). In sharp contrast to the negotiations at the gate, where redemption primarily concerned Elimelech's patrimony, the redeemer here is seen as solely for the benefit of Naomi. The next verse makes clear that the redeemer is the son whom Ruth has borne.

Why then is Boaz not reckoned here as Naomi's redeemer (as per 2:20, when Naomi divulges that Boaz is one of their redeemers)? The likely answer goes back to Naomi's emptiness, so poignantly expressed in 1:19–21. The narrator here addresses her specific loss, her lack of progeny, an emptiness that will be reversed or filled by the redeemer who will care for her. The women soon describe the role of this redeemer in light of such loss.

from you The women are firm in their claim that it is Naomi who is the true beneficiary of this child's birth (not, as some suggest, Elimelech).[226]

May his name be perpetuated in Israel! Hebrew *yikkarei' shemo beyisra'el,* "Let his name be called in Israel." As in 4:11, the verb translated here as "perpetuated" comes from *k-r-'.* "to call," the typical verb for naming, as in the naming of Perez (Gen. 38:29) and Moses (Exod. 2:10). This verb differs from that which Boaz uses in 4:5 and 4:10 (*lehakim*) to denote establishing or perpetuating a name, that is, preserving the legacy of the deceased. This distinction is important because it guards the reader against concluding that Ruth's child is perceived as an heir to the deceased men of the house of Elimelech. The idiom of the women's blessing is virtually identical to that bestowed upon Boaz in verse 11, now cast in the third person. Although grammatically the subject of the verb could be God's name, more likely it refers to the child's name or reputation. As in 4:11, the verb might refer to proclaiming the name of the child publicly as a form of honor.

Israel The women's choice of "Israel" here in place of "Bethlehem" (as in 4:11) broadly expands the scope of their blessings, conferring on the newborn even greater renown than that bestowed upon his father. However, nothing further is known about either Obed or Boaz apart from this book and the genealogy in 1 Chron. 2:11–12.

15. He will renew your life and sustain your old age; for he is born of your daughter-in-law As Trible observes, "the celebration is more than the joy of a male child."[227] The significance of the child's birth centers on what it discloses about Ruth and what it means for Naomi. Furthermore, the women define the term "redeemer" for this specific situation: the redeemer is one who will take care of the aged Naomi. This sustaining role is consistent with the tenor of the redemption laws described in Leviticus 25, even though those laws do not specify a case such as this one. But the defined role differs from the redeemer's task that was earlier depicted at the city's gate (4:5 and 4:10), with Boaz as the legally qualified redeemer. Although the foci of the two groups—men and women—differ completely, they are not perceived as mutually exclusive; on the contrary, the book offers a resolution for both sets of priorities. Oddly, the newborn child's destiny/purpose is disclosed even before his name (which appears only in 4:17), in marked contrast to most other naming in the Bible (e.g., Exod. 2:10). This reverse sequence highlights the child's importance as Naomi's redeemer.

in-law, who loves you and is better to you than seven sons."

אֲשֶׁר־אֲהֵבַתֶךְ יְלָדַתּוּ אֲשֶׁר־הִיא טוֹבָה לָךְ מִשִּׁבְעָה בָּנִים׃

renew your life Hebrew *meshiv nefesh,* "one who restores [or renews] your life/*nefesh.*" The Hebrew contains a wordplay: *meshiv,* "restore" or "renew," derives from the verbal root, *sh-w-b*, meaning "return." Naomi used the same verb earlier when complaining that God had brought her back to Israel (*heshivani*) empty (1:21). The verb also echoes *hishbit,* "bring to an end," used in the previous verse (the similarity in sound is obscured in English; both contain the Hebrew letters *sh-b-t*).

life Hebrew *nefesh.* In the Bible, the word *nefesh* refers to the entire person or simply life, although it is sometimes translated as "soul" (as in the Shema blessing, Deut. 6:5). The normative Bible view understands a human being as a psychophysical unit, an embodied spirituality that cannot be separated into "body" and "soul." God infuses the first human being with breath, making the person "a living being," a *nefesh ḥayah* (Gen. 2:7). The *nefesh,* then, designates the vital self. It is often used to express feelings, as when Jonathan's *nefesh* becomes bound with David's (1 Sam 18:1) or the Psalmist's *nefesh* is consumed with longing for God (Ps. 119:20), both times translated as "soul." Yet *nefesh* is not independent of the physicality of the body. Thus Deut 12:23 prohibits consuming blood, "for the blood is the *nefesh.*"[228]

and sustain your old age As Trible so aptly puts it, the townswomen are concerned with the welfare of living women, not with the names of deceased men. Here they address this issue in socio-economic terms. The child's purpose, as the women interpret it, is twofold. First, he will ensure Naomi's economic survival (although in practical terms, it will be years before the child can support her materially—until then, Naomi presumably will depend on Boaz's and Ruth's generosity). Second, his very existence will sustain Naomi emotionally and spiritually from the day of his birth. In thus characterizing Ruth's child as a source of both economic and emotional sustenance, the women place the child in a larger context of symbolic and cultural meanings, redefining thereby the nature of family. The same verb (*kalkel*) "to sustain" is ascribed to God in the opening lines of the Amidah prayer, addressing God as the one "who sustains (*mekhalkel*) life with *ḥesed.*"

for he is born of your daughter-in-law This sentence makes clear that the redeemer whom the women celebrate is the child, not Boaz, another surprising turn of events, given Boaz's touted role as the redeeming kin (2:20; 3:12; 4:4). But the women's proclamation does more. It credits Ruth the mother with producing the redeemer, not Boaz the father. The declaration thus forges a genealogical link in a new way: not only a daughter or a son, but also a daughter-in-law, can secure redemption and lineage. Whereas at the gate Ruth was portrayed as a means for perpetuating the lifeline of men, here she is a means for perpetuating the lifeline of a woman.

Ruth is not named in this verse. Her identity is inextricably bound up with Naomi as Naomi's daughter-in-law. It is this binding tie that reconstitutes the lineage of Naomi.

who loves you Love is depicted as loyalty and devotion. This is the only time that the root *a-h-v* appears in the Book of Ruth. The Bible rarely mentions a woman's love. Rebekah loves her son Jacob (Gen. 25:28); Michal, King Saul's daughter, loves the young David (1 Sam. 18:20 and 28), and the woman in Song of Songs repeatedly describes her lover as the one she loves (Songs 1:7; 3:1,2,3,4). Love in the Bible ranges from physical or erotic love to love as loyalty, nurturing, or devotion. It is also a covenant term. The most frequent references focus on God as the one who loves and who deserves love, as in the

16 Naomi took the child and held it to her bosom.
She became its foster mother, 17 and the women
neighbors gave him a name, saying, "A son is born to

16 וַתִּקַּח נָעֳמִי אֶת־הַיֶּלֶד וַתְּשִׁתֵהוּ
בְחֵיקָהּ וַתְּהִי־לוֹ לְאֹמֶנֶת׃ 17 וַתִּקְרֶאנָה
לוֹ הַשְּׁכֵנוֹת שֵׁם לֵאמֹר יֻלַּד־בֵּן לְנָעֳמִי

Shema formulation (Deut. 6:4–9). The verb, therefore, usually carries the sense of commitment and complete dedication. Tellingly, the Targum replaces the verb with *reḥimit,* a word for compassion (also related to *reḥem,* "womb").

better to you than seven sons So high is the women's regard for Ruth that they set her even higher than the proverbial seven sons elsewhere understood as the perfect example of a blessed family (see Job 1:2 and 42:13). At the beginning of the book, Naomi bitterly complains about losing the men in her life and sees no future for herself or her daughters-in-law without a son (1:12–13). The women's statement here stands as a radical departure from the perspective that only men can offer security. Affirming a woman's worth as greater than seven sons is itself already a challenge to patriarchal culture, with its emphasis on sons. Affirming the worth of a Moabite woman is an even more astonishing claim. With this proclamation, the women greatly praise the beneficence of Ruth.[229]

16. Naomi took the child and held it to her bosom. She became its foster mother This wordless gesture signals the bonding between Naomi and Ruth's child. With the embracing of new life and future security, a life of loss has now been transformed.[230] Naomi's active engagement with the child is highlighted by the verbs "she took" and "she held." Although the text signals a formal bond between Naomi and the newborn, attempts to discern in the action and words a ritual of adoption in line with biblical and ancient Near Eastern sources have not been successful.[231]

foster mother Hebrew *'omenet,* a term that connotes a trusty caregiver or a parent *in locos* (i.e., a parental surrogate who is not biologically the parent). Mordechai is such an *'omen* to Esther, who is an orphan (Esther 2:7), and Moses refers to this role when he asks God: "Did I conceive all this people, did I bear them, that You should say to me, 'Carry them in your bosom as a nurse [*'omen*] carries an infant'" (Num. 11:12). See also 2 Sam. 4:4, as well as 2 Kings 10:1,5 where the masculine plural form may refer to guardians of the royal children (or so NJPS understands the term).

17. the women neighbors gave him a name In the Bible, a child is typically named by the mother (see Leah and Rachel in Genesis 29–30) or father (see Gen. 16:15 or 21:3). (There is some ambiguity about who bestows the name when midwives are on the scene, as in Gen. 38:27–30 when Tamar gives birth to twins.) Naming rarely functions as an act of authority over a person or a person's destiny. Most often, it discloses the expectations of the one who bestows the name.

women neighbors Hebrew *shekheinot.* This term in the feminine appears elsewhere only in Exod. 3:22 (singular noun there; plural here). Carol Meyers observes that the presence of such neighboring women reflects one of the many ways in which women who lived in adjacent households provided mutual aid and support for each other.[232] Only a few birth narratives mention additional persons present, always women (Gen. 35:17; 38:28; 1 Sam. 4:20, as well as the midwives in Exodus 1). Sasson finds in Ruth's case vestiges of myths familiar from Egyptian and Mesopotamian sources in which midwives or goddesses have "fate-establishing duties."[233] Such motifs are typically associated with royal births.

A son is born to Naomi! The women redefine kinship by providing Naomi with a genealogical lineage where a "blood line" does not exist legally or biologically. (Ibn Ezra

Naomi!" They named him Obed; he was the father of Jesse, father of David.

וַתִּקְרֶ֫אנָה שְׁמוֹ֙ עוֹבֵ֔ד ה֥וּא אֲבִי־יִשַׁ֖י אֲבִ֥י דָוִֽד׃ פ

connects this statement with the relation of Pharaoh's daughter to baby Moses in Exod. 2:10.) Ruth is not mentioned by name in this scene. Some contemporary readers are troubled by the seemingly surrogate position to which Ruth is relegated. Is she, the foreign woman, thus devalued in favor of the Israelite member of the local community, Naomi? Does this scene represent a symbolic adoption by Naomi, designed to remove the stigma of Moabite origin from the child's famed descendant, David?[234] But such interpretations go against the grain of the narrative that shows how *ḥesed* triumphs over loss. As early interpreters already understood, the women are not negating Ruth's role as mother but rather are extending the child's connection to Naomi. The women who once welcomed Naomi and heard her lament of emptiness (1:21) now "intuit the significance of this child in restoring Naomi to her former 'maternal' self.... They recognize that it is Naomi and not Ruth who is fulfilled by the child's birth."[235]

From an anthropological point of view, the non-biological lineage for Naomi and the child is not unusual. Traditional genealogies are subject to retrojection for the purpose of establishing new kinship structures.[236] What is unusual here is that the forging of the new kinship link is done in full view of the community and by means of a woman. No attempt is made to disguise its constructed rather than inherited nature.

born to Hebrew *yulad le-*. This genealogical expression is not common and appears primarily in Genesis (e.g., Gen. 4:26). It is also used in public proclamations of birth announcements: in Isa. 9.5 (followed by "us," referring to the community) and Jer. 20:15 (followed by "you," referring to the father). This is the only place when this expression is applied to a woman.[237]

They named him Obed; he was the father of Jesse, father of David The broken male genealogical line found in 1:1–5 is now symbolically restored, this time highlighting the women. The record continues for three generations. In this context, Naomi becomes the progenitor of this line and the linchpin of continuity.

Obed The name literally means "one who serves" or "one who works," from the root *ʿ-bh-d,* to serve or work. The role that the women assign the new child (4:15) loosely connects to the name, in that they envision him as serving Naomi's needs in her old age. This Obed is mentioned only in Ruth and in the parallel Davidic genealogy in 1 Chron. 2:12.

Jesse... David This comment, usually regarded as integral to the book (in contrast to the genealogy that follows), places a woman at the head of a royal lineage. It also reveals that the story is told from some temporal distance, looking back from the time of David, the most prominent king of Israel, or from an even greater distance. David's name concludes the narrative. The subsequent genealogy embeds the story of Ruth, Naomi, and Boaz in a wider canvas.

EPILOGUE: REWEAVING THE WEB OF LIFE—THE CONCLUDING GENEALOGY (4:18–22)

The Book of Ruth could have ended with the report of David's birth in 4:17. Instead, the author continues with an all-male genealogy, typical of other genealogies in the Bible. This genealogy retraces the family line to an earlier time and concludes with David as its latest member. For an ancient audience, this final genealogy would have been an exhilarating conclusion: good people have been rewarded with the high honor of illustrious progeny. Still, the final list of men, traversing centuries with no reference to the mothers who gave them birth, is jarring in a book so heavily centered on women. From a certain perspective, therefore, this final genealogy seems to co-opt this women's story and subsume it within an all-too-common male-centered lineage.

But from another perspective, looking at the book as a whole, this concluding genealogy actually transforms the patriarchal focus of the male genealogies so prevalent in the Bible. The narrator has carefully traced the arduous (if often elsewhere unacknowledged) work of women, exposing women's active presence behind a statement such as "And Boaz begot Obed" (4:21). By giving a highly textured account of what leads to the forging of a genealogical link, Ruth challenges a simplistic or androcentric interpretation of this genealogical chain—and thus of all others. In addition, this genealogy weaves a story of women back into the larger fabric of Israel's history, thus augmenting and fleshing out both the world of women and the world of men.

Consequently, even if the Book of Ruth is understood (as some suggest) as a mere backdrop to explain King David's lineage, it should also be read as an affirmation of women's roles in bringing him into the world. The final genealogy forces us to recognize and reflect on the lost stories embedded in other biblical genealogies. In addition, this particular genealogy, beginning with Perez, whose name means "breach," signals a subversive dimension to the book, undermining a flat reading of the text (see below "Perez" at 4:18).

The genealogy spans ten generations. In the Bible, ten generations typically demarcate an epoch (e.g., the period from Adam to Noah in Gen. 5:3–32, and from Shem, Noah's son, to Abraham in Gen. 11:10–26). Such genealogies, like other genealogies in the ancient world, do not necessarily preserve accurate historical records but rather are constructed to express a community's ideology about its identity, or to establish the legitimacy of certain structures or persons. In linear genealogies (listing only father and son but not siblings), the names at the beginning and the end mark persons of special prestige or power whose connection with each other needs to be established. The names in between may be obscure, and generations may be telescoped to highlight the important figures.[238] In the case of Ruth 4:18–22, the actual time span stretching between Perez and David would have to be considerably longer than ten generations. An accurate or complete genealogy would thus be expected to include additional names.

Determining the purpose of this concluding genealogy is complicated because it is no longer possible to ascertain whether the genealogy in Ruth was organic to the book or derives from an independent tradition. On the one hand, it is possible that the genealogy was appended to Ruth by a later hand (perhaps to grant the story importance and justify the book's preservation as Scripture).[239] On the other, conceivably, Ruth was composed to provide this genealogy and family history for David, possibly spurred by some challenges to his legitimacy or, conversely, by a cultural tendency to elaborate on the ancestry of national heroes. (In addition, the connection to David may have served to legitimize a counterpoint to the reforms of Ezra and Nehemiah, which exclude Moabite women.) Unfortunately, the similar genealogy in 1 Chron. 2:4–15, which includes all the same names, does not shed light on the matter because 1 Chronicles is late, dated to the fourth century B.C.E. or later.[240] Despite the many uncertainties, it is possible to discern what the genealogy accomplishes in its present canonical location:

• Stylistically, it mirrors and reverses the Prologue (1:1–7), which recorded the death of several men.

• Thematically, by concluding with the birth of David, the book honors those whose efforts led to Israel's most illustrious king and dynast. In particular, the book extols

[18] This is the line of Perez: Perez begot Hezron,
[19] Hezron begot Ram, Ram begot Amminadab,
[20] Amminadab begot Nahshon, Nahshon begot

18 וְאֵ֙לֶּה֙ תּוֹלְד֣וֹת פָּ֔רֶץ פֶּ֖רֶץ הוֹלִ֥יד אֶת־
חֶצְרֽוֹן׃ 19 וְחֶצְרוֹן֙ הוֹלִ֣יד אֶת־רָ֔ם וְרָ֖ם
הוֹלִ֥יד אֶת־עַמִּֽינָדָֽב׃ 20 וְעַמִּֽינָדָב֙ הוֹלִ֣יד
אֶת־נַחְשׁ֔וֹן וְנַחְשׁ֖וֹן הוֹלִ֥יד אֶת־שַׂלְמָֽה׃

the women, the man who responded to their plight, and the virtue of *ḥesed* that made such a birth possible.

• The double emphasis on David as the culmination of the book (4:17 and 4:22) also highlights David's threefold ancestry—as son of Ruth, Naomi, and Boaz.

• It validates a union with a Moabite woman by "splicing" it into an all-male genealogy that "normalizes" and legitimizes it.

But more is at work here: what is usually overlooked in the interpretation of the book is that this genealogy that validates a union with a Moabite woman also acknowledges it as a breach. This point is embedded in the name "Perez" used to begin the genealogy.

18. This is the line of Perez: Perez begot On the meaning of this name and the story behind it, see comment at 4:12. Rashi explains that now, having related David to Ruth the Moabite, the text links him to Judah. But it is significant that the genealogy focuses on Perez, not Judah. The triple mention of Perez's name in this section of Ruth (twice in this verse and once earlier in 4:12) calls special attention to him. The choice to conclude with a genealogy that begins with Perez makes breach and blessings (both of which he represents) an important interpretive key to the book.

the line Hebrew *toledot.* This term is a conjugated form of the verb *y-l-d,* which refers to birth and is here in plural form (lit. "These are the birthings of..."). It is used extensively to bind Genesis together by means of genealogies (e.g., Gen. 2:4; 6:9; 36:1; 36:9; 37:2), and thus connects Ruth to Genesis. It is also common in Numbers and in Chronicles, but only rarely appears elsewhere in this expression (*'eilleh toledot*).

19–20. Hezron The name appears with slight modifications in some ancient versions such as the Septuagint. From 1 Chron. 2:9–10, we learn that Hezron fathered several sons. An editorial expansion about Hezron in 1 Chron. 2:21–24 refers to his marriages.

Ram The name means "high" or "elevated." Ram's name is unique to Ruth and 1 Chronicles. It appears as "Aran" in the Septuagint and takes other forms in other early manuscripts of Ruth.[241]

Amminadab *'ammi* means "my people" (although Sasson connects this name with *ammu* [the Akkadian word for] "uncle" or "kinsman"). The second element means "generous, munificent." According to Exod. 6:23, Amminadab is also Aaron's father-in-law (the father of Elisheba). Elsewhere he is mentioned only as Nahshon's father (see, e.g., Num. 1:7).

20. Nahshon The name resembles the words for "bronze" or "copper" (*neḥoshet*) and "serpent" (*naḥash*). Nahshon appears in the Bible first as Elisheba's brother (Exod. 6:23) and then repeatedly in Numbers as a leader of the Judah clan (Num. 1:7; 2:3; 7:12,17; 10:14). The parallel genealogy in 1 Chron. 2:10 lists him with the title of "prince" (*nasi'*) as does Num. 2:3. Rabbinic tradition credits him with exceptional courage as Israel stands at the Sea of Reeds at the time of the Exodus. According to the Midrash, Nahshon was the first Israelite to enter the sea; only then did the waters part and the Israelites believe that it was safe to cross. He was also the first to bring dedicatory offerings to the

Salmon, [21]Salmon begot Boaz, Boaz begot Obed,
[22]Obed begot Jesse, and Jesse begot David.

21 וְשַׂלְמוֹן הוֹלִיד אֶת־בֹּעַז וּבֹעַז הוֹלִיד
אֶת־עוֹבֵד׃ 22 וְעֹבֵד הוֹלִיד אֶת־יִשָׁי וְיִשַׁי
הוֹלִיד אֶת־דָּוִד׃*

v. 22. סכום הפסוקים של הספר 85 וחציו 2.21

תם ונשלם תהילה לאל בורא עולם

tabernacle, once again acting as a leader and a source of inspiration (B. Sot. 37a and Num. R. 13.9; see also *Mekhilta de-Rabbi Yishmael*).

20–21. Salmon,... Salmon Like Ram, this individual does not appear elsewhere in the Hebrew Bible except for the parallel genealogies in 1 Chron. 2:9–10 and 2:51 and 54. In Ruth, however, his name takes two forms, first listed as *salmah* in verse 20 and then as *salmon* in verse 21. Clearly the same individual is intended, proving that scribal tradition regarding names was comfortable with variant rendering of names. First Chronicles 2:10 uses "Salma" at both points. In the New Testament (Matt. 1:5), Salmon is listed as husband of Rahab, the prostitute mentioned in Josh. 2:1–3, who becomes the mother of Boaz in the New Testament.

Boaz On the name, see comment at 2:1. Boaz occupies the seventh position in the genealogy. Porten and Sasson consider this placement to be deliberate, playing on the number seven in the women's earlier reference to seven sons (4:15).[242]

The parallel list in 1 Chronicles 2, the only other text to mention Boaz, records no other sons. According to Rabbinic tradition, Boaz died the night he consummated the marriage, that is, when Obed was conceived (Ruth Z. 4.14).

Obed On the name, see comment at 4:17. Obed is the pivot upon which this genealogy turns. He complements and completes the lineage in 4:17, where Naomi is listed as the ancestor who leads to David. But the assignation of his lineage to Boaz is somewhat startling in light of Boaz's earlier goal of perpetuating "the name of the deceased upon his estate" and not letting the name of the deceased disappear (4:10; see also 4:5). Elimelech and Mahlon are glaringly absent from this genealogy. This switch in the genealogical track from Elimelech and Mahlon to Boaz is one of several clues that mark Ruth 4 as a trickster tale (see also comment at 4:12 and "Perez" at 4:18, as well as "The Marriage of Boaz and Ruth" in the introduction). It also indicates that the union between Boaz and Ruth is not a levirate marriage, at least not in accordance with the practice described and sanctioned in the Bible (see "Levirate Marriage" in the introduction).

22. Jesse Hebrew *yishai*. The ancestry of David's father is not recorded elsewhere except for the parallel genealogy in 1 Chronicles 2 (where the spelling is longer, with an *aleph* in front of *yishai*). The meaning of the name is uncertain. According to 1 Samuel, Jesse was a Bethlehemite, the father of eight sons, the youngest of whom is David. In 1 Sam. 17:12, he is also called Ephrathite (see "Ephrathite" in Ruth 1:2). Isaiah 11:1 and 10 mention him centuries later as the progenitor of a foretold, just, and powerful ruler. David is sometimes identified simply as the son of Jesse, without reference to his own name (as when King Saul inquires after David in 1 Sam. 20:27).

David The meaning of the name is uncertain, but the name is used in the Bible for this individual only. Ending the book with the name of Israel's most famous king renders the Book of Ruth a prolegomenon to the Israelite monarchy and a bridge from the period of the Judges to the formation of that monarchy. This explains also (along with the time frame given in Ruth 1:1) why the book follows Judges in the Septuagint and leads to 1 Samuel, a tradition preserved in Christian Bibles (on the book's placement in Jewish sources, see "Ruth's Place in the Canon," the introduction).

David's Moabite ancestry is mentioned only in the Book of Ruth. However, 1 Sam. 22:1–4 records that when David was persecuted by King Saul, he requested from the king of Moab (and was granted) asylum for his parents. The readiness of the Moabite king to harbor such refugees may be the link for traditions about David's family connection. Most likely, the report in 1 Samuel influenced the Rabbinic lore about Ruth as the daughter of a Moabite king (see at 1:4).

With this ending, the Book of Ruth probably intends to build on David's good reputation to lend legitimacy to its messages. These are especially relevant to the postexilic and also Hellenistic Jewish communities of the fifth or fourth centuries B.C.E. Texts from that era reveal an internal debate about communal boundaries, as is apparent in Ezra 9–10, Nehemiah 13 (both of which oppose marriage with Moabites and other neighboring peoples), and Isaiah 56 (which envisions the inclusion of foreigners in the community of Israel). The Book of Ruth sides with Isaiah 56, conveying to its readers that Ruth the Moabite is ultimately integrated into the Israelite community and is accepted by that community (the exclusion of Moabites in Deut. 23:4 notwithstanding).

Whereas modern readers might qualify their enthusiasm for the birth of a male hero as the best conclusion to a women's story, such a conclusion in its ancient context signals a happy ending with an abundance of blessings. By ending with David, the book celebrates the rewards granted to Ruth, Naomi, and Boaz because of their virtuous actions. Ruth's practice of *ḥesed* and hutzpah benefits the entire nation by leading to the birth of Israel's most illustrious king and ushers in a new epoch in Israel's history.

NOTES TO THE COMMENTARY

1. On *ʾish,* see D. E. S. Stein, "The Noun *ʾish* in Biblical Hebrew: A Term of Affiliation," *JHS* 8, Article 1 (2008): esp. 16–17.

2. Robert L. Hubbard, Jr., *The Book of Ruth,* The New International Commentary of the Old Testament (Grand Rapids, MI: Eerdmans, 1988), 88n22.

3. For the legal and exegetical nature of the prohibitions in Ezra-Nehemiah in relation to Deut. 23:4–9, see Michael Fishbane, *Biblical Interpretation in Ancient Israel* (Oxford: Clarendon, 1985), 114–29.

4. For details see Edward F. Campbell, *Ruth: A New Translation with Introduction and Commentary.* AB, 7 (Garden City, NY: Doubleday, 1975), 52.

5. See Hubbard, *The Book of Ruth,* 88–90.

6. The use of the verb *n-s-ʾ* for marriage is one of the chief indicators that the Book of Ruth is postexilic. See Frederic W. Bush, *Ruth/Esther,* Word Biblical Commentary 9 (Waco, TX: Word Books, 1996), 26–30.

7. Targum translations are from S. H. Levey, "The Targum to the Book of Ruth: Its Linguistic and Exegetical Character, together with a discussion of the date, a study of the sources, and an idiomatic English translation" in *The Text and I,* ed. S. Chyet, South Florida Studies in the History of Judaism 165 (Atlanta: Scholars, 1998).

8. Hubbard, *The Book of Ruth,* 94n14.

9. Other suggestions: a contraction from *reʿut,* "friendship" (so Syriac and BDB 946); against this view, see Hubbard, *The Book of Ruth,* 94n15.

10. D. N. Fewell and D. M. Gunn, "'A Son Is Born to Naomi!' Literary Allusions and Interpretation in the Book of Ruth," *JSOT* 40 (1988): 99–108.

11. Robert Alter, *The Art of Biblical Narrative* (New York: Basic Books, 1981), 70–87.

12. *Patros* in Greek.

13. Carol Meyers, "Returning Home: Ruth 1:8 and the Gendering of the Book of Ruth," in *A Feminist Companion to Ruth,* ed. Athalya Brenner (Sheffield: Sheffield Academic, 1993), 85–114, 96.

14. See further, Meyers, "Returning Home," 91–94.

15. Naomi uses the verb *ʿ-s-h* "to do," which appears in a *ketiv* (Masoretic spelling) form, *yʿsh*, which is simple future, but the *kerey* (traditional reading) is *yʿs*, which is optative, as the NJPS has it.

16. Rachel Adler, *Engendering Judaism: An Inclusive Theology and Ethics* (Philadelphia: Jewish Publication Society, 1998), 149.

17. See n16 above.

18. On *ḥesed*, see N. Glueck, *Ḥesed in the Bible,* Cincinnati: HUC Press, 1967; and Katherine Doob Sakenfeld, *The Meaning of Ḥesed in the Hebrew Bible: A New Inquiry* (Eugene, OR: Wipf & Stock, 1999).

19. *Gesenius' Hebrew Grammar,* ed. E. Kautzsch §135*o* explains this phenomenon, which occurs more frequently in later biblical books, as the result of the influence of colloquial language on literature. There are seven instances in Ruth where the masculine plural suffix applies to women and four when the feminine dual is used (1:9 and 1:19). See Bush, *Ruth/Esther*, 75. Some argue for a colloquial usage that influenced the present example. Others, like G. Rendsburg, suggest a remnant of an earlier feminine dual suffix that ended also with *m* but was pronounced differently from the masculine ending ("Late Biblical Hebrew and the Date of 'P,'" *JANES* 12 [1980]: 65–80, 77). See also Campbell, *Ruth*, 65.

20. The term is paired with *naḥalah* ("possession, estate") in Deut. 12:9 ("allotted haven"), another source of security (see also Isa. 11:10 and 66:1).

21. See Bush, *Ruth/Esther,* 77.

22. In private communication.

23. See Fewell and Gunn, "'A Son Is Born to Naomi!'" 99–108.

24. For a recent review of levirate unions in the Bible and across cultures, see Dvora E. Weisberg, *Levirate Marriage and the Family in Ancient Judaism* (Waltham, MA: Brandeis University Press, 2009). See also Timothy M. Willis, *The Elders of the City,* SBL Monograph Series 55 (Atlanta: Society of Biblical Literature, 2001) for a good review of ancient Near Eastern material.

25. A Karaite commentary attributed to Salmon ben Yeroḥam has the following as a comment to v. 11: "[E]ven the sages allowed levirate marriage only when the brothers were alive at the same time . . . and here it says 'Have I yet sons in my womb?' to show that this is a rhetorical question" (cited by D. R. G. Beattie, *Jewish Exegesis of the Book of Ruth JSOT* Supp 2 [Sheffield: *JSOT*, 1977]: 57).

26. See Campbell, *Ruth*, 68–69; E. Levine, *The Aramaic Version of Ruth,* Analecta Biblical 58 (Rome, 1975), 21, 54; Bush, *Ruth/Esther,* 79. See also n.19 above.

27. NRSV has "refrain," and the Stone Edition *Tanach* has "tie yourselves."

28. See *The Book of Ruth,* ArtScroll Tanach Series, 76–77.

29. Avivah Gottlieb Zornberg, "The Concealed Alternative," in *Reading Ruth: Contemporary Women Reclaim a Sacred Story,* ed. J. A. Kates and G. T. Reimer (New York: Ballantine, 1994), 65–81, 72.

30. For more on "the hand of the LORD," see Patrick D. Miller, Jr. and J. J. M. Roberts, *The Hand of the Lord: A Reassessment of the "Ark Narrative" of I Samuel* (Baltimore: The Johns Hopkins University Press, 1977).

31. R. Shemuel Uzeda, 16th century, Safed.

32. Tikva Frymer-Kensky, "Ruth on the Royal Way," in *Reading the Women of the Bible: New Interpretations of Their Stories* (New York: Schocken, 2002), 241.

33. Campbell, *Ruth,* 80.

34. Mark S. Smith, "'Your People Shall Be My People': Family and Covenant in Ruth 1:16–17," *CBQ* 69 (2007): 242–58, 254.

35. N. Glover, "Your People, My People: An Exploration of Ethnicity in Ruth," *JSOT* 3 (2009): 293–313.

36. The verb is also mentioned in Gen. 38:3 when Tamar's husband dies and his brother is supposed to impregnate her to produce an heir for his deceased brother.

37. J. A. Kates "Women at the Center: Ruth and Shavuot," in *Reading Ruth*, 187–98, 191.

38. Ibid., 191.

39. N. Glover, "Your People, My People," 293–313.

40. Phyllis Trible, "A Human Comedy," in *God and the Rhetoric of Sexuality* (Philadelphia: Fortress, 1978), 166–99, 173.

41. Fewell and Gunn, "'A Son Is Born to Naomi!'" 100–101.

42. P. Coxon, "Was Naomi a Scold?" *JSOT* 45 (1989): 25–37. Moreover, the narrator's statements that the two went together (1:19 and 22) suggest to Coxon their intimacy.

43. J. A. Kates, "Women at the Center," 192.

44. "Her Mother's House," in Kates and Reimer, *Reading Ruth*, 97–105, 99.

45. Shaddai often parallels the word "God" (*el* or *eloha,* as in Job 31:2), but only a few times does it parallel YHWH (as in Isa. 13:6).

46. See, e.g., Campbell, *Ruth,* 76–77.

47. See also Rashi (on Gen. 17:1), who identifies Shaddai with an aspect of God that is nurturing and nourishing, a sense that fits the present context as well when Naomi bemoans her loss.

48. On similarities between Naomi and Job, see, e.g., Campbell, *Ruth*, 77.

49. See Fewell and Gunn, "'A Son Is Born to Naomi!'" 99–108, esp. 101–3.

50. Reimer writes in this connection: "Readers impressed by Ruth's devotion to Naomi cannot help but be shocked by Naomi's treatment." She goes on to suggest that "Naomi cannot acknowledge or accept the sense of self that Ruth has articulated—a self defined in relation to neither men nor children" ("Her Mother's House," 100).

51. So R. Shemuel Uzeda, *Iggeret Shemuel*.

52. Yehoshua Bachrach, *Mother of Royalty: An Exposition of the Book of Ruth in the Light of the Sources* (Jerusalem: Feldheim, 1973, 1980 ed.), 59.

53. See the poignant treatment of this in Bachrach, *Mother of Royalty,* esp. 51–54. In the translation of this verse there is "Ruth the Moabitess—who returned from the field of Moab" (51).

54. See Lev. 23:10 and B. Levine, *The JPS Torah Commentary: Leviticus* (Philadelphia: Jewish Publication Society, 1989), 157; Deut. 16:1 and J. Tigay, *The JPS Torah Commentary: Deuteronomy* (Philadelphia: Jewish Publication Society, 1996), 152–53; see also N. Sarna, *Exploring Exodus: The Heritage of Biblical Israel* (New York: Schocken, 1986), 88. I thank David E. S. Stein for alerting me to these passages.

55. Frymer-Kensky, "Royal Origins," 238–56, 242.

56. See also Bachrach, *Mother of Royalty,* 62–65.

57. Commenting on 3:13, the midrash uses a wordplay for Boaz's name. Citing a verse from Proverbs: "A wise man is strength [*be'oz*]" (Prov. 24:5), it applies "strength" to Boaz: "A wise man is Boaz [*bo'oz*], in that he conquered his inclination with an oath" (Ruth R. 6.4)

58. See Gesenius, *Hebrew Grammar*, 319–320.

59. Bush, *Ruth/Esther,* 104.

60. As J. D. Schloen writes, "The 'household'... provides the template for social interaction at all levels... Subordinates are either 'sons' or 'servants' of the person in authority, [and] superiors are 'fathers' or 'masters.'" In *The House of the Father as Fact and Symbol: Patrimonialism in Ugarit and the Ancient Near East* (Winona Lake, IN: Eisenbrauns, 2001), 70–71.

61. Fewell and Gunn, "'A Son Is Born to Naomi!'" esp. 100–103.

62. Similar patterns recur in modern representations as well, like Jean-Francois Millet's painting "The Gleaners" (19th century).

63. Tod Linafelt and Timothy K. Beal, *Ruth and Esther,* Berit Olam: Studies in Hebrew Narrative and Poetry (Collegeville, MN: Liturgical, 1999), 30.

64. Hubbard, *The Book of Ruth,* 145n23.

65. E.g., D. N. Fewell and D. M. Gunn explore the possibility that Boaz's interest in Ruth may be of a sexual nature from the start. See *Compromising Redemption: Relating Characters in the Book of Ruth.* Literary Currents in Biblical Interpretation (Louisville: Westminster/John Knox, 1990), 40–44.

66. Ronald A. Simkins, "Patronage and the Political Economy of Monarchic Israel," *Semeia* 87 (1999): 123–44.

67. Lev. 23:9,10,11,15; Deut. 24:19; Job 24:10.

68. Hubbard, *The Book of Ruth,* 148.

69. For example, ibid., 148–50; and Feivel Meltzer, "Ruth" in the *Five Scrolls* (Jerusalem: Mosad Ha-Rav Kook, 1973), 15. Some modern commentators read the Hebrew as *'amirim,* "rows of fallen grain," while others simply omit the word *ba 'omerim* entirely. Neither of these solutions explains Ruth's query. For details, see the lengthy discussions in Campbell, *Ruth,* 94–95; and Bush, *Ruth/Esther,* 113–19, which pertain also to the rest of the verse.

70. The final letter *nun* in this case is what is called "paragogic," a mark of archaic style; so Campbell, *Ruth,* 97.

71. Ibid., 98.

72. Linafelt, *Ruth,* 34.

73. *Ruth: Introduction and Commentary, Mikra Leyisra'el.* Biblical Commentary for Israel (Tel Aviv/Jerusalem: Am Oved/Magnes, 1990), 75 [Hebrew].

74. See Robert Alter, "Biblical Type-Scenes and the Uses of Convention," in *The Art of Biblical Narrative* (New York: Basic Books, 1981), esp. 51–60. Alter observes that this scene has elements from the typical betrothal scene but in reverse, because the woman has come from a foreign land and the man offers water (59).

75. In the following note from the introduction to *Notes on the New Translation of the Torah,* Harry Orlinsky explains some of the difficulties in rendering a sentence such as this one. Orlinsky writes: "It is not always easy to capture the idiom in the Hebrew and at the same time reproduce it adequately in such an entirely different language as English; yet the modern translator may not shirk this task and... content himself with rendering a word for a word.... The expression *maṣa* (or *nathan*) *ḥen be-ene-* is [a] good example.... [NJPS] has made every effort to bring out the nuance of this phrase in the many occurrences of this expression" (Philadelphia: Jewish Publication Society, 1969, 28).

76. So NRSV. NJPS has "accept" instead of "acknowledge."

77. Jack M. Sasson, *Ruth: A New Translation with a Philological Commentary and a Formalist-Folklorist Interpretation,* 2d ed. (Sheffield: *JSOT*, 1989 originally: Baltimore: The John Hopkins University Press, 1979), 51.

78. In Ezra 10:2,10,14,17,18, and 44 and Neh. 13:27, where the majority of feminine forms of the noun are concentrated, these are women to be excluded. In Prov. 2:16; 5:20; 6:24; 7:5; 20:16; and 23:27, these are mostly paired with the "forbidden woman," *'ishah zarah,* who is a dangerous seductress. In Gen. 31:15, Rachel and Leah complain that their father treats them as outsiders (*nokhriyot*).

79. "A Human Comedy," 177.

80. See, for example, Linafelt, *Ruth*, 36–37.

81. Isaac Arama's commentary on the five scrolls (16th century, Italy), *Akedat Yitzchak*.

82. See, e.g., the story of Jacob, which uses "wages" in both senses. Jacob receives his first "wages" as Rachel, and then, his later wages from the flock (Gen. 30:28, 32–33). Leah has a child when she "hires him" with mandrakes and names the child Issachar, for "God has given me my reward" (Gen. 30:16–18).

83. Campbell, *Ruth,* 100.

84. Sasson, *Ruth* 53.

85. 16.1 (Nachamu), cited from the Braude translation of PdRK (Philadelphia: Jewish Publication Society, 2002).

86. Frymer-Kensky, "Royal Origins," 243.

87. Nehama Aschkenasy, "Language as Female Empowerment in Ruth," in *Reading Ruth*, 111–24, 119.

88. See Campbell, *Ruth,* 102. Campbell also links the term with the Septuagint, which suggests "to heap into a mound," like the Hebrew *tz-b-r* (102–3).

89. Admittedly, however, such equivalencies are not altogether certain or precise. Moreover, as ancient readers would have known, the harvest season for barley or wheat lasts about a month each (see Oded Borowski, *Daily Life in Biblical Times,* Society of Biblical Literature Archaeology and Biblical Studies 5 [Leiden: Brill], 28). The gleaned grain would have to provide for future months as well, not merely daily provisions. Nonetheless, in the world of the story, it appears that the narrator emphasizes

the bountifulness of what Ruth brings home. This is more fully expressed in Naomi's elated response when Ruth returns with the day's gleaning. See comment at 2:19.

90. For different options, see Campbell, who reports calculations of 47.5 and of 29 lbs, and prefers the latter (*Ruth,* 104).

91. I owe this observation to my former student Rabbi Mari Chernow.

92. See, e.g., Bush, *Ruth/Esther,* 135–36.

93. See *Numbers 1–20, AB.* I thank David E. S. Stein for the possible application here of Levine's work.

94. Zakovitch takes the opposite view: Ruth still feels herself to be a Moabite as she attempts to digest Naomi's inclusive "we" (*Ruth,* 84).

95. Phyllis Trible, "A Human Comedy," 196. This statement by Trible echoes the roles attributed to Jesus in H. Richard Niebuhr's famous book *Christ and Culture,* 1955; however, Trible does not use this particular verse to make her point.

96. Moreover, Frymer-Kensky argues, the phrases in these books all deal with serious attacks, at times accompanied with verbs meaning to kill (as in Judg. 18:25; 1 Sam. 22:18; 2 Sam. 1:15; 1 Kings 2:21,25,34,46).

97. Borowski, *Daily Life in Biblical Times,* 28.

98. Feivel Melzer associates this three-month period with the time required (according to the Rabbis) before a proselyte may marry an Israelite; see "Ruth" in *The Five Scrolls,* 21.

99. Campbell, *Ruth,* 121; Sasson, *Ruth,* 71.

100. Alsheikh on 3:1–2; Bush, *Ruth/Esther,* 147.

101. E.g., Fewell and Gunn comment that Naomi's chief concern is her own wellbeing (see their interpretation of 3:17 in "'A Son Is Born to Naomi!'" 102).

102. Campbell notes the anomaly of the usage and translates the term as "one of our covenant circle," emphasizing a connection to the notion of redemption in 2:20 (*Ruth,* 117).

103. Excavations in large ancient cities such as Gezer (12th century B.C.E.) show these types of structures adjacent to granaries. See Campbell, *Ruth,* 118–19.

104. The association of threshing floors with cultic sites (see 2 Samuel 24, Hos. 9:1, as well as Gideon's threshing at a sacred site in Judg. 6:11 and the location of the Ark in 2 Sam. 6:6) convinces H. G. May that the threshing floor in Bethlehem was likewise a cultic site and that Boaz remained there to take part in a harvest celebration. See his "Ruth's Visit to the High Place in Bethlehem," *Journal of the Royal Asiatic Society of Great Britain and Ireland* 1 (Jan. 1939): 75–78.

105. S. Greengus, "Old Babylonian Marriage Ceremonies and Rites," *Journal of Cuneiform Studies* (1966): 55–72, 61.

106. One Septuagint ms. explains: "rub yourself with myrrh" (Campbell, *Ruth,* 12).

107. See, e.g., Kristen Nielsen, *Ruth,* Old Testament Library (Louisville: Westminster/John Knox, 1997), 66. Bush translates "put on perfumed oil" (*Ruth/Esther*, 144).

108. David E. S. Stein in a private communication.

109. Nielsen, *Ruth*, 61.

110. See Bush, *Ruth/Esther,* 150.

111. Hillel I. Millgram, *Four Biblical Heroines and the Case for Female Authorship* (Jefferson, NC/London: McFarland, 2007), 56.

112. Bush, *Ruth/Esther*, 145n3b.

113. H. G. May attempts to resolve the issue by suggesting that the verb *y-r-d* is capable of having opposite meanings ("Ruth's Visit," 76).

114. See Jacob L. Wright, "Commensal Politics in Western Asia" *ZAW* 122/2 (2010): 1–22; *ZAW* 122/3 (2010): 1–20.

115. See also 1 Samuel 3 with eight instances, referring to Samuel going to sleep after being called by God.

116. Several modern commentators conclude that the instructions and Ruth's subsequent action involve exposing the genitalia or indicating nudity. E.g., Nielsen writes, "She [Ruth] uncovers her sexual organ and invites Boaz to cover her with the corner of his garment" (*Ruth,* 70), a highly improbable situation given biblical narrative and the description in this section.

117. Note a wordplay in the Hebrew: *gilit margelotav*.

118. Harold Fisch, "Ruth and the Structure of Covenant History," *VT* 32/4 (1982): 425–37, closely compares the story of Lot's daughters in Genesis 19 along with the Judah and Tamar story in Genesis 38 with Boaz and Ruth at the threshing floor in Ruth 3 to show how they function as commentary on each other. He notes a development from an extreme act of incest in Genesis 19 to a slightly less serious violation in the case of Judah and Tamar (Judah is only the father-in-law). In the Book of Ruth it has been muted and transformed into a union sanctioned by established custom (429–30). See "The Relation of the Book of Ruth to Other Biblical Books" in the introduction.

119. See also, e.g., Bachrach, *Mother of Royalty,* 51.

120. As David E. S. Stein writes (in a private communication), "the expression *ke-khol 'asher tzivvah* (or similar conjugation of that verb) occurs 34 times in the Bible. Meanwhile, *kol 'asher tzivvah* and the like occurs only 17 times—not counting instances of additional prefixed prepositions—and, therefore, the longer formula with *ke-* is arguably the normative one. Thus, God is depicted as using the term *ke-khol 'asher* in instructions to Moses (Exod. 29:35; 31:6,11), and in so doing surely God is expecting complete compliance. So, also, the declaration of obedience in Deut. 26:14, which surely cannot be claiming that "I followed God's directions, more or less." I thank David E. S. Stein for correcting my earlier conclusion about *ke-khol* as indicating an ambiguity.

121. This appears to be the normal verb for a head of household or administrator's instructions to the household members (not only its servants or slaves); David E. S. Stein in a private communication. See Gen. 27:8; 28:1; 49:29; 50:16; 1 Sam. 17:20; 20:29; 1 Kings 2:1; Jer. 35:6,8,10,14,16; Esther 2:10,20.

122. So, too, Sasson in *Ruth,* 73.

123. Millgram, *Four Biblical Heroines,* 57n15.

124. Nielsen, *Ruth,* 70.

125. Linafelt, *Ruth,* 51.

126. Linafelt contemplates the possibility of yet another allusion to Lot and his daughters in *balat,* which sounds like the word *be-lot* ("against Lot"), a word that appears conspicuously in a Genesis episode (19:9). And in both stories, a woman wants something from a man who has been drinking; after having conferred with another woman in her household, she violates convention by "coming" to "lie (down)" at night with him, in such a way that he does not "know" it, and, which later results in the birth of a boy (*Ruth*, 52).

127. One instance is active, *va-yilpot,* when Samson brings the temple down in Judg. 16:29; the *niph'al* occurs in Job 6:18 *yillaphetu* and here. The first is generally translated as "Samson grabbed" the pillars; the latter that the paths were winding. In the context of Ruth, it might mean that Boaz pulled back, as translated here; or "he turned over" (so the NRSV), or he doubled over (as Ibn Ezra suggests), or "groped about" (so Campbell). The verb *lapatu* is common in Akkadian when it means "to touch." Frymer-Kensky suggests that the *niph'al* would be "to be touched" or "to startle as if touched" (notes).

128. D. N. Fewell and D. M. Gunn therefore suggest that Boaz's unease is prompted also by the uncertainty whether Ruth has exploited the situation in the mode of Lot's daughters (*Compromising Redemption,* 86–87).

129. Potiphar's wife attempts unsuccessfully to seduce Joseph in Genesis 39.

130. In 1 Sam. 25:44, King Saul gives his daughter Michal, wife of David, to Palti (or Paltiel). In 2 Sam. 3:13–16, Michal is taken back to David. The Rabbinic sages reconcile this reunion between David and Michal and the laws of Deut. 24:1–4 (which forbids a remarriage with the first wife after she was married to another) by insisting that the marriage between Michal and Palti

was never consummated. He had kept a sword between them to avoid "crossing the line" (B. Sanh. 19b).

131. These terms apply to a woman's state during her menstruation cycle, and the time of month when she can have physical contact with a man. See, e.g., the laws of menstruation in Lev. 15:19–24. Rabbinic tradition develops these laws extensively.

132. Lit., *'amah* refers to the forearm. When applied to a woman, it carries the sense of someone who functions as an extension of another's hand; hence, "handmaid" is an apt translation. By extension, *'amah* is also a body-based measurement, translated usually as "cubit," analogous to the English use of "foot" as a measure.

133. The terms are at times used interchangeably in biblical texts (as Abigail does in 1 Sam. 25:27–28).

134. Hubbard, *Book of Ruth,* 211 (so too Sasson, *Ruth,* 80–81). Campbell thinks the terms are synonymous in Ruth (*Ruth,* 123).

135. See E. M. Meyers, "The Shelomith Seal and the Judean Restoration: Some Additional Considerations," *Eretz Israel* 18 (1985): 33–38.

136. E.g., the Targum and the Midrash.

137. E.g., Bush, *Ruth/Esther*, 164–65; Campbell, *Ruth*, 123; and Hubbard, *The Book of Ruth*, 212–213.

138. Bush, *Ruth/Esther,* 165.

139. Sasson discerns two separate requests: first Ruth asks to be taken into Boaz's family (whether as wife or concubine is not clear); and second, she asks or affirms Boaz's role as redeemer, a role unrelated to the first request. To reach this view, Sasson argues that the conjunction *ki,* elsewhere translated as "for," need not be interpreted in this manner. He cites Paul Joüon, *A Grammar of Biblical Hebrew* (1947) 164b (503), as one of his sources for justifying this possibility for *ki* (*Ruth*, 83–84).

140. D. R. G. Beattie, likewise, speaks of a hint ("there shall probably be found a gentle hint of marriage") but also adds that it "is not that Ruth demanded or even explicitly requested marriage but rather that Naomi conceived a plan of putting the idea into Boaz's head by putting Ruth into Boaz's bed" ("Ruth III," *JSOT* 5 [1978]: 39–48, 43). Bush considers this conclusion incompatible with the biblical portraits of the women and with Boaz's reasons to Ruth (*Ruth/Esther,* 165).

141. Only Isaiah, with its 66 chapters, has more occurrences of the term (25 times; cf. 21 in the 4 chapters of Ruth)! Leviticus, with 27 chapters, mentions *g-'-l* 22/21 times.

142. Shlomo Bahar, "What Is the Difference between חלץ (ḥalas) and שלף (šalap)? The Purpose of Recalling the 'Form of Attestation' in the Scroll of Ruth (4:7)," *Shnaton: An Annual for Bible and Ancient Near East Studies* 20 (2010): 69–85, 75 [Hebrew].

143. A fourth set of laws regulates the redemption of items dedicated to the sanctuary. See Lev. 27:11–23.

144. The laws of person and land redemption are most fully developed in Leviticus 25. The Bible casts a wide net as to who can act as redeeming kin (Lev. 25:49–50; see also Ezek. 11:15). Leviticus 25:48–50 specifies the kinship sequence of responsibility, which includes: uncle, cousin, and then any other family member. Baruch A. Levine writes in his comment to Num. 5:8 [*AB* 4A]): "According to Lev. 25:48–49, one's clan relatives . . . included . . . [a smaller body of] 'flesh' relatives [which] are, in turn, listed in Lev. 21:2. They include one's mother, father, son, daughter, and brother" (*Numbers 1–20,* 100).

145. *Iggeret Shemuel;* Malbim on 3:10; Hubbard, *Book of Ruth,* 213–14.

146. Campbell, *Ruth,* 124.

147. A work complied by the 11th-century Jewish commentator R. Toviah ben Eliezer Hagadol (Greece and Bulgaria).

148. The translation as "a woman of valor" captures the militant sense of *ḥayil,* a word associated with warriors as well as power. The Septuagint also reflects that sense by translating *ḥayil* forms of *dunamis* (here and at 2:1).

149. Frymer-Kensky suggests that one should read both instances of *ki* as separate particles. Some modern scholars have suggested omitting the first or the second *ki* or the whole second phrase. There is no reason to omit the first *ki.* As for *'omnam,* it comes from the root *'-m-n,* "be true" and can appear alone as "truly, verily" (2 Kings 19:17) or as a question *ha'umnam* (Num. 22:37; Ps. 58:2). The addition of *'af* or *ki* seems purely stylistic, whether in questions such as *ki ha'umnam* (1 Kings 8:27) and *ha'af umnam* (Gen. 18:13); as emphatic asseverations, *'af 'omnam* (Job 19:4; 34:12); or, as here and in Job 36:4, *ki 'omnam.* Job also reverses the order *'omnam ki* (Job 12:2) with no appreciable difference. As for *ki 'im,* it does not seem likely that this is the well-known compound conjunction, for the compound *ki 'im* comes after a negative statement and means "but rather," "except for," a sense that does not fit here (Frymer-Kensky; notes).

150. This last possibility was suggested by David E. S. Stein in a private communication.

151. Bush, *Ruth/Esther,* 177.

152. However we interpret the scene, Ruth is in a compromising situation. Ancient Near Eastern mores considered it a disgrace to a woman (and her family) if she engaged in sexual relations outside of marriage, regardless of whether she had consented.

153. Hubbard, *Book of Ruth,* 221.

154. To some interpreters, the pouring out symbolizes sexual relations. Linafelt elaborates on the double meaning of Boaz's gift. Both the heap of grain beside which Boaz reclines and the gift of grain with which he sends Ruth back to the city "are the products of 'seed,' a word used in the Hebrew Bible in its literal sense, as well as in a metaphorical sense of semen and by extension of offspring. Boaz . . . is the possessor of seed" (*Ruth,* 59–60). As Linafelt points out, the women need food, hence seed, but they also need seed if they are to continue the family line (59–60). B. Porten puts it more boldly: "the seed that fills the stomach was promise of the seed to fill the womb" ("The Scroll of Ruth: A Rhetorical Study," *Gratz College Annual* 7 [1978]: 40, cited by Linafelt, *Ruth,* 60 n16). Yet these comments are problematic because the narrator here has chosen to speak of barley, not *zera'* ("seed"). (See comment at 3:17 for possible explanations for why "seed" is not used here.)

155. About 58–95 lbs. See Hubbard, *Book of Ruth,* 222.

156. See ibid., 224–25; Sasson, *Ruth,* 99–100.

157. 1 Sam. 26:14, Isa. 51:12, Zech. 4:7; cf. *ben mi 'attah* in 1 Sam. 17:58 in light of 16:19. The answers to the same question *mi 'attem* (with a masculine plural pronoun) in Josh. 9:8 and 2 Kings 10:13 treat it as a demand for explanation rather than mere identification. Thus it is distinct from the similar but more specific question *mah shemekha,* "What is your name?" (Gen. 32:28; Judg. 13:17; cf. Exod. 3:13; Prov. 30:4).

158. André LaCocque, *Ruth: A Continental Commentary* (Minneapolis: Fortress, 2004), 3.

159. The NJPS regularly conveys the repetition of the verb *a-m-r,* "said," by means of "he/she added" after a character has already been speaking (Gen. 15:5; 21:7; 27:36; 38:25; Exod. 4:26; 2 Sam. 24:23). The resumptive repetition of the verb indicates that the person continued to speak after a pause.

160. Fewell and Gunn, "'A Son Is Born to Naomi!'"

161. See P. Coxon, "Was Naomi a Scold?" 25–37.

162. Ibid., 29.

163. Bush, *Ruth/Esther,* 189.

164. Linafelt, *Ruth,* 61.

165. Ibid.

166. Ibid, 61–62.

167. For "seed," see "through the offspring" at 4:12.

168. Linafelt mentions "dissatisfaction about the fact that the story of Ruth and Naomi seems to be usurped" (*Ruth*, 79). His interpretation of the concluding genealogy, however, suggests

that the Book of Ruth rectifies the history of failure depicted in Judges and as well the failed Davidic household (80–81).

169. Campbell, *Ruth,* 141–42; 157–58.

170. Beattie translates the Aramaic as "O man whose paths are modest" (Targum).

171. See Campbell, *Ruth,* 142.

172. For discussion and for examples of this sense of *'anashim,* see David E. S. Stein's essay, "The Noun *'ish* in Biblical Hebrew," 17–18.

173. For a detailed study of elders, see Willis, *The Elders of the City*. See also Bush, *Ruth/Esther,* 198.

174. *In the Service of the King: Officialdom in Ancient Israel and Judah* (Cincinnati: HUC Press, 2000), 63. A detailed analysis can also be found in Willis, *The Elders of the City*. See also David E. S. Stein's entry on elders in "Dictionary of Gender in the Torah," in *The Contemporary Torah* (Philadelphia: Jewish Publication Society, 2006), 397–398.

175. So Bush, *Ruth/Esther*, 211.

176. Linafelt, *Ruth,* 67.

177. Bush, *Ruth/Esther,* 215.

178. Naomi, Bush argues, could not actually own the land at present. "Naomi and Ruth have been living throughout the story as paupers dependent on the largesse of Boaz, as noted above. Surely the coherence and credibility of the story precludes the possibility that Naomi had either the right to or the actual possession and usufruct of such land" (*Ruth/Esther,* 213). One other possible explanation is that the land in question is the parcel upon which Naomi and Ruth now live.

179. Naomi's silence concerning the land convinces Fewell and Gunn that Naomi deliberately withholds information from Ruth ("'A Son Is Born to Naomi!'" 101); Linafelt, however, suspects that Boaz fabricates the story of the land as a subterfuge in order to justify marriage to Ruth. "It gives him the cover he needs to pursue in public his desire to marry Ruth: while everyone is focused on the noble duties of land-redemption, Boaz can slip in the fact that he is also 'acquiring' Ruth" (*Ruth,* 67). But such conjectures, based on ascribing a great deal of deviousness to the protagonists, stand in tension with the rest of the narrative in Ruth. Still, they highlight the provocative irregularities in the story.

180. Bush, who thoroughly investigates the legal and narrative issues involved, has concluded that the apparent obscurity is a result of our cultural distance as readers. He states that our uncertainty results from "our lack of knowledge of the socio-legal customs and traditions that regulated such real estate transactions and family obligations in ancient Israel rather than from the narrator's ignorance, ineptitude, or deliberate (albeit 'artful') manipulation of legal principles" (*Ruth/Esther*, 211; so, too, Campbell, *Ruth,* 158).

181. It is possible that if the land had been "sold," it is only now that it can be reclaimed, once the harvest is over, and one can negotiate with the person who has been using the usufruct.

182. The Shunammite widow of 2 Kings 8 appears to have a young son (in 2 Kings 4), who presumably can inherit. In the case of Elimelech's patrimony, the presumed inheritance lines are unclear, given the sequence of deaths. Did Naomi or his sons inherit the patrimony? And upon the sons' death, did Naomi or their wives inherit? See "Redemption" and "Inheritance" in the introduction.

183. Several contracts from the Jewish colony in Elephantine, Egypt, show that women could own and dispose of property. See, e.g., Kraeling 6 and 12 in the *Brooklyn Museum Aramaic Papyri: New Documents of the Fifth Century* B.C. *from the Jewish Colony at Elephantine* (New Haven: Yale University Press, 1953).

184. Campbell, *Ruth,* 145; Bush, *Ruth/Esther,* 207.

185. Linafelt, *Ruth*, 66; Sasson, *Ruth*, 118.

186. For episodes that highlight the value of a household or clan holding on to its patrimony, see 1 Kings 21:1–3; Numbers 36.

187. The risk of settling non-Israelite women upon the land is construed as a major crisis in Ezra-Nehemiah (see especially Ezra 9–10). For details, see Tamara Cohn Eskenazi, "The Missions of Ezra and Nehemiah" in O. Liphschits and M. Oeming, *Judah and the Judeans in the Persian Period* (Winona Lake, IN: Eisenbrauns, 2006), 509–529, esp. 518–24.

188. "So far in the conversation between Boaz and the other redeemer Ruth has not been mentioned in a single word.... In a masterstroke of dramatic irony it is only the reader who has an inkling of what is afoot. But even for the reader it is a twist in the plot..." (Nielsen, *Ruth*, 84).

189. Such ambiguities may not simply be by-products of our distance from the world of the narrative. They may have an interpretive role as part of the message of the book. See "The Theology of the Book of Ruth" in the introduction.

190. In this case, precedent for the reading *kanita,* "you acquire(d)," is found in Naomi's speech in Ruth 3:3 and 4, when the form of first person verb "go down" in the *ketiv* is best read with the *kerey* as second person. This usage can be the author's way of showing Naomi and Boaz as cohort, using an older linguistic form. However, Boaz uses *kaniti* (I acquire(d)) in 4:10.

191. For discussions about the force of *ketiv* and *kerey* in biblical texts, see Ziony Zevit, "Dating Ruth: Legal, Linguistic and Historical Observations," *ZAW* 117/4 (2005): 574–600; as well as R. Gordis, *The Biblical Text in the Making: A Study of the Kethib-Qere* (Philadelphia: Dropsie College, 1937), 152–54; and H. A. Orlinsky, "The Origin of the Kethib-Qere System: A New Approach," *VT*Supp 4 (Leiden: Brill, 1960): 184–192; see also W. S. Morrow, "Kethib and Qere," in the *ABD* IV, ed. D. N. Freedman (New York: Doubleday, 1992), 27 ff.

192. Frymer-Kensky, "Royal Origins," 251.

193. Zevit, "Dating Ruth," 581.

194. An indication that no legal ruling applies is evident throughout because no one in the narrative till this point acts as if Ruth was obliged to marry a relative in Bethlehem. Naomi never brings up that option when she encourages the younger women to return home. Boaz's words in 3:10 make clear that Ruth is free to choose a man. See also Bush, 223. Bush concedes that there is no legal obligation under levirate law, but claims that there must have been a moral obligation (Bush, *Ruth/Esther*, 226). On this complex and contested subject, see Bush, "Excursus: Levirate Marriage in the Old Testament" (*Ruth/Esther,* 221–29); see also for a different opinion "Levirate Marriage" and "The Marriage of Boaz and Ruth" in the introduction.

195. A version of this intriguing possibility appears in Linda Earle Bertenthal, "*Chesed* and *Chayil: Geulah* and Halakhah" (Rabbinic thesis, HUC-JIR, Los Angeles, 1999), 40–41.

196. See, e.g., Ruth R., Malbim.

197. Translation as per Levey's n14.

198. See Linafelt (*Ruth*, 69), Nielsen (*Ruth*), and Zevit, who prefer the *ketiv.* See Zevit's "Dating Ruth," 574–600. Zevit also explains the past tense form of the verb, *kaniti* ("I acquired") as a peculiarity of ancient Hebrew idiom, which often uses a past tense verb in formal *locutions* during the course of legal transactions. Zevit adds that it is used to express intent, "The rhetorical convention represents something being done or about to be done as having been accomplished already" (595–96). He mentions Gen. 23:11, 48:22; Judg. 1:2; 1,2; 2 Sam 14:21; and 24:23 as examples.

199. See D. H. Weiss, "The use of קנה in Connection with Marriage," *Harvard Theological Review* 57 (1964): 243–48. Likewise, David E.S. Stein (private communication, citing an agency sense of *'ish/'ishah* and Gen. 4:1; 39:1; Lev. 22:11) suggests that the expression *'eshet ha-meit kanita/kaniti* may denote a formal assignment of agency: Ruth had been acting in Mahlon's behalf, and now her agency will be "acquired" by the redeemer.

200. H. C. Brichto, "Kin, Cult, Land and Afterlife—A Biblical Complex," *HUCA* 44 (1973): 9–24, 15.

201. Ibid., 18.

202. Brichto suggests that "redemption" and "exchange" be read as a hendiadys for "transfer of the right to redemption" (ibid., 18). As Brichto observes, no property whatsoever is traded in this exchange, only the rights to engage in acquisition (19).

203. Elsewhere in the Bible, references to removing a shoe or a sandal constitute signs of mourning (Ezek. 24:17), defeat (Isa. 20:2–4), or humility (Exod. 3:5).

204. E. Speiser claimed to find comparable references to sandals in some tablets from Nuzi (Mesopotamia/Northern Iraq, 14th century B.C.E.); see E. Speiser, "Of Shoes and Shekels," *BASOR* 77 (1940): 151–56. But the reading of the tablets is uncertain, and his conclusions have subsequently been challenged; see T. D. Thompson and T. Thompson, "Some Legal Problems in the Book of Ruth," *VT* 18 (1968): 79–99. See also the criticism by Brichto, "Kin, Cult, Land and Afterlife," 19. E. Lachemann notes that the Nuzi archives do record that setting one's foot ritually on the property counts as a ratification of a land sale; see his "A Note on Ruth 4:7–8," *JBL* 56 (1937): 53–56; however, that is a different kind of transaction.

205. Susanne Klingstein, "Circle of Kinship: Samuel's Family Romance," in *Reading Ruth*, 199–210, 206.

206. Campbell, *Ruth*, 151.

207. Brichto, "Kin, Cult, Land and Afterlife," 15–19; D. H. Weiss, "The Use of קנה in Connection with Marriage," 243–48.

208. In the Mishnah, the term *k-n-h* appears right at the beginning of the tractate *Kiddushim* (1.1), listing the three ways in which a woman is "acquired." There it arguably refers elliptically to acquiring the bundle of responsibilities that define husbandhood. Significantly, *k-n-h* is not the term in the Mishnah that designates the marriage itself.

209. On the literal meaning of *'ish/'ishah* in marital contexts, see David E. S. Stein, "The Noun *'ish* in Biblical Hebrew," 12–13.

210. "The Concealed Alternative," *Reading Ruth,* 65–81, 74.

211. On the creation of legal fiction in the case of Zelophehad's daughters, see Michael Fishbane, *Biblical Interpretation in Ancient Israel* (Oxford: Clarendon, 1985), 104–5.

212. *Leviticus: A Book of Ritual and Ethics.* A Continental Commentary (Minneapolis: Fortress, 2004), 65.

213. Ibid., 65–67.

214. Glover, "Your People, My People," 293–313.

215. PdRK, 16.1.

216. I. Fischer, "The Book of Ruth as Exegetical Literature," *Bible Forum* (2006): 1–7, 3.

217. This is Malbim's final comment in the English version of his commentary, *Malbim on the Book of Ruth: The Commentary of Rabbi Meir Leibush Malbim* (Jerusalem/New York: Feldheim, 1999), 133.

218. Brichto, "Kin, Cult, Land and Afterlife," 22.

219. Adler, *Engendering Judaism*, 154–55.

220. Although the Bible offers no definition of the processes that legalize marriage, it does specify the terms of divorce (Deut. 24:1–4).

221. See, e.g., Kraeling 7, *Brooklyn Museum Aramaic Papyri* 7.

222. See, e.g., ibid. and Cowley, 9. See further "The Family" in the introduction.

223. The one possible exception in Judg. 21:23 is often ascribed to a late hand. It describes marriage to kidnapped brides.

224. The formula appears in a few other cases as well: Gen. 24:51,67 with regard to Rebekah, whose implicit right to refuse is mentioned in 24:58, and Gen. 20:12 and Deut. 21:13, which do not offer a clear picture.

225. Note that "A Human Comedy" is Trible's title for the chapter on Ruth in *God and the Rhetoric of Sexuality,* 160–99.

226. See, e.g., I. Bettan, *The Five Scrolls: A Commentary on Ruth, Song of Songs, Lamentations, Ecclesiastes, and Esther* (Cincinnati: UAHC, 1950), 47–72, 71; and Sasson, *Ruth*, 163.

227. Trible, "A Human Comedy," 194.

228. See H. Seebass, *Nepesh* in *The Theological Dictionary of the Old Testament,* Vol. 9, ed. J. Bollerweck, H. Ringgren, H-J Fabry (Grand Rapids, MI: Wm B. Eerdmans, 1998), 497–519. The separation of "body" and "soul" emerges in Judaism later, under Greek (especially Platonic) influence. The divine origin of the *nefesh* in Gen 2:7, prompted later views that, like God, the *nefesh,* or "soul," transcends temporal and spatial limitations. It is eternal, only temporarily lodged in a person's body, and constitutes the higher self. Kabbalistic and other mystical traditions theorize about the structure of a person's soul as a mirror of the cosmos and teach that the soul's intimate connection with God enables it to have an impact on all reality. These traditions, therefore, develop processes for cultivating the soul, to enable it to repair the world.

229. A similar comparison (but to a very different effect) is pronounced by Hannah's husband, Elkanah, in 1 Sam. 1:8, who seeks to comfort his wife by asking, "Am I not more devoted to you than ten sons?"

230. Fewell and Gunn, however, consider Naomi's silence here as one of the five that indicate Naomi's ambivalence about Ruth ("'A Child Is Born to Naomi!'" 102).

231. See, e.g., Campbell, *Ruth,* 165. R. De Vaux (*Ancient Israel: Its Life and Institutions* [London, 1961], 42) links this ritual with the placing of a child on the knees as a sign of adoption (Gen. 30:3–8; 48:5–12; 50:23). Sasson reviews the evidence and rejects this conclusion (as do Rudolph and Campbell). Sasson also notes the Hittite practice of placing the child on the knees as acknowledgement of adoption. But neither of these examples—biblical and extra-biblical adoption practices—conform to the present action (Sasson, *Ruth*, 170–72). Instead, Sasson considers vestiges of mythical motifs associated with a goddess. See further comment at 4:17.

232. Carol Meyers, "'Women of the Neighborhood' (Ruth 4:17)—Informal Female Networks in Ancient Israel" in A. Brenner, *A Feminist Companion to the Bible: Ruth and Esther*, 2d Series (Sheffield: Sheffield Academic, 1999), 110–27.

233. Sasson, *Ruth*, 233–39.

234. G. Gerleman supposes that the purpose of this statement and the gesture that follows is to supply the child with a genuinely Judaic mother (*Rut: Das Hohelied* [BKAT 18. Neukirchen: Neukirchener, 1965], 37–38). It seems less than convincing that the book goes to such an extent to give the child a Moabite mother only to eliminate this link at this point and in such a manner by displacing the mother. In the Bible, the noun *ben* carries a wide semantic range of kinship, including that of a grandchild (Gen. 31:43; 2 Chron. 22:9). It is this sense that best fits the women's statement. The women's emphasis rests on providing continuity for Naomi. Actually, one could make a case that the person displaced by this statement is Boaz the father, not Ruth: elsewhere, whenever this formulaic statement "was born to," is used, it typically mentions the father (see, e.g., Gen. 10:21).

235. Reimer, "Her Mother's House," 97–105. Reimer rightly underscores the collaborative nature of this birth. One can note (as Ibn Ezra already implies) that other biblical texts also highlight the collaborative aspect of women around the birth of a child, with Exod. 2:1–10 as an example.

236. See M. D. Johnson, *The Purpose of the Biblical Genealogies,* 2d ed. (Cambridge, 1988); and R. R. Wilson, *Genealogy and History in the Biblical World* (New Haven: Yale University Press, 1977).

237. Sasson, *Ruth,* 176–77 underscores the significance of this usage.

238. Wilson, *Genealogy and History in the Biblical World*, 33–34, 133–34.

239. The superscription to Song of Songs, which ascribes the book to Solomon, is usually viewed as an example of attribution for the sake of securing the book a place in the revered tradition. The majority of earlier scholars tended to see the genealogy in Ruth as an independent document appended later to

Ruth. See Bush, *Ruth/Esther*, 13–16 and Sasson, *Ruth,* 178–86 for a discussion of the options. But opinions shifted with newer studies of genealogies and their function. Sasson believes that Ruth 4:18–22 is contemporary with the rest of the Book of Ruth (*Ruth*, 186), and Bush considers it integral to the story (*Ruth/ Esther,* 16).

240. The genealogy in 1 Chron. 2:4–15 includes all the same names that Ruth 4:18–22 has, and in the same order, but also spreads horizontally to include siblings in each generation. It is also but a segment of a much longer genealogy that begins with Adam in 1 Chron. 1:1 and continues the line of David for several centuries after him (see 1 Chron. 3:19). Evidently, the genealogy in Chronicles is constructed to expresses different emphases from what we have in Ruth. Some of the same names also appear in a second unit, 1 Chron. 2:16–54, with other details that are not always clear or consistent.

241. Sasson relies on the instability of the name to argue that 1 Chron. 2:9–10 and 2:25–27 is derived from the genealogy of Ruth (*Ruth,* 187–188).

242. B. Porten, "The Scroll of Ruth: A Rhetorical Study," *GCA* 7 (1978): 48; and Sasson, *Ruth,* 182–84. Among other things, Sasson suggests that beginning with Perez was necessitated to place Boaz in the seventh position (*Ruth*, 182–84). But as noted above, the genealogy likely telescopes names. It could have started elsewhere to achieve this particular goal. For this and other reasons, as I suggest when discussing Perez in 4:18, it is more plausible that Perez's story and name are important to the author.